The UK Church Fundraising

Revd Maggie Durran works as a freelance adviser on development, planning and fundraising for churches to facilitate funding of repairs, alterations, outreach and sustainability for the future.

Her professional career began with teaching Maths in a comprehensive school; followed by working in church renewal with the Community of Celebration and Fisherfolk in the 1970s and 1980s. With the ordination of women as deacons she trained on the Southwark Ordination Course and became curate at St Matthew's Church, Brixton, and St Leonard's Church, Streatham, South London, and once ordained priest became the Vicar of St Christopher's Church in Walworth, South London, for four years. Maggie has an MSc in Management for Ministry.

The UK Church Fundraising Handbook

A practical manual and directory of sources

Maggie Durran

CANTERBURY PRESS

Norwich

First published by the Canterbury Press in 2003

This second edition published in 2010 by the Canterbury Press Norwich
Editorial office
13–17 Long Lane,
London, EC1A 9PN, UK

Canterbury Press is an imprint of Hymns Ancient and Modern Ltd
(a registered charity)
St Mary's Works, St Mary's Plain,
Norwich, NR3 3BH, UK

www.scm-canterburypress.co.uk

British Library Cataloguing in Publication data

A catalogue record for this book is available
from the British Library

ISBN 978 1 84825 002 4

Typeset by Regent Typesetting, London
Printed and bound by
Antony Rowe, Chippenham, SN14 6LH

Contents

Appendices

Foreword

Many churches and hard-pressed vicars and churchwardens cheerfully testify to the good fortune of the Diocese of London in being able to call upon the services of the Reverend Maggie Durran. As Historic Churches Project Officer she has made all the difference in unlocking the potential and the hope in a number of seemingly intractable situations. She has always married faith and finance in an intelligent way, and the results of many successful campaigns can be appreciated in the pages of this book. Now she has distilled the experience she has gained in the field and produced a book which should enable a much wider public to benefit from her knowledge and approach.

This is a very timely exercise. In many ways, the law of the country and the attitudes of communities, trenchantly expressed whenever there is a threat to the local church, reveal that the Church of England in particular is treated as if it were a public utility. There is reason in this attitude. Even beyond the constituency of the 37 million people who declared themselves to be Christians in the recent census, there is a sense that church buildings belong to the whole community. They are so very often a treasury of vernacular culture and local memory.

In the past this sense of ownership by the local community has been expressed in tangible ways. St Paul's Cathedral is a brilliant edition of this truth. It was financed out of the proceeds of the tax on coal entering the Port of London, and if it had been left to the worshippers unaided it would never have been built. Now, however, we have got into a situation where responsibility is firmly assigned to the worshipping community within a regulative framework set by others.

In addition, the Church of England, among European churches with comparable responsibilities, is the most financially disestablished of them all.

The Eckstein Report (1999), which was produced to provide some statistical basis for the VAT campaign, did a survey of the average annual cost of repairs to church buildings at that time. This evidence, corrected by more recent enquiries like the Archdeacon of Middlesex's articles for 2002, suggests that the cost of repairing church buildings over the coming five years will be not less than three-quarters of a billion pounds. We have indications that grants from various public sources may be as much as two hundred and fifty million, leaving us with a contribution of half a billion to find from private donations, principally of course the faithful.

We have to communicate the fact of the cost-effective way in which the Church of England cares for such a large part of the community's cultural inheritance, the huge achievements of tens of thousands of volunteers and the generosity of worshippers. The results of this effort can be seen in the state of most of our cathedrals and churches, which can challenge comparison with the more lavishly funded regimes on the Continent of Europe.

Are we jealous of the fact that all church buildings in France before 1904 are the responsibility of public authorities, or are we wingeing about the church tax regimes enjoyed by our partner churches in Northern Europe? Not at all. We are proud of our voluntary character and we know that the effort of looking after our churches and cathedrals can often bring benefits in quickening church community life.

But facts must be faced. In the financial revolution through which we are passing, increasing responsibilities are falling to dioceses and parishes, and a reassessment of the asymmetrical relationship between church attenders and the wider community, with respect to maintaining such a vital part of the nation's inheritance of art and culture, is now urgent.

Churches have a key part to play in various aspects of the present government's agenda. There is clearly an educational role, and many places like Southwark Cathedral and Canterbury have recently completed new educational centres.

There is a role in urban regeneration. St John's Hoxton in Hackney, one of Britain's poorest boroughs, has received a good deal of publicity as it brings together new facilities for the community, including an employment project for the disabled and a facility for families under stress.

Tourism is one of the most significant economic activities in the country and a huge employer. In a recent debate in the House of Lords, I was able to say some very obvious things about the contribution to the regional economy of places like York Minster. I was puzzled by the suggestion from other speakers that this was a novel perspective.

In the meantime Maggie Durran helps us to see what is possible even now in enlisting allies and tapping the hard-pressed resources of grantmaking trusts and generous individuals. Some of the answer to our present challenges lies with others, but we can do much for ourselves, and this book helps us to see how.

Richard Londin
September 2003

Introduction

These days many of our churches are struggling to remain financially solvent. Even while they try to be socially responsible in their giving, the demands for cash are rising – for central church contributions, for repairs, for gas, electricity and water, and for insurance. Income dwindles if congregations decline and costs continue to rise. *The Church Fundraising Handbook* tackles this dilemma from the viewpoint of the people of the church, both clergy and lay, paid and volunteer. It analyses not just the many tried and tested ways of raising extra funding, but also how to manage finances better, to cut costs and to capitalize on assets as well as on time and other scarce resources.

> Fundraising must not be simply about generating resources but about creating a viable and strong organization which is able to sustain itself in the future. The church's plan for mission is the journey; finance is merely the vehicle.

How to use this book

Most people will not read this book from cover to cover. However, it is important to use the early chapters to inform the work that is undertaken in later chapters. So Chapters 1, 2, 3 and 4 are about getting your house in order, especially the church's finances as the foundation for effective fundraising. Chapters 5, 6 and 7 are essential principles about setting a strategy, learning the language of the funders and creating the church's own unique strategy. The following chapters work systematically through a number of potential funding sources and ways the church may develop them.

The key to good fundraising is in the skills of the key fundraiser, especially the ability to communicate clearly and succinctly in a relaxed but informative way. They should understand thoroughly all the financial management and targets, the strategy for the future, and have access to all the key officers and members of the church council. They must be able to focus on administrative detail and detailed follow-through as well as the big picture.

One of the key factors in successful fundraising is to create a space (time and place) where your fundraiser (ordained/lay, volunteer or paid) can concentrate without interruption for good blocks of time, with all the equipment and materials they need.

The Church Fundraising Handbook suggests many simple, practical strategies that have been tried and tested in a number of churches, especially in the Diocese of London.

I

Becoming a Fundraising Church

Many churches around the country are struggling with the tension between raising revenue funds to keep the church going, raising capital funds for repairs and building and raising funds for wider Christian mission and ministry. Why?

Over the past half-century the numbers of people attending church regularly, their patterns of attendance and their style of loyalty have changed. For the Church of England, traditional endowments have been unable to raise sufficient capital to keep pace with inflation, more realistic salaries for clergy and other church workers, and changing provision for pensions. For other denominations the same pressures to meet spiralling costs have challenged traditional styles of income generation.

There are many lessons to be learned from churches and other charities that are breaking through and finding new ways to become sustainable. Many historic churches are national treasures and can attract funding from outside their regular congregation or their parish, but many others are challenged by buildings that are way beyond their financial means but that still have a meaningful role for them and for local people. Sometimes the building is replaced by a modern and more manageable building; sometimes its inherent value is sufficient to keep it going by providing additional service to local people.

But the more painless way to tackle the issues depends on understanding the church itself with all its aspects: the congregation, the liturgy and sacraments, the building, the beneficiaries, the mission, money, and the spiritual journey on which both church and members are engaged. Many aspects of the church's life are means to facilitate and enable the journey. Money is one of these. Therefore to count money as outside the spiritual life of the church and not an issue that we discuss together easily and tackle along with our plans for worship, prayer and mission, is to cut one leg from our three-legged stool. The fact that the Gospel writers recorded so much of Jesus' teaching about money and recorded stories of money issues indicates its significance in the spiritual journey and rightful place in our consideration. From honesty and integrity about money in the early chapters of the Acts of the Apostles to Jesus pointing out the place of generosity in discipleship, as in the parable of the Widow's Mite, money features all the way through teaching on the Christian life.

Churches have a number of strengths in regard to fundraising. The commitment of worshippers to gather week after week (though many committed people nowadays are more likely to attend two or three times each month); the tradition of giving on a regular basis (some churches are stronger at this than others); many conspicuous and picturesque locations that make them a local attraction and bring in many people with a variety of interests; they have a pool of experience and expertise that if not present in every congregation is often shared among the denomination. Often the key to effective fundraising is to harness and focus what is already happening, to ensure that energy is spent effectively, to challenge a wider group of people to become involved and to find the means to turn ideas and opportunities into effective and achievable strategies.

Attempting to create a culture in which the financial implications of all decisions are considered is the beginning of developing a strategy for finance that supports mission and every aspect of the church's work.

In the chapters that follow the first stage is to understand the church's finance and ensure that all money is well managed. As a foundation to raising new money inside and outside the church it is vital that everyone understands the church's mission and its action plan for mission. Why? Because people give to people. Even when we fundraise for building works, the gifts are about people: loving a beautiful building and wanting it to be there for themselves and others for worship, wanting it to be there for their children and grandchildren, wanting more and more people to have access to their architectural and spiritual heritage.

As the book progresses we shall consider many challenges that fundraising can present, and how to face them:

Develop a fundraising subcommittee of the church council.
- Fill key positions (a champion, etc.).
- Set the committee SMART objectives within the fundraising strategy, delegating responsibility to those who can do the job and do it well.
- Keep records.

Build fundraising into the worship life of the church.
- Teach discipleship and create an atmosphere of responsibility and generosity.
- Make opportunity in liturgy and teaching to encourage financial responsibility.

Deliver the message.
- Learn how to write attractive leaflets and posters.
- Learn how, and develop programmes, to publicize and advertise the fact that the church is fundraising.

Design a fundraising strategy around the church's existing relationships and the relationships it could have.

Learn the languages and the cultures of the people and sectors among whom the fundraising committee will venture when fundraising outside the church.

Build relationships with local celebrities, local dignitaries, local politicians, officers of the council, other churches, and network with people of all backgrounds who care about local people and their concerns.

Prepare the ground through understanding the person or organization the church is contacting or meeting. Do not require them to understand the church.

Prepare the ground through dialogue and listening – and asking other churches how they made their contacts. Talk with voluntary sector groups, local workers and members of the congregation who are involved in those other sectors.

Prepare the congregation and church council members to get the message right when meeting outside potential funders.

The professional fundraiser

It is possible to get a professional fundraiser to do the work for your church. Local churches who may be unsure of how to develop a strategy and work on it effectively may be far better off with a fundraising consultant who will join their meetings and help steer the work through. This latter course will be far less expensive and usually more effective as so much of the work depends on local knowledge and networks.

Starting Fundraising with a Mission Plan

Mission must come before money, but putting mission into practice will need at least some money.

Most churches engaging in ministry have a set of biblical understandings, either implicit or explicit, that determine the actual activities they undertake. Equally, most have a set of primary activities that they are already providing. Yet the reason for reading a book on fundraising is usually a mismatch between resources for existing activities and total resources needed for new and targeted activities. The aim of this chapter is to provide the church with a way of undertaking its own overview programme, ensuring that the church is really doing what it wants to do to fulfil its Christian mission without wasting time and energy. Additionally, the chapter aims to ensure that as the church sets out on new activity for which it wishes to get new resources, it will know why and how it will undertake that activity *before* asking others to help financially. Deciding to fundraise because of a financial crisis and a desperate wish to avoid calamity will not, on its own, result in successful fundraising. Similarly, setting up a new and worthy project for local people without fully counting the cost of time, money, commitment and other resources will be unsuccessful.

The simple business model in Figure 2.1 may help to lay out some fundamental questions in order. This is an adaptation of a model that has the value of being much softer and more adaptable than many models from the business sector as it asks open-ended questions that have qualitative aspects more applicable to the church sector.

I suggest a starting point on a system that becomes circular – we keep revisiting the questions as the church grows and changes over the years. Some of the information to answer questions posed here is traditionally presented in the church's annual report. But the element added here is to review where the church wants to go in a way that is specific enough for an assessment of what it will cost to get there – in use of time, use of money and even use of buildings.

In other words the foundation for financial strength is the church's mission plan. Questions start with both understanding where the church is now and deciding where the church wants to go in the future. How is the church progressing on its journey? Monitor its progress to ensure that once the plan is under way the adaptations needed to cope with all sorts of minor and major changes are dealt with before they derail the whole plan. Questions link mission and money, because most

Monitor	Understand where you are now	What activities are we undertaking, why and for whom? What resources do we have (people and money)? What is our current financial position and what is our current financial performance?
	Look ahead and see what's in front of you	What commitments have we already made, for activity that will cost time and/or money? What additional resources do we anticipate generating and when? What spare resources will we therefore have available?
Aim	Decide where you want to go	What are we looking to achieve? Describe this in terms of outcomes. What would these outcomes look like in financial terms?
Plan	Decide how you intend to get to what you want to achieve	What resources have we already committed to continuing current activity? What resources can we commit to both present and new activity, from reserves or future income? What are our priorities in order of importance? What additional commitments is it appropriate to make or stop making now?
Act	Set off in your intended direction	

Figure 2.1 A simple business model[1]

[1] Taken from *Charity Finance*, July 2001 issue, and adapted from the SSI model.

of the activities we undertake in our churches have a financial implication and it is essential that we ensure we can afford something before spending either time or money. And if we have insufficient money we either cut back our mission plan or seek to raise sufficient money through one or another form of fundraising.

Turn this into a circular process so that when the action is under way you start again at the top and begin monitoring.

Tackling the questions

Aim: Decide where you want to go

Most churches undertake a variety of activities that provide for Christian worship and pastoral care, and serve a variety of the needs of local people. Most churches want to be generous to people in need in the wider world. For these there are clear biblical imperatives. Most churches also are based in a particular building that is the home for and the focus of activity. Most serve a limited geographical area and are not in a position to plan to preach the gospel throughout the world.

Our purpose is to serve the people who live, work, visit or worship in ——— Town through the regeneration of St Michael's Church.

We will provide a sustainable future for St Michael's Church in its liturgical and pastoral ministry, its service to its parish and in opening the building to use by a wider public.

St Michael's Church is a vast, beautiful building in poor repair. A few years ago a new vicar set out to revitalize the church, bringing in new people, going out to local people and tackling the issues of the church building as the centre of mission and ministry. The ten to twelve regular members at the time had concluded that their church had very little future and that the best plan would be to stop their few activities and walk away from the building. The new vicar brought new commitment to mission and ministry and was sufficiently pragmatic to develop a financial strategy alongside the mission strategy. The new strategy included repairing the dilapidated building.

The main door was opened as often as possible and always for services (even though there was no heating) so everyone would know they were welcome even if they just wanted to drop in off the street as visitors. The empty and decaying church hall was opened to a project working with homeless people.

After five years, part of the church hall has been leased out to a major charity

– so raising money to pay for heating in the church – and the remainder of the hall is used by the congregation and let out to local voluntary groups and organizations, and let out on a daily basis.

As one of the largest public spaces in the town centre, St Michael's Church decided that they could not keep the building busy all the time and would like to share the space with other local people for a variety of activities. A set of values that the church held at first implicitly and more lately has stated in writing, indicates how they would do this. ('In writing' so that they could present themselves openly and clearly as they sought outside funding for building repairs and new activities.)

VALUES

1 Worship Heritage

- We aim to provide a vibrant centre of Christian worship and prayer at the heart of ———— Town.
- We will support additional uses which respect and relate to the building's Christian heritage.

2 Architectural and Historic Heritage

- We are committed to safeguarding and sharing our heritage.
- We seek an appropriate restoration and conservation of the church.
- We wish to preserve the building's flexibility as a community space.

3 Community Use

- We want to ensure that as many groups and individuals as possible have access to the space.
- We wish the church to contribute to the community development of ———— Town.
- We aim to offer a welcome to all, recognizing people of other faiths and none.

4 Event Use

- We seek to encourage music and arts events that celebrate or interpret the Christian tradition, the life of ———— Town or those who live in, work in or visit it.
- We want to provide an opportunity for those who do not have ready access to the arts and to provide those working in the arts with access to a local community.

These statements of Purpose and Values lead readily to a set of Activities, some of which already happen and some of which are looking to the future. So St Michael's can now make out a list of activities that fulfil their purpose and assess what resources they have to enable these to happen. Over five years the finances have improved. Gradually increasing giving, renewed stewardship programmes and small-scale fundraising have taken care of running costs. Some capital work has been undertaken with money raised from small grants for repair; the sale of a lease is paying for heating installation; and partnerships with other agencies have provided finance to pay for new staff.

The outcomes at St Michael's are a full programme of worship services, on Sundays and festivals, programmes for the church school, having the church open to the public several days a week (they are aiming for every day), encouraging local forums to use the church as a meeting place, and arts events by choirs and drama students. The church still has other outcomes to achieve – as soon as they can afford them. So the church is still planning for increasing income and capital fundraising.

The development of mission and ministry has led to a parallel need for finance, and the church has carefully prepared itself, on a regular basis, to consider what it could afford to do in the next phase of working towards achieving its aims.

Task

Summarize your purpose and values and discuss this with church members to see if they agree, and determine what they would like to add or subtract.

This should result in a list of actual activities the church wishes to provide in the future.

Task

Make a list of activities the church now provides, and ones the church would like to provide. Then work on the answer to the second question.

What would these outcomes and activities look like in financial terms?
For example:

Activity	Resources used/needed	Finance used/needed
Sunday and festival worship, daily prayers, weddings, baptisms, funerals	Mostly provided by parish clergy with volunteer help Finance provided by congregational giving (mostly)	Clergy (diocese provides salary and house) Clergy costs Service costs – printing Advertising Insurance, heat and light . . .

Activity	Resources used/needed	Finance used/needed
Pastoral care		
Visiting local people		
Parent and Toddler group	Organizer/church's child protection officer Volunteer?	Volunteer expenses, running costs Actual cost . . .
Youth programme	Paid youth workers Management committee of volunteers	Salaries and running costs Actual cost . . .
Building repairs and increased use by church and local people		

Each of the church's activities can now be assessed in terms of what it will take to get them going, who is able to do what. In the third column write the budget for each activity and get the treasurer to help bring these items into the projected budget for the church.

Plan

Are the church's resources adequate for all the church's activities?

What resources are tied up in continuing present activity? Is there any present activity that can be cut back to fund something new?

Does the church have any reserves that might be committed to new activities or any new income that it expects to receive that is available for the activities?

Discuss these possibilities and then question priorities (pp. 12ff.) before going further in planning. For a church, the number one priority will be provision of regular public worship and the church council probably will not wish to cut that back in any way. Pastoral work with local people as well as church members may be the second priority, but for this there may already be limitations of available time, and more could not be done without more staff. Is the provision of church-based groups for parents with toddlers or for pensioners higher or lower in priority than home visiting? Clergy running church-based groups will be engaged in pastoral care while working with groups, but will do less visiting. To extend either pastoral care or activities may include the costs of extra staff.

So the last question of the planning section asks what additional commitment we can make now. Should we be stopping some commitments or putting them on hold? Make the decisions, taking carefully into account the time people have available and the money that will be needed.

Clearly some activities will continue with the current income, and for some activities the church will be able to say, 'We will do this as soon as we have the money for the work, be it repair or providing staff.' For the provision of staff the next question is to look at who will find the money, how they will do it (will they need to give up some other commitment in order to fundraise?) and how much it will cost. Some existing activity will have to go on hold if an already busy person (such as one of the clergy or a volunteer) is going to take up fundraising.

As the church plans, it will be able to look at each existing and new activity and organize preparation for time and money as small steps on the way to the big picture. 'In the first three months we will . . . Then our next step is to . . . When we have a worker or volunteer in place we will . . . When our group is running we will . . .'

At each stage the church council can mark progress and affirm direction. Each activity then becomes a series of small achievable steps. The smaller the resources that are available at the start, the more this approach of steps and stages will assist the church as members will be able to see they are actually making progress.

Act: Set off in the chosen direction

Set out on the planned programme of activity, comparing your progress with your objectives and making necessary adaptations to changing circumstances through monitoring and new action.

Monitor: Understand where you are now

After three months the church is now in a position to ask questions about progress against its targets. How is the financial position, not just cash in the bank today, but in paying for the new activities that the church wants to start? How is people's time working out? Like St Michael's some of the church's targets may take a long time to reach. The church will need to review the targeted activities and priorities as it progresses. Is the heating of the building more important than the disabled-access toilet, as we have raised funds for one but not both? But since the church does know its long-term aim, everyone knows that eventually it will do both.

Key points

- Understand where you want to go.
- Plan your activities and actions in the light of money and time.
- Act upon your plans.
- Monitor and review how your plans work out in the light of where you want to go and then plan new actions.

3

Conducting a Review of Church Finances

Church members may be working through this book because they are already aware that the income *is* going downwards and there is an unrelenting upward path on expenses. Later chapters of the book cover many different ways, internal and external, to increase income, and the internal ways must be addressed first when the need is revenue income.

We shall start by breaking down in order to build up again. Remember the stories of Ezra and Nehemiah who returned to Jerusalem after the exile in Babylon to rebuild the city and rebuild the temple. The people looked at the wrecked walls of their ancient city and decided to rebuild it, and not to start again elsewhere, and I can easily imagine them picking stones and rubble out of the streets, assessing their value, lining them up by kind and recycling them into new walls, new gates and new homes. The church may need just such a review as it sets out to face its financial challenge. The church's aim is to be in charge and use its resources to support and encourage its chosen ministry.

Most of church income and expenditure is repeated, year after year. It's normally fairly straightforward to investigate and review if we know what we are looking for. There is very little rocket science involved, and a tiny amount of science will take members a long way. Writing up financial records in a form that is required by the Charity Commissioners is a little more complicated, and the work of the accountant or experienced treasurer may be needed. But what we are seeking here is a way for most of the church members, and all of the church council and clergy, to be able to see the common sense in what is being done.

Setting priorities

The principle needed for setting priorities is not much different from the age-old method of putting the week's cash into labelled jam jars so that when the bills come the money has been set aside to pay for them. The sensible housewife put money in the RENT jar first, then probably, the HEAT, LIGHT AND WATER, and

FOOD. Only after these essentials come luxuries such as SWEETS, HOLIDAYS, and LEISURE ACTIVITY. When money is short the latter jars go empty, not the former.

What are the equivalent essential and luxury categories for jam jars for the church?

Essential (the roof over our heads)

- building maintenance
- building insurance
- staff costs (contractual)
- Common Fund (to the diocese for clergy costs and pensions and housing)
- savings for major items of building repair (replacing the boiler, rewiring, etc.)

Important (but not essential to survival)

- heat and light (there are churches surviving without these)
- books and service sheets
- candles, wine and wafers

Desirable (but not essential)

- leaflets and notice sheets
- flowers
- cleaning
- donations to others

Set out the church's chart that responds to the church council's particular set of priorities. These choices will inform the way the church deals with money pressures, so it is important for the church council to look at these priorities together.

Work together as a church council to decide which items are *essential*, which are *important*, and which are *desirable* in looking at how money is spent.

Why do this? Because if the church has no set of stated priorities, the money will be spent on the first thing that *demands* money rather than on the essential but less-demanding items. This is exactly how many churches fail to put aside money for running repairs to the building and then repairs are not addressed until there is a *crisis*, of stone falling or rain gushing in.

In the light of the church's priorities, the church council can then begin to assess whether its finances are in good order to achieve what they want. When we come to budgeting (below) we will return to the jam jar imagery, as this will enable the church to plan to use its money to fulfil the targeted priorities.

How can you tell if your financial state is good or bad?

By working through a series of simple review tasks you will be able to assess the following. Is the church's income sufficient to pay for its expenses? Or is the church regularly in crisis wondering where the money will be found to pay the next bill? Is the church always trying to cut the costs of ministry in case there is not enough money?

Perhaps the following can be a method for the church to plan spending so that essentials are covered and staff know which *desirable* items can be bought.

How can the church tell whether it is financially healthy at present? If someone reads the church's bank statement for the current balance to get the answer to the financial state, the church is not in a good state.

Can you tell whether the church is financially sustainable? That is, will the church be able to pay its way over the next ten years with or without a major crisis? If you have no idea, then you need a good review followed by thorough financial planning for the future.

The review

At a meeting of the church council start the review, working on the information together. Have available last year's levels of income and expenditure. Using each category of expenditure in turn ask the group to set what they believe to be an adequate sum for the church to achieve its mission targets. Against this set a parallel target for types of giving. Look at these alongside each other. Will the income comfortably and sufficiently meet the needs for expenditure on mission? If all is well and income is sufficient to meet all the targeted expenditure with a calculated surplus going into the savings account for the rainy day (when the church roof leaks), then all may be relatively healthy. *Or if it isn't, how shall we proceed?*

From the group elicit a brief list of all the *types* of income you expect to get every year. Such as:

Sunday cash collection
Sunday stewardship envelopes

donations at special services
income from weddings, baptisms, funerals in church
other donations

Now list income earned through fundraising events:

jumble sales
Christmas fair
summer fete

Now list 'unearned income':

interest on savings or investment account
church charities

The church needs a healthy surplus of income over expenditure and enough reserves to see the church through the foreseeable future. It is not at all uncommon that the church does not show enough income to pay for even regular spending, as churches juggle with tight finances. What we have is called budget deficit. Normally the church, or any organization, now has two choices. Either, cut some expenses so they fit the income (using the priorities in the jam jar exercise, the church knows which end of the list to start cutting) or consider how to increase income. As a struggling church, first look at how you might increase your income, because cost-cutting will tend to cut down on mission also. Increasing the income to cover expenditure is *fundraising*.

Is cost-cutting the way forward? If the church makes cuts without doing the priority exercise first it may find itself making choices by default that jeopardize long-term priorities. A building becomes shabby, dilapidated and leaky in small, almost invisible, increments. So it is relatively easy for regular maintenance and minor repairs to be considered less demanding than a heating bill from the gas board. But the problem grows. If the church does not maintain the boiler it breaks down, the church has no money to repair or replace it, and then who needs a gas bill – they cannot run the heating anyway. If the gutters are not cleaned and slipped slates replaced, before long the water will not be able to get down the downpipes, it will pool up in the roof and run down the inside of the walls, rotting the wood and damaging the plaster and decorative finishes, and when the next quinquennial report comes the church will find it needs £100,000 for work that would have cost only £2–3,000 per year if done annually.

The art of budgeting

Why set a budget? Each church council member[2] is one trustee of a charitable organization even if it does not have a charity registration number – it is an excepted charity. The chief of its responsibilities is ensuring that the activities of the charity and the finances of the charity have been used to fulfil the charity's objects and nothing else, and that these activities have been undertaken within the parameters of good practice. The Annual Report of the charity, required by the Charity Commissioners, contains material that shows that the trustees have done their job.

The budget is the management tool that most readily enables trustees to plan for proper use of finance over the year and to ensure that expenditure will not exceed income and is used on appropriate expenditure. So *how* does a budget help that to happen? The year's projected budget is set up for or by the trustees and approved early in the year. Or even better *before* the financial year begins.

First (usually led by the treasurer), the church council members, as the trustees, agree what the predictable anticipated income of the year will be. This will be sensibly based on the previous years' levels with a very good justification given for any significant change up or down from previous years. So each member/ trustee can confidently agree that this is reasonable and realistic.

Second, the church council agrees how that income will be broken down into the elements of the projected expenditure. It's a good idea to list the categories of expenditure in order of priority – see the example above – so the most essential cost is allocated first. Discuss the various projected levels till the projected income is just above the expenditure. *It is very unwise for you to set a budget for deficit, as you are not legally allowed to function in deficit. In practice, to run in the red means you are using someone else's money not the charity's to do your work, and that's not a choice the church is legally allowed to make.*

The budget you have set is now used to control anyone spending church money. Under any specific category the treasurer or staff may now only authorize payments that are within the money allocated to that category. So if the church has allocated £100 for candles this year, no-one can buy candles that will take the expenditure on candles above the allowance that has been set. If this were cash, the church would just put £100 in the jam jar for candle money, and when that cash had been used there would be no more to spend on candles. If staff want to spend more on candles they then need the church council to approve that item through ascertaining that money has been saved elsewhere. Any non-budget item has to be individually approved by the church council. Without an approved budget *every* item should be approved individually by the church council.

[2] Here 'church council' is used as in the Church of England.

Income to date	Budgeted income for year
. . .	. . .
. . .	. . .
. . .	. . .
Expenditure to date	Budgeted expenditure for year
. . .	. . .
. . .	. . .
. . .	. . .

Figure 3.1 A simple report

If you are a church with an income over about £15,000 it is wise to bring a report on progress to each meeting of the church council (see Figure 3.1 for an example).

Add notes that tell if the church's levels are running too high or low on each item.

To make it more complicated, where more money is involved, report on a quarterly basis. But always report by calendar months – not, as in a few churches I have visited, from meeting date to meeting date.

Reporting on a monthly basis is a more detailed alternative, but remember to include notes that show that some expenditure, such as on the phone and the utilities, are on a quarterly system, and that insurance is annual.

Income				
Category	Income to date	Budgeted to date	Surplus to date	Deficit to date
Expenditure				
Category	Spent to date	Budgeted to date	Surplus to date	Deficit to date

Figure 3.2 Income and expenditure

Spending to budget

It remains for those people who have access to spending to keep within these figures. And remember that every item is the responsibility of the church council members.

By having a budget that everyone has agreed is reasonable, the church's staff can now use that budget to guide them. Any time that money is to be spent the person concerned can look at the church budget to check that money is available for that item. Anything that is not in the budget cannot be spent without going back to the church council and asking for permission, and the church council in turn will ask where, from within the limited income, that money will be taken. It is like running out of money in the jam jar for candles but agreeing together that candles are more important than flowers, so you will take money from the flowers jam jar to pay for candles. *No* category can exceed its budgeted amount unless you all agree the change because you can see where that excess will come from. If one item goes up then another must go down.

As the church and staff get used to the system they will over the year be able to assess each category more readily and make informed decisions. In this way the church will have more control in keeping spending within income over the year.

To go back to the example at Figure 3.2, you will find that you can anticipate the problem of expenses being a little higher in some areas and make adjustments as you go along, so you don't end up with a crisis. Alternatively you will see that the things you really want to achieve are going to require more income, and again you become a fundraising church – you will set out to achieve the income you need for the things you want to do. You will plan, not just blindly hope things turn out OK.

Preparing staff to operate with budgets

Set up a meeting of those who incur expenditure on the church's behalf to explore what it means to work with a budget, how it will affect what they can do, what information will enable them to know they are within budget, what they can do when something unplanned arises (other than panic or go ahead blindly!), how they will avoid miscommunication about who is spending what (e.g. whether it is the clergy or the administrator who is initiating spending on stationery), and keep to budget without confusion between them.

Discuss how to deal with items like utility costs if they stray above budget and how the church might expect bills to occur over the year. To help keep the budget clear, the church could set up a monthly standing order agreement for items like gas and electricity so that seasonal highs and lows are more controlled.

Using IT in financial administration

Most personal computers with home office programmes have the means available to run the church's budgeting system very easily on a spreadsheet. Programmes such as Lotus 123 or Microsoft Excel (in the standard Microsoft Office package) would be ideal. Only a very large organization needs something more expansive.

In the example in Appendix 18, the spreadsheet gives a grid into which all the categories of income and expenditure are typed. In the next column are all amounts projected. At the bottom of income will be a TOTAL box into which the computer will add the column – as instructed. Beneath that the computer has been instructed to indicate whether TOTAL INCOME minus TOTAL EXPENDITURE is positive or negative. The budget figures may be replaced by the actual figures on a regular basis and the bottom line continues to indicate surplus or deficit.

Minor repairs must have a figure in the budget, as do regular building maintenance figures. The church's particular repair and maintenance figures may be obtained in two ways.

(a) The quinquennial report from many architects lists annual or twice-yearly building care tasks. Take the list to a church council meeting and on this care list place a name next to each task so you know who is going to see that each task is completed on time and at what cost.

(b) If you have on the whole done regular maintenance and minor repairs over the years, add together the repair total for three years, divide the sum by three and use that figure as your budget figure for repairs.

> **Task**
> Summarize the picture to the church congregation. People who are well informed as well as committed are more likely to make realistic contributions to the church's running costs. See the stewardship section in Chapter 8.

Long-term finance

Using a budget to control finances year on year is the beginning. The church that intends to turn a corner in being viable and sustainable in the long term will wish to create a financial system that safeguards the future mission and ministry.

Therefore, it may be time to create a fund to cover depreciating assets such as heating systems. Nearly every church I visit that is unheated has the dilapidated remains of an old system that finally gave up the ghost, and the church in question had not saved up the money for refurbishment or replacement.

The long-term budget in Appendix 20 addresses major maintenance, and has come from a Grade I listed church that is attempting to address its future maintenance after the current major structural repair programme. There are built-in assumptions, based on the work of the architect and other professionals who assessed the life-span of major items and the accrual that would be necessary to have money in hand to replace them when the time came. This will enable the church council to target new income sources that would enable it to prepare for the long term. The budget is prepared without allowance for inflation, and the treasurer will need to upgrade these figures regularly, and particularly to increase the savings or building fund figure in line with inflation each year. A five-year review of the figures alongside the quinquennial report will allow appropriate updates so the church can adjust its targeted income. These figures were prepared to justify a fundraising application to the Heritage Lottery Fund for several million pounds and were built into the Business Plan. They also represent good stewardship of funds for any church that wishes to be realistic in developing its finances to support present and future mission.

The role of the treasurer[3]

The treasurer's role is to record the financial transactions and take care of the probity of the financial procedures on behalf of the church council. The treasurer will normally prepare regular financial reports, help prepare the budget and prepare annually for the records to be given to the external examiner of accounts. However the church council sets out the financial strategy and the budget, the treasurer administers it. The church council is responsible for financial procedures and the treasurer will follow them. The buck stops with the church council, *not with the treasurer*.

Recording and review

- A cash-book should be kept up-to-date, and should include a record of all receipts and payments and a cash-book balance for the parish.

[3] From the June 2002 newsletter of Robert Hardy, Director of Finance and IT for the Diocese of London.

- The cash-book balance should be reconciled to the bank statement on a monthly basis and reviewed by someone in addition to the treasurer.
- All supporting paperwork including vouchers, invoices and receipts should be retained and filed in an orderly manner and cross-referenced to the cash book.
- At the start of each year a projected budget (including cash flow) should be presented to the church council for review and adoption.
- The church council (or a sub-committee) should consider the current and projected future cash position of the parish at each meeting of the church council. This would be part of the wider presentation of the financial position to the church council.
- The treasurer should have meetings with the clergy and the churchwardens on a regular basis (for example, monthly) to review the finances and the cash position.
- The annual accounts should be reviewed/audited by an independent examiner/ auditor. The church council should ensure that the independent examiner/ auditor is suitably independent and has the requisite ability.

Cash collections

- Any cash (including money in weekly or Gift Aid envelopes) should always be counted by two people together, and this role should be rotated among a group of people.
- Collections should be counted as soon as possible after the service.
- The amount should be entered into the service register at the time of counting and be initialled by the two counters.
- Money should be banked as soon as practicable and kept in the safe until it can be banked.
- Never leave cash unattended in church.

Reasonable financial procedures

The following summary of procedures is taken from a book by Kate Sayer.[4] It is recommended that this summary is turned into a Handbook by each church on the principles of how the church runs its finances. Each church council member

---

[4] *A Practical Guide to Financial Management* by Kate Sayer, published by Directory of Social Change, 1998.

can then have a copy and understand how well (or not) the church runs its finances. It is very important that potential trustees or church council members know this *before* they accept office.

1. *Introduction* on what the handbook covers.

2. *Organization chart* saying who is responsible for what aspects of finance. Include how to contact, for example, those authorized to sign cheques.

3. *Budgets*: when each year's budget is set and who is responsible for ensuring that it is set and brings the draft budget to the church council for approval.

4. *Financial reports*: how often reports are made to the church council and what is contained in them.

5. *Bank accounts*: a list of all bank accounts and the appropriate signatories. If the church has an investment account held through the diocesan Board of Finance, detail how that money is managed and if necessary accessed.

6. *Income*: how to deal with the various forms of income:
   - opening the post that may/will contain money
   - banking receipts of all kinds
   - invoicing and payments against invoices
   - handling cash.

7. *Expenditure*:
   - spending limits for Church Council approved items
   - procedures for authorizing expenditure on large items
   - systems for approving and paying invoices
   - ordering items
   - procedure for items not on the annual budget.

8. *Payroll*:
   - method of payment for staff and authorization of payment
   - changes in pay rate, how they are calculated and instigated.

9. *Petty cash*:
   - levels and types of expenditure that can go through petty cash
   - who can authorize petty cash expenditure
   - how reimbursements will be done *and not done*
   - system of record-keeping.

10. *Staff expenses*
   - how these will be reimbursed
   - for what types and levels of expenditure (for example, travel, stationery, stamps, clergy phone, etc.)

- who may authorize staff expenditure
- policy on computers, equipment and software.

Risk assessment

As a matter of recent charity law, trustees are required to undertake a financial risk analysis if the turnover is more than £100,000. The items listed here are the financial risks to be addressed. Further work is needed on, for example, health and safety risks. In undertaking a risk assessment as a church council it is normal to list the risk, assess the likelihood of the risk happening, the level of impact if the risk materialized and finally what mitigating action the church council is taking to avoid that risk materializing. See Appendix 15 and further information on risk assessments in Chapter 20.

Internal risks

- Failure to keep expenditure down to the level of income (budgeting and a policy for exceptional payments are means of mitigating this risk)
- Incompetence in following budgets and procedures (training staff will reduce the risk)
- Misappropriation of cash (embezzlement and theft are mitigated by good cash procedures)
- Failure to anticipate essential repairs (better use of quinquennial reports and basic maintenance work will tend to keep crises to a minimum and have money set aside for them)
- Making invoice payments only when goods have been received (good financial administration procedures will save mishaps)

Task

The risk assessment required of trustees by the Charity Commissioners is a way for charities to review their finances, but in doing so it would be wise to review financial procedures as well. In particular

- Make sure that none of the church's money goes into a personal account of one of the trustees – review how you run the vicar's discretionary account.

- Petty cash should run on an imprest system[5] and with a maximum cash payment of perhaps £50.

- All cheques should require two signatures and no-one should ever sign a blank cheque. If a holiday is coming and a key signatory will be away, the church should add more signatories!

- What is your purchasing system? Can anyone order something in the church's name for which the church cannot make payment? How can you ensure that purchases are all within budgeted levels? Set up a simple ordering/purchasing system, checking the budget before ordering, not just when payment is due.

External risks

Planning can minimize threats by:

- a spread of sources of income (so if one source of income fails the effect is less drastic)

- minimizing fixed costs (the photocopier and other contracts can be stifling and unnecessary)

- detailed consideration of contingency plans (it is easier to brainstorm solutions before the crisis happens then resort to a pre-planned strategy as required)

- insuring against some risks – check with your insurance provider

- time-limited commitments to staff, and for groups' lettings and leases (so notice can be given as needed)

- building up an appropriate financial reserve (of months for running costs and for years for building repair)

- establishing proper maintenance and repair strategies.

Key points
- Review the church's finances and sustainability.
- Set priorities.
- Begin budgeting.
- Understand the treasurer's role. Set up good procedures.
- Sort out the risks.

---

[5] An initial float is topped up by repayments against actual receipts.

4

Making the Most of What You've Got
Income Generation

In north London the new vicar arrived at a sad-looking Grade II listed church. Water leaked in regularly, grass had been overwhelmed by rubbish dumped by local people, the church cottage was occupied by squatters and in very bad repair. The adjacent church hall was let on a full-repairing lease to another church who had made income by letting out the space but never did any repairs.

What comes first? The vicar first tackled the air of decay, cleaning and removing rubbish inside and outside the building. The congregation were encouraged to join in and a few did. Over a year his friendly manner encouraged more local people into the church, notably people from ethnic minorities. The demand for meeting space in the area, which has good transport links, is high, so immediate income was raised by letting the church itself to two other independent churches on Sunday afternoons and weekdays. This income was sufficient to pay for repairs to the church cottage, which was then let out commercially until such time as the church needed it for church staff. The income from all these sources is now contributing to regular building maintenance and tackling the accumulation of repairs. The lease of the church is rather more difficult as it has no break clauses. You receive less rent with break clauses in place, but you have the benefit of more readily regaining possession.

Using your assets

Fundraising is not simply about generating resources for the immediate crisis but about creating a viable and strong organization, which is able to sustain itself into the future. During the course of this book each church is encouraged to develop financial stability that will be a steady and firm foundation for future mission and ministry.

In the model for this chapter, the ailing St Jude's is a rambling Victorian church with even more rambling Victorian vicarage and a scruffy dilapidated church hall that is not well used apart from an occasional jumble sale. What is the mood of the congregation? Regardless of whether there are 15 people or 50, there is a struggle to keep out the water, a struggle to keep warm and to keep members, a struggle to pay the Diocesan Common Fund and some resentment! The mood fits the general state of the place. And the vicar on an average clergy salary has the same struggle in the vicarage; it's cold and uninviting. The situation is not effective in mission, not efficient in using resources, and not sustainable (it's running down). The archdeacon sees this as a potential church for a *cut*! The pressure is great. What can we do? Now! *Or even sooner!*

Edward de Bono, in his ideas about thinking, stated that all decisions are ultimately emotional and that we should do as much reasonable and rational thinking as we can before making a decision. The best decisions take time and forethought, even though in the end our emotions will make the choice. The lesson for us is to open up possibilities and hold off the decision. St Jude's is in a despondent mood and will under the present pressure make a decision that reflects the current despondent state and will thereby reinforce the view that the future is unpromising. Intense emotional pressure says do something quickly. Instead, it is advisable to spend a significant amount of time thinking first. For comparison: an IMMEDIATE NEED is a funeral as these don't and can't wait; an URGENT NEED is the phone or the doorbell ringing. But IMPORTANT NEEDS cannot be left pending; IMPORTANT changes the future; IMPORTANT has to be done and done well. IMPORTANT can often be neither immediate nor urgent. The church's financial sustainability is IMPORTANT and it is LONG-TERM.

If we look at the church's assets as an IMMEDIATE or URGENT problem we can summarize:

Church	Hall
Has no value as an asset. Needs £250,000 for roof repairs.	Too shabby, not worth repairing as this would cost £60,000 that we don't have. We could sell it for £150,000 and spend the money on the church roof.
Vicarage	**People**
It's not ours, it belongs to the diocese.	Tired. Have been struggling with this too long.

The IMMEDIATE decision might be to sell the hall and apply for grants for £100,000. But if the church can move its thinking from the IMMEDIATE/URGENT to IMPORTANT/LONG-TERM, there is much more to be taken into consideration. If the church were to go with the IMMEDIATE/URGENT route, where might the church be in 20 years' time?

Church after 20 years	Hall after 20 years
Needs major repairs again! There's no money for repairs.	We don't have a hall as we sold it and we have spent all the money from its sale on church repairs 20 years ago.
Vicarage	**People**
It's not ours.	It's the same people and they're older and still struggling!

After 20 years, the church has nothing to negotiate with, no hall to sell again, so what can be done next? Further diminishing of physical resources is obvious. So if the church *today* were able to start by thinking about IMPORTANT and LONG-TERM stability and sustainability, might it make different choices? Can St Jude's tend its assets more wisely and more fruitfully?

Consider a stewardship programme. Each person commits £5 per week on the stewardship programme.

Each year	After 5 years	After 10 years	After 60 years
@ £5 for 52 weeks	@ £5 per week for 5 years	@ £5 per week for 10 years	@ £5 per week for 60 years
total £260	total £1,300	total £2,600	total £15,600

Once you have established a good stewardship programme as the norm for the congregation and *with increases each year for inflation* each member of the congregation has become a major donor. The only difference between this and a major grant is that this money is received in increments. With increases of 3 per cent per annum for inflation (not shown on this table) the value of the lifetime contribution becomes considerable; add to the sum the interest from the savings account with compound interest and the sum is even larger. This is an incredibly valuable donor to the church. And this lifetime of commitment may be later reflected in a legacy.

If St Jude's could put aside in savings the stewardship contribution of 10 per cent of the congregation and get the weekly spending money from the remaining donations, St Jude's would have a major contribution towards the building repairs in 20 years.

Consider the hall:

Current income	Income if repaired and let out	Income accumulated after 5 years[6]	Income accumulated after 10 years	Income accumulated after 20 years
£3,000 p.a.	£35,000	£185,000	£385,000	£900,000
Current sale value	Invested @ 3%[7]	After 5 years compounded	After 10 years compounded	After 20 years compounded
£150,000		£173,891	£ 201,587	£ 270,917
Current sale with capital then spent on church repair	Spend £150,000 and some more	After 5 years	After 10 years	After 20 years
£150,000		No value	No value	Need more capital for major repairs to the church

Clearly more detail may be drawn into the picture, such as spending some of the hall income over the years on hall repairs and caretaking. But still the scenario is one in which the hall can contribute significantly to the financial stability of the church. Additionally, if the church gets busier with greater financial security in the future it can re-establish its own programmes in the hall, no longer requiring the income from hall letting in order to survive. So, if the church decided to repair the hall in order to raise money to sustain the mission and ministry of the church and help with the repair fund – what could the picture be? (See table opposite.)

At the end of twenty years the church has been repaired and has maintained the buildings each year so there are few major repair costs.

The hall is in use and it still belongs to the church who can regain its use if needed for ministry.

Significantly: the church now has a sustainable income stream.

[6] These figures include approximately 3% increase p.a. for inflation.
[7] Rate of interest available in 2002.

	Income	Expenditure
Year 1: Get a loan towards hall repairs and repair hall	Income: £60,000 from loan	Spend £60,000 on hall repairs
Year 2: Lease the hall out commercially	Income: £35,000 per annum from hall revenue income	Begin to repay loan with £25,000 per annum and later contribute income to church repairs
By year 3: Raise grants for church roof repair	Income: £250,000 grant income plus hall income of £35,000	£250,000 to church repairs £25,000 loan payment £10,000 to church running costs
Year 4: Establish maintenance programmes on church and hall using hall income		Repair the church roof
Year 5: Complete the roof repairs and continue to use hall income to pay off the loans		£10,000 to church revenue for repairs £25,000 for repair fund covering maintenance and future repairs
Ten years from the first loan, the capital is paid off, major grants can be raised for further works to the now well-maintained historic church.	Accumulating income for future work as well as covering maintenance costs	

Looking at a broad plan in this way can really make it clear to St Jude's that by using its resources carefully the church may be able to make the future rather better than the present.

Sometimes, the first steps are the hardest. For example, while the church hall is being repaired the church may be short of the £3,000 income with which it was temporarily scraping by. One solution is to let the church space to other church groups for a realistic – not a give-away – price. A well-looked-after church will get a good letting fee per hour even in a deprived area where other facilities may be less amenable. Many schools will make a contribution for the use of a church space that doubles as a school hall. In 2003, £25 per hour was a common figure. Many churches can earn £5,000 each year from sharing with other churches. As soon as the church is more comfortable financially it may revisit and review these choices and do differently.

So in making a decision about its assets the church is well advised to consider the *longer-term and SUSTAINABLE* and make that the context for short-term decisions. Once the church has established a long-term view it can then look at the short-term pressures as steps toward a sustainable future. In the short term, with the future well mapped out, the church can seek grant help towards repairs, get the hall into shape to earn income, and get church members to respect and appreciate their own financial contributions and consider ways they may help over the long haul, such as with a legacy.

Summary

Raising funds for repairs should be addressed with the long-term view of passing improved assets to future generations of the church, so they too can make decisions about how to use these assets to advance the gospel mission. In particular, the church will not dispose of its assets to meet pressing immediate needs. *We will take a considered view and endeavour to use our assets to provide effectively and efficiently for a sustainable future.*

Becoming entrepreneurial with assets and resources can enable us to find our way out of using only long-standing traditional styles of managing money and finding ways to collectively steward our assets in ways that adapt to contemporary financial culture. *But* it is wise to seek advice from appropriate professionals and assess all risks fully so that mitigating policies can be in place.

Postscript

One suburban church was offered £50,000 for a piece of land on which the diocese wanted to build a new vicarage. A commercial surveyor then valued the land at £750,000. The former would have been a helpful contribution to the church's development budget; the latter paid for the whole development.

Think laterally, and *if you are going to sell anything, land or buildings, get external valuations from a commercial surveyor*. Diocesan surveyors may not be up to date with the speed of change in the value of assets in every part of a large diocese, though they may be great in helping you with the processes.

5

People Give to People

Why do people give to charities, good causes or churches? Why might people inside and outside the church contribute to the church's fundraising programme?

Individuals give to a charitable organization because it will achieve their object – the object of the donor, usually one that the donor is not in a position to achieve themselves or on their own. When we consider in Chapter 15 funding contributions from government sources, we find that the object of the donor is a factor surrounded by terms and conditions on how that object should be fulfilled. But inherent even with that apparently impersonal process lies the same truth that we will unfold here that *People give to beneficiaries* and that the art of fundraising is all about *Relationships with donors*.

People give to beneficiaries

People give to those who benefit from charitable work. Donors are not very interested in the organization or the agency through whom the gift travels, except to determine its effectiveness, its efficiency and its appropriateness in delivering help.

In the world of big national and international charities, it is well known that published figures on the percentage of each donation that is spent on internal administration affects the numbers of people who give to that charity. If only 18 per cent of charitable giving is used in the charity office to pay staff, and other internal costs, then donors are more interested than if the charity uses 30 per cent of received donations on internal costs. Donors are trying to make a difference for the beneficiaries, not for the charity itself. So the significance lies in *how* the organization is going to help beneficiaries. Does it do the job well and in a way that is fitting to the context?

At the local level we find that although charities that receive donations often gain a personal allegiance from donors through mutual interest, even local donors would stop giving if they thought that little of their money was going to their targeted beneficiaries, whether it was a children's holiday scheme or a local hospice. They may well be aware, from local knowledge, whether the holiday really was fun or if the hospice is badly run. Churches seeking funds face the same questions. So your church, as the organization or charity that needs money, exists to meet the mutual needs of the donor and the beneficiary.

Nationally, in Britain, 40 per cent of people in the 55 to 70 age group already give regularly to charity. Many make standing orders and use Gift Aid. It is worth considering the members of the congregation who are in this age group – they have more disposable income than any other age group – so what is their pattern of giving? The church will not be able to fulfil all the charitable interests of these people, but it might do more than at present. But why might they give more and why might they think of a major gift towards the church's financial concerns.

> The Church of England collectively is the envy of the voluntary sector as its many members contribute £417 million each year through weekly committed giving.

Why people make a particular donation

Again in national reviews, it has been found that people choose to give to beneficiaries through a particular charity because they recognize and respect its name. For example, what springs to people's mind when the words 'Church of England' are mentioned? What associations does the name draw for outsiders? We all tend to hear from outsiders that the Church of England is well-to-do, run by the white middle class . . . and we do not hear of identifiable beneficiaries. Like most, your church has to think about how to improve its image and use its name effectively. It is possible in both published materials and information to give a very different impression of your church and effectively to change the image.

Is your church an easy name to use in fundraising? The name of a local church can have a very particular resonance for local people. 'My mum got married there', 'They did a really nice funeral for my grandmother', 'They are very active in caring for homeless people (or people with mental health problems . . .)'. In other words, there are very likely to be local church names that have good associations with clear beneficiaries, so that local people might become contributors. Notice how these perceptions are based on people as beneficiaries and on relationships already made, and this is the church's highest-value local link.

Churches of national heritage significance or even international significance may get particular grants that are not open to all churches. If your church's original architect was Wren or Hawksmoor or one of the fine Victorian architects it may gain some outside grants on that name alone. But regardless of name and significance, for major grants each church will have to show that its building is being well cared for, that it is open to those interested in heritage and that it will be passed on to future generations in good shape.

As mentioned above, the percentage of donations that is spent on the internal business of the organization rather than on the target benefit is also important. A charity such as Oxfam spends something like 18 per cent of its incoming donations on running its organization and the remaining 82 per cent goes to the beneficiaries. How does your church compare: running costs? religious activity? building repair? donations to others? Consider the proportion of the church budget that is spent on various aspects of mission and understand how to attribute them. After all, mission is the charitable purpose of the church.

On fundraising challenge events – running a marathon, abseiling down the tower, a sponsored walk, or a bunjee jump – people contribute to the runner/jumper and don't so much care which charity is going to benefit; people are committed to the brave soul who has a go. Get the church's most gregarious and popular people to run, jump or walk, especially those who work in companies that have lots of co-workers as potential sponsors. The bus driver who works from a major bus station, a pub landlord, a company receptionist. It is the church's task to win over the smaller group who will take up the challenge and let those who are doing the challenge gather their own sponsors from their circle of friends and acquaintances.

As the church progresses to thinking about promoting its fundraising outside the church circle, consider the *faces* that appeal on the publications. It is well known that the Royal National Lifeboat Institution uses the image of working lifeboatmen, as people also like to give to the heroes. Some of the people who deliver aid to the needy can be the 'heroes' of the church's promotion. Very seldom will a church figure such as the vicar appeal to people outside the church as a worthy beneficiary or 'hero' figure. So bear in mind that outside the immediate circle of your church the vicar may be neither a hero nor an attractive beneficiary; the dog-collared minister is not necessarily a good image in contemporary culture. Use a hero figure only if you have a natural one. And putting the photo of some of your beneficiaries into fundraising material can be a good move.

Many churches use a promotional photo of the church and its setting. It is extremely unlikely to generate donations *except* from people who have already made a relationship with the church or have a local interest in it as a place that meets a spiritual need, or as a potential location for a wedding or any additional service for which the church is already known in its community. Later in this book there is detail on planning the materials, but bear in mind that photos of people are more appealing.

Then, *how* you ask is important – *the more pressure and obligation you create the less people want to give.* The key to giving will be the quality of relationship people have with the church and its members, the quality of the project for which the church is fundraising and its beneficiaries in the eyes of both internal and external potential donors. Asking must be a simple unpressurizing request in a well-prepared relationship. *And* use the telephone only for saying thankyou. *Never* ask over the phone.

As the church prepares to communicate its fundraising project, list fully the beneficiaries of its work and mission and the benefit each receives. For example:

Sunday congregation	Opportunity to give to others Mutual support on the spiritual journey
Children	Grounding in faith in a Christian community context
Teenagers	Peer fellowship Targeted education and youth programmes
Elderly	Fellowship, friendship and support Extended Christian family
Passers-by	Streetscape, conservation and heritage value Drop-in help
Residents in the area	A brighter environment with occasional services
Tourists	Opportunity to appreciate and learn about the heritage of a living church in a historic building
Community groups	Meeting places Financial support Understanding

Task
Create your own table.

As the church considers outside grantmakers for its project, what are the key facts and images that will enable outsiders to see the effect of their grant on *their* target beneficiaries?

English Heritage	Church and members of the general public having access to the national heritage
Government-sponsored Regeneration Board	Disadvantaged residents of your neighbourhood gaining support, training and education
Grantmaking Trusts	Access for disabled people Preservation of architectural heritage Provision for disadvantaged people Tackling social exclusion

Directly or indirectly, always include information on the people who already benefit from the church's work as well as those who will benefit in the future. Don't just say lots or many – use actual numbers as far as possible, so remember to keep records of services (in the usual service book) but also keep records of types of groups and of numbers of people in each meeting and event in the church, hall or other facilities. There is more detail in later chapters of this book on making applications.

Fundraising relationships

In the general world of fundraisers it is considered that 10 per cent of the work is the preparation for fundraising, 80 per cent is making and developing relationships and 10 per cent is asking.

Giving money to a good cause is about relationships not transactions. Imagine the church members, and what comes to mind will be faces, feelings, commitments, families, moods and lots of other human qualities. You will not first think of church members as donors making a weekly transaction with your church, *even though* if the church were to add up the lifetime value of someone who contributes £5 each week the total would be a considerable level of giving. Long-standing members of the church give money because of their relationship; they love the church, its mission, its building, its spiritual life, its history and its people. Both members and close neighbours give because they have common aims and objectives and they enjoy working with the church as friends.

Local people, residents, workers and visitors give because they think the church has a particular place in their neighbourhood. Maybe they like a bargain and maybe the church is offering one. The church matters to their environment and quality of life, either because of the quality of the building, or the contribution it makes to local life. You will be able to come up with a list of other ways in which local people have a relationship with the church that may be important to them.

Outside agencies give money because they have come to know the church well enough to know that it will achieve their objectives if they give the church money.

> **Task**
> Make a list of the various elements, Capital or Revenue, for which the church needs to raise funds. Against this list note people or organizations who might have a personal commitment to that element.

Stained-glass repairs	The Glaziers Trust – as they have cared for fine glass for centuries
Sunday school	Parents and grandparents of pupils and potential pupils
Mental health project	Individuals who have mental illness in their families, or trusts and agencies who want to help those with mental health problems
New vestments	Worshippers in your church
Spire repairs	Local people who can see the spire from their windows or who may be at risk if it falls
Churchyard improvements	Environment and nature groups locally Local authority Heritage Lottery Fund
New chairs	Those regular and occasional church attendees who have to sit on them

While such an exercise can be quite amusing, it is the first step towards developing a unique fundraising strategy. It also leads to some interesting ways to raise quite large sums of money. Individuals or families or even members of a music group that rehearses in the church for an occasional concert may each be prepared to sponsor an element of the church project.

When churches begin to look for outside agencies as sources of money, it is critical that they understand the agencies and their objectives. Think out carefully how, in achieving the church's target, it will be achieving the potential funder's target. If there is a common objective then the church may be able to build a partnership! For example,

- In preserving our common heritage
- In protecting and conserving a heritage building
- In providing community programmes for local people
- In providing meeting and event space for local people
- In providing programmes of arts and culture for local people
- In providing space for much needed local neighbourhood programmes

Maintaining relationships internally throughout fundraising

It is common and probably advisable for a small executive group of people to create the fundraising strategy, to put together action plans and to head up new initiatives. But it is extremely important to keep all church members engaged in and owning the process. So the fundraising group needs members who are financially minded but also those who are involved in relating to all members of the congregation and will know whether the fundraising group's communications are really getting through to everyone.

The working group should summarize the fundraising strategy in writing and then present it to all the church members, engaging them in aspects of work, in developing new avenues such as local fundraising and identifying how they may help in the overall scheme, perhaps by offering time or skills or money. Above all, use those with leadership skills to keep the whole church pulling in the same direction. The efforts to raise funds externally will be relatively ineffective without the wholehearted support of the church.

Build in a programme for updating people, even celebrating major milestones towards the target as a way of re-energizing people; collect new ideas as you go along. Set out a plan in which everyone knows when and how they can contribute. Nothing brings people together as well as a common challenge or a common enemy. The effort can then be reported and appreciated in a funding newsletter. Use photos as well as reports, so people can feel appreciated for what they have done (more on this in Chapter 10). As outside funders visit and consider whether to help the church, they will assimilate the overall enthusiasm and commitment and be more interested in helping.

Outside funders, including grantmaking trusts and local authorities, should receive regular written reports and the church's fundraising newsletter. Keep all contributors in the picture, so loyalty is maintained, and invite everyone who has contributed to a celebratory event when the project is achieved. Look carefully at how relationships are needed to achieve results, and how relationships will be built through involvement in this challenge of fundraising. These will be friendships that will last into the future. Then invest time carefully.

General appeals and relationships

If the church's members, friends and previous donors are giving generously and sacrificially, then it may be time to consider a general appeal.

It is widely accepted among fundraisers that a general public appeal ought not to start until the organization has reached 60 per cent of the target sum. Consider the fundraising project: What will the fund purchase and for whom? Is this something that passers-by, local residents and local businesses would recognize and be attracted to?

First, the project is going to be a success (if the church already has 60 per cent, it is a 'winner'), so it will not be embarrassing for local people to be identified with the project. People like to be part of success. Yet even the nicest passers-by do not give randomly. How many volunteers can the church muster to become the 'face' of the project, to ask for contributions? What is the strap-line (the message in a few key words) that will catch their attention? Does the church have a catchy message for them? Relate that phrase to what their target beneficiaries might be. Think of the church's beneficiaries and what might appeal to local people about them. 'Providing for churchgoers' sounds like self-interest, not local interest, but 'providing for the children of the future' or 'protecting our village's heritage' may well appeal to local people. When you have explored every kind of potential donor – individual or group – you will be able to set some priorities and plan your preparation.

Priorities

Insiders – members and church council – are targeted as donors, regardless of how much they can give. Lead from inside.

Next, determine where the big donations are most likely to come from. These are the targets for the most skilled, most careful, most considered attention. Each of these targets merits an appropriate amount of time from the church's best communicators and planners. If an application form will take two people a week to plan and write, but might contribute £500,000, every hour is well invested. A jumble sale that will bring in lots of goodwill but less than £1,000 does not justify the same time investment from the most skilled fundraising people. From the relationship or mission point of view the visitors to the jumble sale are extremely important, but they do not need the fundraiser's time. If she or he can spend the same amount of time raising tens of thousands then that is the work on which that person should focus.

Work your way through each and every diagram in Chapter 6, making a note of how each and every relationship will be developed, and how each donor will be encouraged to give again and give more and more consistently.

Identify potential sources of big grants and donations with whom the church has no contact and begin to plan how you will make your initial contact, that is a relationship-building contact. In these cases start with the language, messages and targets that those potential donors want to hear. Later chapters of this book cover communication with specific target donors and their objectives.

Gradually the ideas and targets will turn into a systematic action plan of things to be done, people to see and letters to write. That plan will always begin with the people already most committed to the church. (See Appendix 1, 'Communicating with potential donors'.)

Key points

Know precisely what you need to achieve, why, how, when and how much:
- for yourselves
- for local people
- for people in need
- for outside agencies and funders.

6

Setting Your Church's Unique Fundraising Strategy

All churches' needs, locations and relationships are different, so each church has a unique fundraising strategy.

We can imagine the church to be like rings around the sun, as in Figure 6.1. Those who are warmest to your cause (the centre circle) and the most likely to contribute to your church are your parochial church council and electoral roll members. Many are already very committed donors. Many are members of stewardship schemes and volunteer for work as sidespeople, gardeners and stall-holders at the Christmas fair; they clean, arrange flowers and look after children. In the long-term view of the church you will never get donors that are more committed.

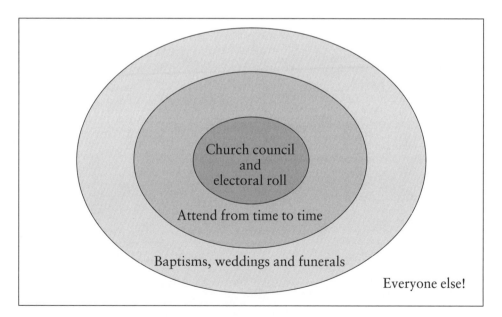

Figure 6.1 Targeting and developing potential donations and grants

The second circle (middle circle) are the church's less committed people. Perhaps they give when they attend church, but not when they are not there, and they don't attend every Sunday. They help on work tasks when the sun shines or when something else is not happening. But they are valued.

The outer circle is people who contribute occasionally when they need the church or when an event attracts them. They may attend church for a wedding or baptism or enjoy church jumble sales and church fairs. The church cannot really count on them, but they make a valuable contribution from time to time.

Outside of these are all the other people in the world. They have no particular connection to the church and no history of giving to it.

This descriptive model is used in other ways too. When we are considering evangelism, we might see the central circle as really committed disciples who take responsibility for the church. The next circle enjoy being involved, but if the central circle do not organize and make the event happen then this circle will not do it either. And the outer circle might be sorry that the church has disappeared but soon replace it with something else – kind of fair-weather friends (see Figure 6.2).

When we tackle fundraising we use the same set of circles and spread them out a little. This will help us to understand an aspect of fundraising. That is, that *people who have already given before are more likely to give again.* They have already made their first decision to give – the church has attracted them as

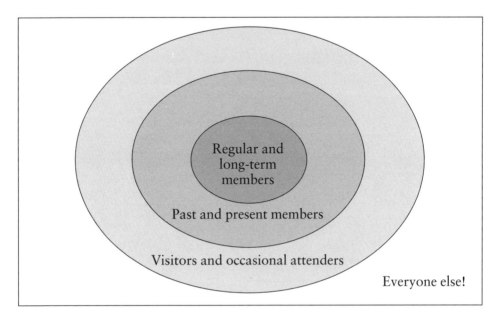

Figure 6.2 People who have given in past years are the most likely to give now

committed or occasional donors. They are much, much more likely to make a donation to an appeal than people who have never been interested in the past. As people get more involved and committed they will give sacrificially. This is illustrated by separating the circles and stacking them up (see Figure 6.3).

The top circle is those who 'own' the project; they work hard and give sacrificially. The church can depend on their contribution.

The second circle is those who give time and money when they have leadership that carries them forward. The church is fairly sure that if it gets the message right these people will contribute, but not to the same sacrificial level.

The third circle give something if the church project achieves something for them, whether it is fun, prizes, a better environment or another personal objective. They give as a one-off decision but are interested in what the church achieves; they may or may not give again.

And the fourth circle is those people who have never given. They are clearly the hardest group to interest in giving to the church.

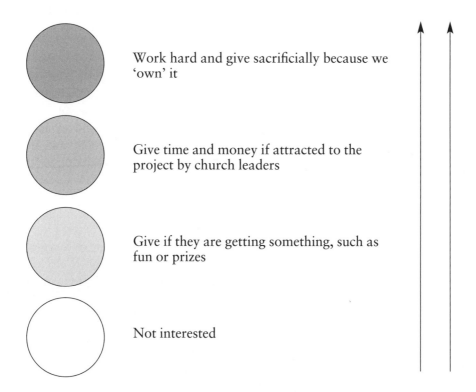

Figure 6.3 Turn each kind of donor into a more committed donor

As fundraisers it is our job to get people to move up the circles, to move from never giving to a one-off gift, then to get the one-off people to give again and a larger contribution. To get those who gave when others provided the leadership to become the pace-setters and become people who make sacrifices and will go on giving. When we consider grantmaking trusts we may want to move them into the circle of giving for the first time. If trusts have made grants before, they are ideal targets in the first round of trust fundraising.

So when we set out on a new project needing a new fundraising strategy we look first to understand ourselves, our friends, our past contributors and then everyone else. It is a mistake – even if the church has to find a million pounds for major church repairs – not to ask the regular and committed donors to contribute first. They are the church's 'owners' and will give leadership to others. The size of the donation will fit their circumstances, but they want to give sacrificially; they expect it of themselves. After all why should unknown outsiders, even if they are rich individuals or major grantmakers, give of their hard-earned funds if the church members do not set the example themselves?

Our second task is to identify who, other than churchgoers, might go from a lower circle to a higher circle. Then, thirdly, we will identify those who have never given before but who might move to a contribution now.

A new donor sent £10 to a major charity who replied with a polite form letter saying 'thankyou'. Within days a larger donation was sent and the donor received a letter that was specially written. Then came a new larger donation and a personal thank-you letter was sent by the director. After a subsequent extremely large donation, the donor was invited to the HQ for a personal thankyou, and to meet staff and beneficiaries of the charity's work. A lifetime generous supporter was born; caring for the relationship – understanding the *person* who gives – was critical. There are trusts who operate the same kind of system. Never forget the relationship and how to maintain it (and see Chapter 13).

There are many potential sources of funds. Each of the groups and types of donation shown in Figures 6.4 and 6.5 needs to be explored. Who is already a committed donor? Who has given before – is already warm? And who is outside but might be interested?

We can look at the potential donor groups one by one. Photocopy these pages for your church so that the fundraising team can consider each of these carefully. And fill in the church's actual details so that the fundraising group can map out the action plan fully. Keep your worked examples so that as you work through successive chapters you may add more ideas of your church's specific targets.

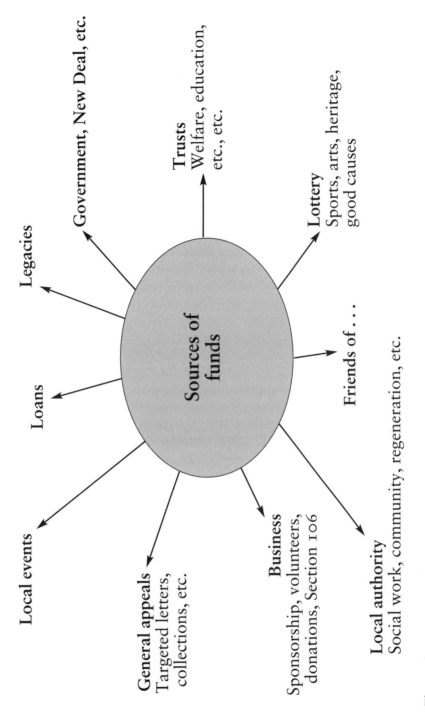

Sources of funds

Government, New Deal, etc.

Trusts
Welfare, education, etc., etc.

Legacies

Lottery
Sports, arts, heritage, good causes

Loans

Friends of . . .

Local events

General appeals
Targeted letters, collections, etc.

Business
Sponsorship, volunteers, donations, Section 106

Local authority
Social work, community, regeneration, etc.

Figure 6.4

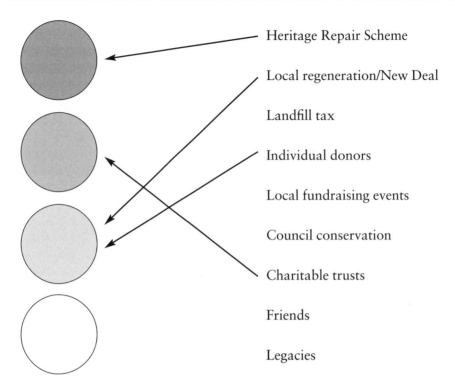

Heritage Repair Scheme

Local regeneration/New Deal

Landfill tax

Individual donors

Local fundraising events

Council conservation

Charitable trusts

Friends

Legacies

Use arrows to identify your most committed partners

Figure 6.5

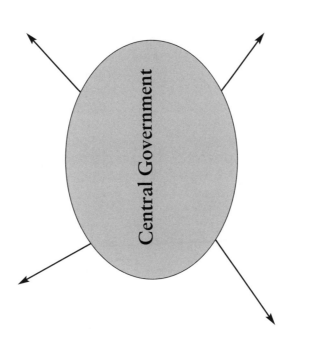

Identify your connections

Central Government

Use RED for existing and BLUE for potential

Figure 6.6

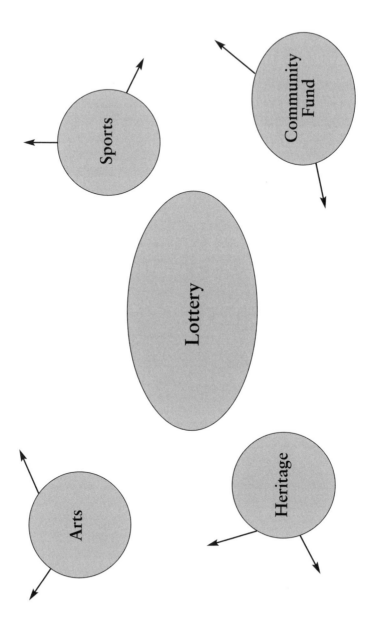

Figure 6.7

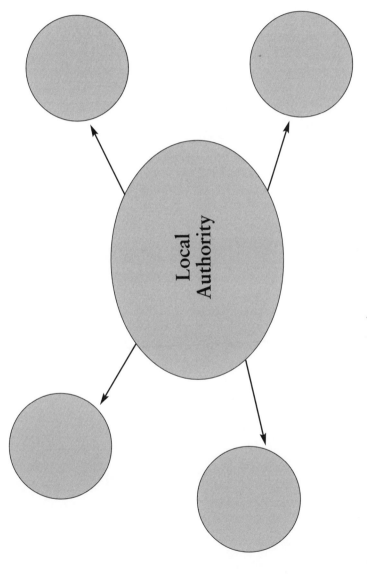

Identify departments you have contact with in RED
Departments you see as potential in BLUE

Figure 6.8

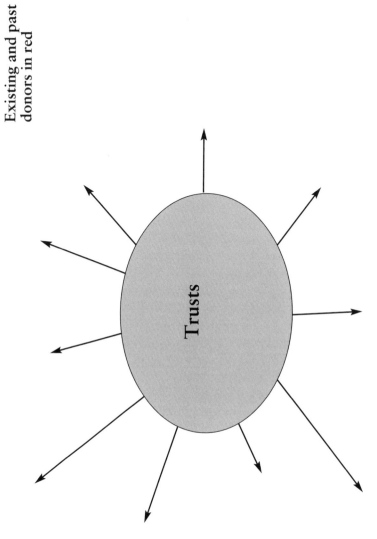

Existing and past donors in red

Potential new donors in blue

Trusts

Figure 6.9

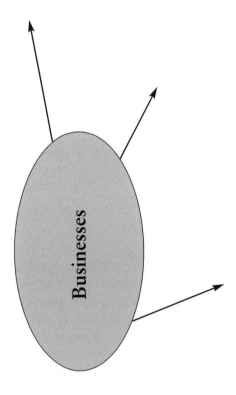

Potential links and contacts for building a relationship

Businesses

Figure 6.10

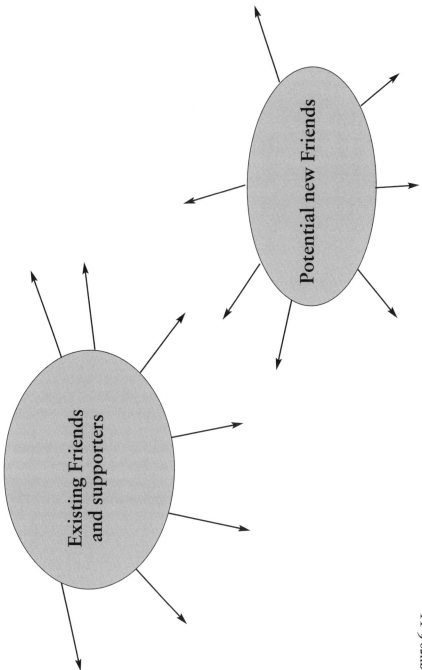

Figure 6.11

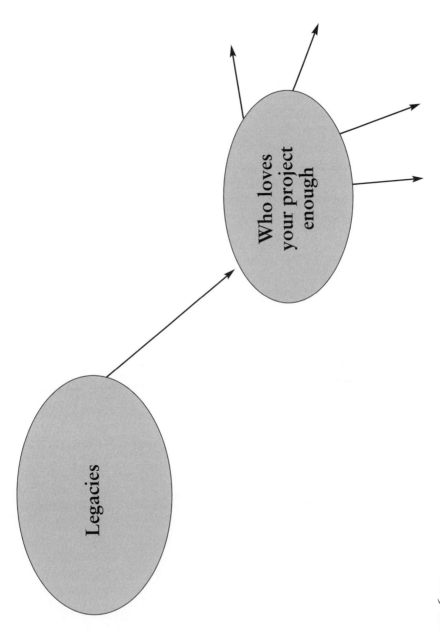

Figure 6.12

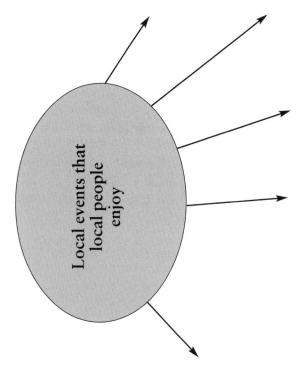

Figure 6.13

What does a worked-out plan look like in practice? Figure 6.1 gave the example from one London church that explored each of the groups of people who were beneficiaries of the church's work. Appendix 2 shows the example of another church that explored each of its target groups and decided what action might bring each closer to becoming donors. These became an action plan with names against each group indicating which members of the fundraising group were going to take the contact forward.

One year later the same church had progressed the work on several fronts and employed a part-time fundraiser who first summarized with the group what had been achieved (nearly £200,000 of the first £330,000 phase of works).[8]

Overall purpose

> We will provide a sustainable future for the Church of St Augustine in its liturgical and pastoral ministry, and its service to the parish and wider community.

Review of the current position

Strengths	Weaknesses
Large congregation with good fundraising track record Large network of contacts through school, Anglo-Catholic circles, lovers of Victorian architecture, etc. £95,000 already in the bank Grant offer of £120,000 from Joint Repair Scheme £5,000 to pay for fundraiser Strong patrons	Worsening condition of south aisle subsidence damage Cost of works to remove asbestos from the organ has eaten into the funds
Opportunities	Threats
Archdeacon's committee likely to offer funding Historic Churches Preservation Trust likely to offer funding	No large community projects – this is principally a Christian/heritage cause Currently not eligible for Lottery funding

[8] Courtesy of Giles Semper and St Augustine's Church.

Fundraising purpose

We will raise £1.5 million to cover the restoration, cleaning and conservation needs of the church over the next five years, together with some new works. All the relevant works are listed in the Quantity Surveyor's Indicative Budget.

Values

- We believe that the repair of the fabric of our church is achieved to glorify God and enhance our worship.

- We will try to ensure that as many of the general public as possible have access to the building, during and after renovation works.

- We will not allow congregational giving to the appeal to detract from regular Christian stewardship.

- We will make it our policy to thank everyone who gives to the appeal.

- We will seek to give credit – to all those who give or fundraise significant amounts.

Strategic aims and objectives

We will establish a base and an identity for the whole appeal – in both its private and its public phases:

- design a relevant and attractive logo and strapline
- design and produce appeal stationery
- create the appeal office
- appoint an appeal president
- appoint appeal patrons
- strengthen and resource the restoration group so that it becomes the engine of the appeal work.

We will seek up to 50 per cent of the money from grant funding, from both private and public sources, i.e. trusts, corporates, national heritage funding, local regeneration funding. We shall

- undertake careful research into the most likely grant funders
- explore personal connections and other routes into these funders
- approach relevant funders using their guidelines and our contacts.

We will seek to raise the remaining 50 per cent from public appeal. We shall

- identify audiences with personal experience of St Augustine's
- seek to understand why each of these audiences is likely to give.

We will produce a plan showing how each audience will be reached:

- create a website
- develop targeted mailings
- press and PR campaign
- create a simple set of incentives towards individual giving and individual fundraising
- buy-a-brick campaign
- make it easy for audiences to make their donations
- create a facility for credit card transactions
- standing orders to be established
- freepost facility
- charity card donation facility
- payroll giving
- collecting tins
- run a legacy campaign
- run a programme of fundraising events and other community fundraising initiatives such as raffles and fairs.

Action Plan for 2002

2002	Action
July	• write all fundraising materials • commission design and print • finish first applications to archdeacon's committee and Historic Churches Preservation Trust
August	• fundraising materials go to press • website goes live • letters go to trusts and corporates
September	• PR and press campaign • mailings to individuals
October	• service at church to launch appeal
November	• major donors event
December	

Key points

Identify each of the church's key donors at present, potential donors already known and complete strangers. Set an action plan for contacting each of them.

7

The Language of Fundraising

People will give to beneficiaries through a church or community project. They have a choice about whether to give the church money. In the end they do so because they believe the church will spend the money well and they trust the church to spend their money the way they agreed with the church that it would be spent. *But*, first the church has to apply to them in ways that the funders understand, indicating that the church fits in with their language and culture and will be spending the money in accordance with the funders' guidelines.

Some of what the church will need to include will seem like empty 'political correctness' but it is seldom that. What may be blatantly clear to the church will be unknown to the outside funder, and the church will need to state the obvious. For example, the church will need to state that it applies equal opportunities to people of all backgrounds and sorts. It is not just that churches have a patchy reputation of racism and sexism – every organization has to openly practice equality and be seen to be offering equality.

Similarly, the church will be asked how it monitors and reviews its work. This is to ensure that the church continues to fulfil its purpose, and if it never reviews the objectives of the church at all, how can outside funders be sure the church is still focused and doing good work?

This is not the usual language of churches, but it is the language of fundraising. There are several aspects of the language and culture of funders that are common to all outside funders; some aspects are more specialized. Getting familiar with potential funders through handbooks and other sources will give a clearer idea of what is needed in communicating with them, and this book will also tell you a great deal about how to communicate, and includes many examples. For some funders, as with regeneration projects, the only way to understand in detail will be to attend the meetings locally and read all the paperwork that regeneration boards produce.

See Figure 7.1 for an idea of some of the grant sectors and the languages with which you should become familiar. How do you start to communicate to the funders in the language and culture they understand?

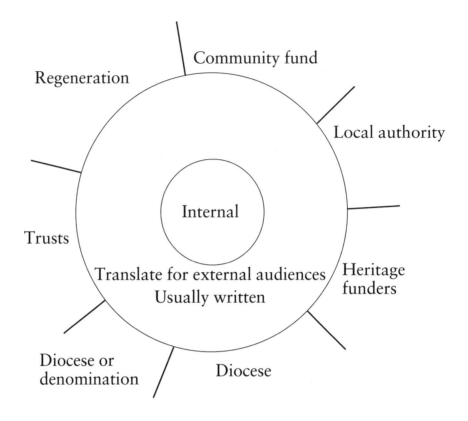

Figure 7.1

First note the church's target beneficiaries and list how it will meet their needs. There may be many different kinds of beneficiaries; list them all. Do these beneficiaries and targets correspond with any of the trusts and funders that were identified in earlier chapters? For example, the Main Grants Programme of the Heritage Lottery Fund targets heritage projects that offer increased access to heritage, education and new audiences to heritage. It is quite a disciplined way of thinking that translates what the church does and what it wants to do in the future into a particular language framework. If the project is really not going to benefit those targeted in the funder's objectives, however worthy the cause, it is not worth applying.

Trustworthy

So what is it in the church's communication to potential donors that shows that the church can be trusted to deliver the project? The answer is not in passionate declaration of worthiness but in quantifiable facts.

Every outside funder will ask to see the annual accounts, sometimes two or three years of accounts. Every church or charity is required to produce an annual report and accounts for the Charity Commissioners. These affirm the charity's basic credibility – that it has fulfilled its purposes to date. Church of England parish churches are required to send their annual report and accounts to their diocese as each local church is registered as an *excepted charity*;* this means it is counted as a charity by the Charity Commissioners but does not have an individual charity registration number (though increasingly churches are being required to register individually). Within the whole charity sector the annual returns are the first evidence of trustworthiness.

Is the project *needed*? How will the church show this to outside funders? If the church wants to help homeless people then it will need actual evidence that homelessness is a problem in the area. Give the statistics and show the demand is there. (See 'Resources and Connections' for the web address for local statistics on need.) Similarly, if the church wants to repair the building it will be expected to produce a professional assessment that identifies the need and the urgency of the repair – summed up in a quinquennial inspection report or something similar.

Evidence that the project is *justified* may be shown by the church setting up the only project for homeless people in the neighbourhood. If there are already several such projects – despite the statistics – the project may not be justified. If the church is asking for a major grant for building repairs but cannot show it is doing a reasonable job with regular maintenance and repairs, the project is not justified. The latter is shown from your accounts and annual report, and from the churchwardens' report on the building fabric.

The project must be *appropriate* to the problem and the context. For community-work projects, compare the way the church delivers its provision with similar projects elsewhere. Is the church providing a service that suits the needs and uses the best ways to deliver help? Neither too large and undersubscribed nor too small to be financially realistic? In later chapters the appropriateness of repairs to listed buildings is considered with statements of need and statements of significance (see Appendix 7); these are entirely about appropriateness.

Then the church will need to show the project is *viable*. The evidence for this is in the projected cashflow and budgets. For the community project, the church will need to show that it has sufficient income to run the project well (when the requested grant is included). For the building project the church will need to produce budgets and cashflow projections to show that once the building is repaired it will continue to be maintained. The more money asked from a funder, the more the church will need to submit evidence of viability through its financial projections.

If all the above are acceptable, then the question that enables the funder to select good projects to fund is about the church's effectiveness and efficiency. *Effectiveness* is shown by numbers of people for whom the project achieves the benefit targeted. That is, numbers of actual homes for homeless people; numbers of people counselled; numbers of local people who have actually visited the building; numbers of job trainees actually leaving the project and getting jobs. Funders dislike projects that create dependence, such as a job training project that gives IT training for 12 people at a time, but at the end of the year still has the same 12: this tells them that the project has not been effectively training its clients. Much of the information on this aspect will be evident in a well-produced annual report and accounts that include numbers appropriately. A new project will give target numbers, but over the first year or two will be closely scrutinized as to whether it is achieving those targets.

The church's *efficiency* will be compared to other projects. The cost per beneficiary must be comparable to other similar projects. The number of beneficiaries combined with the annual cost tells this. If the project is expensive in comparison, is there a straightforward and acceptable reason? The same question will apply to church repairs – being much cheaper or more expensive than other similar buildings for similar work will be questioned. This is particularly relevant to common factors in church.

Especially for community projects the church should show it is well managed by sector standards. The policies and practices of management are evidence of this. Health and Safety, child protection, staff safety, and other aspects are evidence of good management. Similarly, the project should fit well into the premises and location. A children's project is not adjacent to a drug project. A pensioner project is adjacent to good bus links and so on. Again the project should fit with the demography of the area; that this is not a homeless project where there are no homeless people. Then the project must ensure that staff are professionally qualified to do the job well. On this point, a building project must be led by a suitably qualified professional, and their names and details should be included. Even when volunteers undertake maintenance and repair work it should be clear they are getting professional advice before working on a heritage building to ensure that materials and workmanship are of an acceptable standard.

The community project or the church must be seen to be sustainable. Will the grant/donation be a good investment? Is there a good return for the beneficiaries? Will the project be well maintained, well run and develop constructively over the coming years? The church's and staff's past record will tell. It would be hard for example for a potential funder to be sure the church will maintain its building if it has failed to do so in recent years.

What does the church have planned for the next five years or ten years? Is the long-term strategy well founded? Is there evidence that good delivery can continue to be assured? The answer is partly in the quality of the management committee and the church council. Include the professional skills of the church council members, so that outsiders can see that the church has the requisite management skills to maintain good delivery. See Chapter 20, p. 182 for an example.

More and more funders are asking organizations to produce a Risk Assessment. This is designed to look at the potential for failure and address the risk of failure by setting up a strategy to prevent the failure happening. (For more detail, see Chapter 20 and Appendix 15.) Charity Law now requires that all charities with an annual turnover of more than £100,000 produce a risk assessment, and churches should also be doing that.

When contacting outside organizations remember too that the language of the church may not describe the project to the church's best advantage (see Figure 7.2). Members and churchgoers may know what a vicar, churchwarden or archdeacon is – but who else will understand if they are outside the church circle? So consider some other words. If asked about the management committee, don't say 'we don't have one'; the church does have one, but it's called the church council.

Translate your language as necessary

White	Black-majority
Anglican	Faith group
Church of England	Voluntary sector
Parish	Local initiative
Tradition	User-led
Mission	Purpose
Vicar	Aims
PCC	Chair of management
	Neighbourhood project
	Partnership
	Management Committee
	Trustees

Figure 7.2

Key points

- Understand each of the audiences and individuals to whom you need to speak.
- Learn how to speak to each of them in the language with which they are familiar, both the words and the concepts.
- Learn from other local groups in the voluntary sector.

8

Giving Begins with Us!
The Church's Warmest Audience

Giving money is about relationships and goodwill – not transactions. Think of your own church members: their faces, their smiles, feelings, commitments, families and moods. It is not a picture of them primarily as donors making a weekly financial contribution to the church; yet they do, and most are major donors.

Discipleship includes giving. Taking adult responsibility to each and every member, even considering the priesthood of all believers, means fundamentally that we are equally responsible for being the church. So we choose to give of our own resources – time, skills and money – to fulfil our responsibility. We will not have a mature church if we do not take seriously the need of all our members to play their part as adults in their commitment and their giving. The lesson of the widow's coins in the Gospel is not that she is poor and need not have given, rather it is that even though poor she gave sacrificially.

Most churches have a tradition of tithing. In recent centuries in the Church of England this was overtaken by historic endowments. More recently these endowments have proved insufficient to pay for mission and ministry in contemporary life. A new phase of tithing and sacrificial giving is needed, and this may actually result in more focused Christian discipleship.

Yet church history has many stories of generous donors making gifts and leaving legacies for the ministry of the church. In the fourteenth century, Mr Tavie left a bequest to St Andrew's Church, Holborn. The money was invested and income used for maintaining the church building for successive generations. Wisely invested capital still produces sufficient income for building maintenance and assistant staff. Several later benefactors left sums of money that were invested for the income to be used to make donations to the poor of the parish. Eight charities under the umbrella of St Andrew's Church still make donations and provide pensions for the poor of the area. Today's discipleship in giving may further the church's ministry in the future, through legacies that create endowment funds and committed giving that funds current mission and ministry.

Stewardship in churches

Church stewardship programmes are about giving systematically, regularly and in a committed way to the church to which we belong and which therefore we value. Without a system to which we are committed, our giving will tend to be haphazard or impulsive, and we will normally only give when we are attending church. A stewardship programme encourages us to be more consistent.

Many churches are viable financially because they have developed a culture of stewardship. In all traditions, from evangelical (where such a culture has commonly had a higher profile) to Anglo-Catholic, churches that develop an ongoing regular and systematic approach to stewardship are financially more stable and more viable.

Key aspects of the culture requiring planned activity are: annual thanks to everyone who has been giving in a committed programme; an annual review of progress over the year with planning for the year to come; and an annual presentation to the church. These more specific events are reinforced throughout the year.[9] The more a church creates an atmosphere of thanksgiving, responsibility and generosity about money the less that congregation will be plagued by financial problems.

The culture of planned giving

'Thank you for your generosity' is an uncommon phrase in our churches. Speaking to the church and affirming the importance of their giving, explaining what their gifts have paid for and offering the opportunity for a new commitment will bring a positive response. If church leaders only mention money when it has become a problem they easily adopt a threatening or pushy approach which has regularly been proven to be counterproductive.

An annual letter can be sent to each person on the committed giving programme. (See outline opposite.)

Clearly, each letter will be personally prepared and signed, not duplicated, though most of the content is common to all.

Regular information rather than the occasional financial bombshell keeps everyone alert to the financial situation. Information channels that are common to the church can be used to keep the finances open and known. As awareness grows, individuals will more easily consider the situation in terms of 'What can I

---

[9] Notes on a Culture of Stewardship were given by Larry Bain, Stewardship and Resources Officer in the Anglican Diocese of Southwark, and Finance Advisers in the Anglican Diocese of London.

Annual letter to members who undertake committed giving:

Thank you . . .
You promised . . .
You gave . . .
We did . . . (highlights)
We want to do . . . (plans)
Vision . . . (we are)
New promise for the year ahead . . . (up or down)
Thanks again! . . .

do to help and to what will I commit myself?' It is helpful to include stewardship information in a variety of ways throughout the church's communication material.

Approaching potential committed givers
- Welcome packs for new members include information on how the church is financed.
- Welcome events from time to time include the same information.
- Enquiry leaflets and cards inform potential members.
- The stewardship officer of the church is identified, perhaps by a photo on the noticeboard but also by personal introduction at times throughout the year.

Include stewardship in every aspect of the church's life. How the church receives donations and the respect and affirmation afforded the donor will have enormous impact on future giving. A major donation that is publicly appreciated (even if anonymously) will bring more donations. As the church considers many teachings of Jesus on the subject of money it will find many ways to appreciate this financial discipleship in its spirituality and its liturgy. Consider how the church takes up the collection. Is it carried forward in sight of the congregation and offered to God with a prayer or is it simply tucked away till it is counted after the service? The former will increase generosity and be part of openness about the place of stewardship in Christian discipleship.

Modelling the place of money in our spirituality
- Watch what you say
- Watch what you write
- Watch what you do
- Consider whether you are doing enough.

There are plenty of opportunities in the Common Lectionary for preaching on money, discipleship and committed giving. Doing so regularly will enable everyone to reconsider their giving to the church, away from the pressure of the annual renewal programme.

A Church of England leaflet on 'Christian Giving at your Local Church'[10] includes lots of biblical references that encourage giving.

2 Corinthians 8.9	1 Corinthians 16.1, 2
Matthew 10.8	2 Corinthians 8.12
Luke 10.36, 37	Deuteronomy 16.17
Ephesians 2.10	2 Corinthians 9.8
2 Corinthians 8.7	Deuteronomy 14.22–9
Haggai 2.8, 9	1 Chronicles 29.10–13
Malachi 3.10	Matthew 6.19–21
Luke 16.10–13	2 Corinthians 8.14, 15
2 Corinthians 9.10	2 Corinthians 9.11, 12

The same leaflet, which could be circulated at the annual renewal of stewardship, includes a ready reckoner on percentages of various income levels and fill-in boxes on levels of giving. (It should be extended to include a church's particular funding information, Gift Aid and standing order forms.)

Preaching about money and wealth
- When you don't want any money
- Be led by the lectionary/Spirit
- Two-thirds of Jesus' parables address money and its place in discipleship.

On any particular day, whether a Sunday service or a weekday event, most churches have one-off visitors or people who attend on an irregular basis. Many are happy to contribute financially. Use the weekly notice sheet to give basic information on giving, so newcomers know how to get involved.

It is becoming more common for small envelopes printed with Gift Aid forms to be handed out with the service sheet. Leave some cheap biros in the pews so people can fill in the box even if they didn't bring a pen. Ensure the explanation on how to give is straightforward and clear to outsiders (test the wording on non-churchgoers to check). If possible give brief up-to-date information with the envelope – a leaflet maybe – that will encourage people to put more than the minimum inside. Most will put a £5 or £10 note in the envelope, but if they are told how £25 or larger gifts will be spent the church may receive a larger gift. The general truth is that what people see others doing is what they do themselves.

[10] Published in 2002 by Birmingham Diocesan Stewardship Adviser, Canon Jim Pendorf.

The large plastic money collecting chests by cathedral doors are always littered with £1 coins, £5 and £10 notes, so that's what people post in through the top. If cathedrals could find a way to model much larger donations, many people would be far more generous.

> **Helping the 'one-off' donor**
> • How easy is it to understand and to give?
> • Where is information on where the money goes?
> • Where are the one-off envelopes?
> • Can I borrow your pen?

Cash in envelopes has several shortcomings in the fundraising church. It takes time for the donor to find the right change before bringing the envelope. It takes more time to count, record and bank. Most people carry very little cash in their pockets or bags for more than small one-off gifts, and certainly very few now regularly carry chequebooks. People are used to more mechanized systems. Churches are beginning to use systems that enable individual churches to receive credit card payments. (The Charities Aid Foundation runs a credit card scheme that registered charities and churches can use. Note that Anglican churches who do not have individual charity registration numbers can have a credit card account with Charities Aid Foundation.[11]) This will allow donors – one-off or regular – to fill in a credit card payment form as well as Gift Aid information on the donation envelope. Once received in the offertory the church will send these to the agency (such as Charities Aid Foundation) and transfer the cash value back to the church's account. Donations can thus be of higher value than present systems encourage. A similar service is increasingly being offered to charities for receiving Internet payments through secure links from a webpage or email.

For week-by-week stewardship, many churches now encourage Standing Orders, distributing new Standing Order forms each year with the stewardship renewal programme. (If new forms are not distributed then old standing orders may continue at a lower donation level than if updated.)

> **Standing Orders**
> • Maintain regular giving
> • Help the book-keeper
> • Reduce the cash for banking.
> Issue cards to maintain liturgical symbolism and to avoid embarrassment.
> Issue bank details to other donors of one-off special gifts.

[11] See 'Resources and Connections', p. 267, for contact details for the Charities Aid Foundation.

Since the money is received relatively invisibly the participation in the liturgical ritual of putting an envelope or cash in the plate is gone. There is a resultant loss of participation in the sacramental action. Similarly the occasional visitor may see a regular member putting nothing in the collection plate and will follow the example. To counter these issues churches encouraging Standing Orders are beginning to give regular Standing Order donors envelope-sized cards to put in the plate as it circulates.

St Jude's Church

I contribute to St Jude's Church through making regular payments from my bank. I thank God for the opportunity to contribute to the life and well-being of the church and its mission to our neighbourhood.

The annual stewardship programme renewal

A well-prepared programme annually will generate additional commitment and generosity. Involve members of the church council in the personal collection of commitment cards and slips, as this will add to both affirmation and efficiency in seeing everyone. Setting up the programme in the autumn will encourage new contributions to begin for the new financial year in January.

Suggested programme

- The clergy and church council prepare the programme, and agree new leaflets, such as in Appendix 3, and action plans.
- The presentation to the church is planned. A well-respected lay person is often the best presenter as they 'model' a committed discipline of giving. Clergy can represent a confused imagery as 'recipients' of the money – even though they don't receive it for themselves.
- Prepare and send the thankyou letters for the past year's committed giving.
- Prepare lists of all regular worshippers. Allocate a list of names to each church council member so that person may follow up the responses to the letter from those on their list.
- Draft and agree letters (see below).
- Prepare letters entering names and signatures *by hand* and addressing envelopes individually. Enclose either a reply card or a response slip. Enclose a legacy leaflet. Enclose a stamped addressed envelope.

- Make the presentation.

- Mail the letters and collect the response cards or slips.

- Three weeks later check with all members of the church council on responses received from people on their lists. Agree to chase up non-responders by sending a second letter.

- Continue to preach about money if there are relevant readings in the lectionary.

- Debrief with the church council. Ask each collector for their comments and ask the treasurer to give results. Review, noting changes and additions for the programme for next year.

- Thanksgiving at church services, report on the success and level of commitments – congratulate and thank everyone.

Sample first letter to congregation members:

[individual name]

We are writing to everyone who is a regular worshipper at St ———— and to whom our church means so much. We do so because we believe our financial responsibilities belong to all of us and therefore financial support needs to come from all of us. So at the beginning of this new year, we believe it is the right time for each one of us to renew/review our common commitment to pay for our local church work.

In order that we do not spend too much time in months ahead focusing on fundraising, we are asking you to consider carefully what you can give for God's work in and through our church. So that we can plan properly, it would help if you could let us know your intentions on the enclosed card, returning it, if possible, by the end of the month either using the enclosed s.a.e. or including it in the offertory plate one Sunday.

For your information, our current weekly 'direct giving' is an average of almost £10 from 86 regular contributors. To continue and develop our mission and our many church activities this needs to increase; it also needs to include more of us as regular contributors. As you can see, we are doing our part and are sure you will want to do yours as well. The presentation on Sunday ———— and Sunday ————[12] will explain further how we manage and spend the church money on our mission and ministry.

None of us wants our historic church to go up in smoke; however, it is a sobering thought to realize that no-one at the moment is giving as much as – let alone more than – a tankful of petrol for the average car, costing as much as £30! We

---

[12] Two presentations on consecutive Sundays make sure that everyone gets the message.

hope this will change. There are also a number of people coming to church services and events these days who have as yet not become involved in planned giving. We hope that their response will be readily forthcoming.

We are enclosing a legacy leaflet, as we do each year, to enable you to consider our church in the future, as you write or update your will. Legacies will safeguard our church for future generations, our grandchildren. As members we all want to do the best for our church and for all those people who are part of it – either directly or indirectly. That means making sure that what we give realistically reflects our faith in God and our discipleship. Accordingly, we thank the Lord for all the exciting opportunities we have here together and for the thoughtful and committed way we know you will respond to the letter.

[signatures of vicar and churchwardens]

This card is enclosed for replies:

Dear Vicar and Churchwardens,
[ ] Yes, you can count on my/our financial support. Until further notice, you can expect from me/us on average £___ per week. Please give me/us details of Standing Orders.
[ ] I/We want the church to reclaim tax on our donations, and I/we will tell the church if I/we do not pay an amount of tax that at least equals the tax deducted from what I/we give.
[ ] I/We would like to know more about leaving a legacy in my will.

From: _____

Draft follow up letter:

[individual name]
Just a few weeks ago you received a letter sent to almost 200 members of St ——— Church whom we believe have a particular interest in regard to our parish church. Approximately two-thirds [?] have generously responded with commitment to becoming regular contributors.

So far it looks as if we can count on an additional £___ per week to meet our financial obligations over the next twelve months. We are of course deeply grateful to all those who have already responded.

Unfortunately, there is no record of you having returned the card provided. Perhaps this has been overlooked or mislaid. Accordingly, below is a special tear-off section for you to indicate what your intentions are now, as we do not want any-one to feel left out or ignored.

It is important for us to know what we can expect in the way of support from everyone who cares for and values the village church. Therefore, would you please be kind enough in the next day or so to complete the slip and either use the s.a.e. or drop it off at church.

If you would like to speak to someone personally about this, please let any of us know, and an arrangement will happily be made. In the meantime, your time and thought in such a matter is very greatly appreciated indeed.

Yours sincerely

. . . .

[tear-off slip]

Reply slip from: _____

[ ] I/We are/are not currently able to make a regular financial commitment to God's work in and through ――― Parish Church.

[ ] I/We will make an offering on the collection plate when I/we come to church.

[ ] I/We would like/would not like a box of weekly/monthly offering envelopes.

[ ] I/We want our church to reclaim tax on all my/our donations and will let you know if my/our tax paid is less that the tax deducted from what I/we give.

Key point

As many organizations are beginning to post up their mission statements and codes of operation, the Diocese of London finance advisers have begun to work on just such a postable statement about stewardship in churches. It summarizes the work of being a stewardship church.

**St Agatha's Church
Working hard to be
a stewardship church**

- There is a regular teaching and preaching on giving and stewardship in the context of Christian discipleship.
- We believe that each of us should prayerfully give a proportion of our income to the mission of the Church.
- Everyone, including those new to the church, is given an annual opportunity to review their committed giving and make a new financial pledge.
- We thank each giver in writing at least annually for their regular giving to the mission of our church.

- Good-quality information on tax-efficient giving and regular giving methods is readily available, and Gift Aid envelopes are available for visitors at services and events.
- We are committed to increasing dependence on committed giving rather than other forms of fundraising to pay for our running costs.
- As responsible stewards the church council prepares, publishes and monitors an annual budget to support the mission aims of our church.
- We are prayerfully committed to giving away at least [10 per cent] of general income to others less fortunate than ourselves.
- We are joyfully committed to paying all our bills on time and the parish shares (to the diocese) promptly each month.

9

Legacies

Legacies have been a means of giving in the Church for hundreds of years. As an aspect of fundraising we find ourselves needing to reintroduce it because in the last two or three decades many major charities have promoted legacy fundraising while the churches have stayed silent. So those leaving legacies have moved towards those other charities saying they need the contributions!

After general donations, legacies are the second most common form of charitable giving. A legacy programme is cheap to run and most people are less embarrassed than one might first think. More people talk about money more openly than they did in years past.

All fundraising is about relationships and people. Loyalty and commitment are built up slowly and people need to be sure that their legacy is going to be well spent with all the criteria we have mentioned earlier (pp. 59–64). Look over that section as you prepare for legacy fundraising if you are going to be able to do it well. Just as with other fundraising, the key stages are *preparation*, *building the relationship* and then *asking*.

A legacy is a way of giving that is painless to the giver; nothing happens till after their death. Often the legacy gives access to assets which, for most individuals, who are homeowners, are far greater than their regular income. Many people do not need to leave their home to their children – who have their own houses – and the inherited house would be sold for cash by those who inherit.

There are two key kinds of legacies. A pecuniary legacy names a specific sum of money that is to go to the beneficiary. A residuary legacy is usually a percentage of assets or a particular named asset. In 2000, the average pecuniary legacy was £3,200 and the average residuary legacy was £24,000. When the church begins to talk to people about legacies, remember that time passes between writing a will and the money being received, and the actual amount named in a pecuniary legacy will have reduced in value because of inflation, while the residuary legacy – often a percentage of a house value – will have kept its real value over the years. Unless there is a major downturn in the property market this will continue to be true. Legacies from church members will be slower in being paid out in future years as the average age of death rises.

Who gives a legacy?

Two-thirds of legators are women. Generally they have been living alone. Many are widows (women still tend to live longer than men). The average estate is valued at £138,000 (year 2000) with their house being the main asset. Many elderly widows are cash poor and asset rich. They may have small work-related pensions but own their own home. During their life many such church members are able to give very little to the church financially, and their contribution to stewardship programmes may be very small, despite their dedication. Many are glad to know their church will benefit later.

Most legators name up to three charities in their will, reflecting different areas of interest during their lifetime. Of the key charities benefiting from legacies, religion comes fifth after health and social welfare, medical research, animal welfare, and disabilities. Notably, most legators use a solicitor to help them make out their will and generally do not tell those who will benefit.

What are the ethical issues?

Discuss the issues among the church council before preparing material to communicate about legacies. Try out potential messages on each other or on a few willing volunteers. On the whole people do not mind talking about death; they may even find it helpful to talk about how their interest in the church may continue after their own death. A Church of England leaflet (2002), featuring the TV gardener Alan Titchmarsh, may be suitable for most churches to use.

Communication must not prompt either fear or guilt, and for this reason consider any leaflet produced about legacies as backup information, not as the main communication. Make a public presentation, such as using a sermon time, so that everyone understands the principles. Then follow this up with conversations as appropriate, after which leaflets can be given to summarize the key points. In this way you will be able to pick up and alleviate fears or a sense of guilt. Ensure that the particular people who will talk to others about legacies know how to communicate with sensitivity and without pressure and without generating guilt.

The people who will be most vulnerable to pressure, to feel guilt, will be the church's more dependent people. Those who are old enough to need care rather than being able to care for others may feel that the request is 'to make them pay' for the care they receive. Detach the care which is theirs through the unconditional love of Christians from the gift they may make which is equally unconditional.

Those who are bereaved, or emotionally vulnerable, should not be pressurized in any way. It is neither ethical nor legal to create any pressure for people who are, because of present circumstances or health reasons, not 'of sound mind'. In any case if the church proceeds to seek a legacy from someone in this state it may well be disputed by other legatees later. It should not be done. The best kind of legacy fundraising programme is ongoing anyway and should, in a quiet way, be part of the church's regular programme, in the way that stewardship programmes are. It is a good idea to simply add the talking about legacies, and the leaflets, to your annual programme of renewing stewardship. This gives the additional opportunity from time to time to suggest that people update their wills.

The church and church council members should *not* offer to get the will written for a church member, although they may suggest the way to find a solicitor. In fact, they should keep clear of anything that may seem prejudicial or manipulative. Be aware that any will may be contested by other potential beneficiaries later, and it is not advisable to have any appearance of pressure on a legator. Family disputes about a will can and do happen – it is not worth being involved in the acrimony that can ensue. Any such dispute could result in bringing the church into disrepute from negative criticism – warranted or not. The church may be best advised to just wait till all the arguments are over and gratefully receive anything it does get.

Presenting the case for legacies in your church

Prepare carefully in your committee, remembering that most people consider a legacy as a gift for the long term, and some legacies actually will be endowments from which the church can only take the interest. Consider ways in which legacies can support the church, avoiding short-term projects. Bear in mind that many specific social welfare projects may be short-term. Homelessness or unemployment may be short-term, poverty or disability will be long-term. Repair and maintenance of the building may be long-term, while replacing the heating is short-term.

Recollect what legacies have done for the church in the past, or if you are unaware of the history of legacies in the church see what other local churches have received. Build up the story so people can see models of what might be achieved.

In legacy communications, both written and verbal, give examples of what future legacies will be able to do for the church. Remember to phrase this in terms of beneficiaries with whom the potential legators might identify – future generations of children . . . grandchildren . . . local residents . . . those who worship in the continuing tradition of the church and appreciate its heritage . . .

Since the memory of the person is important, consider carefully how the church will 'recognize' the gift. A name may be put on a plaque, a project may be named, or the gift recorded on a noticeboard. A legacy from which only interest may be spent can be named each year in the church accounts. While a particular legator may not be around to see their gift remembered in this way, there will be other potential legators who would see that the promise of being remembered is kept and this will influence their decision. There is a particular kind of respect involved in making a commitment to someone who will not be around for the delivery of your half of the trust equation.

Tips on legacy fundraising
- Make the campaign a regular feature of church life.
- Do not expect income in the next three years!
- Do recruit a steering group of volunteers.
- Do set an objective and write a plan of action and budget for such items as printing brochures, numbers of people to 'visit', and timescales.
- Do consider all your audiences for the programme: regular worshippers, occasional (Christmas only?) worshippers, neighbours and local interest groups. Remember the most positive contacts will be with elderly people.
- Focus on face-to-face conversations, but don't make too many assumptions about who can give or who will give. You may be surprised.

Setting up the legacy communication campaign

Written material on legacies

First, run over key communication points that will be used in all written material or publications. This will ensure that the message is neither too apologetic nor too pushy, and that it is coherent and has the right appeal for those most likely to need the information. Remember to say who the beneficiaries will be and what will be funded by legacies.

The design should reflect the fact that most people including a legacy to the church as they update their will are elderly. The design, pictures, layout, language, print size and information should reflect this.

Plan an *Updating your Will* brochure that summarizes the key issues, including how to make a legacy and how the legacy will be used by the church. Give information on the person with whom the potential legator can discuss any questions. The emphasis on updating is important. Many people already have a will that may be very old, and they may be advised to review it anyway. Even if a church member has in the past written the church into their will, an update may result in a legacy that is more realistic in the light of present financial needs in the church.

Include information on legacies in the church's regular communications, from newsletters to notice sheets, information packs to financial reports, and stewardship programmes. Display posters that encourage legacies.

An exhibition can display material about how legacies and donations have made a difference to the church in the past, how stewardship and other schemes help now and how legacies can help towards stability in the future.

Within the church council agree a period of time during which face-to-face meetings may be needed, such as after a stewardship programme that includes legacies. Prepare those who are going to talk to members direct so that they can run over the messages, discuss ethical issues and know what to do if a counselling or pastoral issue arises that is outside their scope.

Face-to-face meetings

Most people in local churches know one another well enough for face-to-face meetings to be successful. It is far harder for charities who have little or no regular personal contact with donors and potential legators. Those churches that plan annual presentations and one-to-one meetings about stewardship plan to include legacies as a topic. Talk to as many members as possible, include rather than exclude, making sure that the reasons for excluding are completely obvious and make no assumptions about relative wealth and likelihood of contributing. Remember the widow's mite.

In each meeting, give information backed up by the information brochure, answer points of information and communicate the church's sense of vision for the future.

Find points of interest from the potential legator; they may be more concerned with some aspects of church life in the future rather than others. For example, their interest might be children of the future, the continuing tradition of churchmanship, safeguarding a beautiful building or continued funding for priestly ministry. A legacy can have restricted use according to the wishes of the donor, and this can be encouraged.

Use this opportunity to build up a relationship that continues as friendship in the future.

Follow-up

Just as the overall strategy should be the subject of a report on the church council minutes for future information, each individual meeting should be briefly noted in a file about legacies. This will, as time passes, keep those informed who are responsible for the legacy programme and for following up appropriate action points.

Write a letter thanking the potential legator for their interest and spending the time in meeting with a church council member. This may seem a rather formal step to take in the context of church relationships that are relatively informal, but you will not be able to express appreciation after the church receives the legacy. Reduce it to a note-card if you wish, but do bear in mind that churches are on the whole very poor at saying thank you to their own members, and as a result members can feel used. If the potential donor would find it helpful, send in writing details of the church's name in full, so that they can take it to a solicitor.

Some charities use pledge cards so that those who write a legacy into their will can let the church know what to expect. If the church uses pledge cards these give an opportunity to care for the pledgers, making sure that over the years they don't begin to feel the church is no longer interested. Don't forget they can write the church out of their will as easily as they put the church in. Given the experience of major charities like Christian Aid, there is no need to be embarrassed over pledge cards. Most people are happy to give the charity information about a possible legacy.

After the meeting make a note against each person 'visited', under such categories as:

- casual and probably not interested
- potentially interested but not yet
- interested but hasn't got round to it
- definite, may return a pledge card.

Important legal points

1. Legacies must be properly worded where charitable bequests are concerned. Keep a list of solicitors who do wills, from which the individual can choose for themselves. *Do not recommend one.*

2. Ensure that your brochure contains *the correct current name* of your church.

> One church had changed its name over the years since an ex-member had made her will. The church lost its £50,000 bequest. It's a cogent reminder that regular updating of information about legacies and updating wills should be on each church's annual programme.

3. If an asset has to be sold to pay for a legacy it may be preferable to transfer the asset and then sell it. This may avoid capital gains tax.

Key points

- Invite every member of the congregation and close associates of the church to give sacrificially.
- Invite everyone who directly and indirectly benefits from the church to be a committed donor.
- Invite people to become regular donors so that the church can count on their contributions.
- Promote and invite legacies.
- Say thank you and acknowledge legacies positively.

10

Put the *Fun* in *Fun*draising

Many local people seek out opportunities for social events, and many of the local fundraising events the church may set up can appeal to local people's social needs. The need for friendship, fun and a place to belong can all be focused around church, including many people who do not see themselves as church-goers, but who want to participate in developing the social well-being of their neighbourhood. Some people find social cohesion in the local pub or the football club, or a club for the elderly. The warp and weft of local life needs maintaining, and the church, being a key player in this kind of extended family, will win the loyalty and commitment of many people. Such loyalty and commitment will result in people raising money for the church when that becomes necessary.

The local council are important locally but bear in mind that local councillors are easier to get involved but often have less power than officers of the council, even though the theory says otherwise. Sometimes it is helpful to invite council-lors to consultation or information briefings, as their personal understanding will result in their support of the church's project on the committees in which they take part. Perhaps more importantly, they will be helpful in saying whether the church is presenting itself well in the communications or applications you make to council departments. Local MPs are useful supporters, particularly if they rep-resent the same party as the council leaders.

Strange and unusual challenges, fun and games, bargains and new opportuni-ties can all be elements of local fundraising. Different people will join in different events, and some people may just want the chance to be bystanders and watch others do the challenges.

Put the *Fun* in *Fun*draising

Local fundraising events and programmes develop and support fellowship, as well as mission, networks and links between local groups.

As the church includes everyone in the activity, local people will feel ownership of the whole project. Then the church can use the fundraising programme to inform and build new partnerships that are not just about money but are about increased participation as the church prepares for new engagement in serving the local people.

Local fundraising is the best description for the amazing mixture of programmes, events and challenges that make up a key element of a major fundraising project. Even if it were possible for a church to raise all its funds from completely external sources, this local activity should still form an essential element of the programme. The local church or the parish church so often is an essential feature of the built environment, one indomitable factor in the fabric of local society. While not every urban church has that pride of place felt by village churches, very few are without some sense of local community ownership. In the Old Kent Road in south London a Victorian Gin Palace painted a gaudy blue and yellow, with massive chandeliers and gloomy windows, was recently demolished. There is a huge crater in the sense of continuity people felt from having the building always there. And though many of us had never been inside, someone has demolished a local building that belonged to us. Local fundraising gives an opportunity to take local pride and build it into a common sense of purpose, of working for what belongs to all of us.

The parish church's history means that it belongs in one way or another to all those who live in the parish; it certainly does not belong solely to those who go to church. Even in the complex set of custodian trustee structures that mean the Church Commissioners have rights over the building, if your church is sold part of the proceeds go not to the Church Commissioners but to the parish – usually that parish into which the parish of the sold-off church now is incorporated, to continue to work for local people. That sense of ownership and partnership is the basis of local fundraising. 'This is our local church, let's work together to repair it!' can be said by local people, churchgoers and non-churchgoers alike.

Engagement

When the time comes to build a network of individual donors beyond the congregation, who might these donors be? What messages will appeal to each group? What will make it easier for them to give?

Fundamental to success is the quality of relationships the church has collectively and individually with local people – or that members are prepared to have. If the local pub will hold a challenge darts match to raise funds for a project, will members continue to drop in from time to time or hold the occasional match in the future? Above all, local fundraising does create a level of loyalty and friendliness that can be the foundation of future goodwill and ministry for the church.

In preparing the fundraising project, begin to consider the view that others have of the church building as they pass. Where does it fit into their social and cultural environment and for what objective might they be willing to get involved? Different people will get involved for different reasons and in different ways.

The fundraising strategy of a west London parish church has won it two Direct Marketing Industry awards for cost-effectiveness (£744 raised for every £1 spent), and for its use of databases.

The strategy was devised for the St James Norlands restoration appeal by two parishioners, Pan Craik and Jon Boelkel, who raised £150,000 with one accurately targeted mailshot. Ninety per cent of donors had never given to the church before.

'We are simply amazed at the church's achievement,' said the chairman of the awards committee, Fabienne Tyler. 'These awards are the Oscars of the direct-marketing world.'

St James Norlands, a Grade II listed nineteenth-century church in gardens in the centre of a square, has been threatened with closure, and needed £300,000 for its rescue plan. The object of the mailshot was to raise the first half of this.

The fundraisers compiled a database that segmented the parish by wealth (based on the value of houses and flats), location, and by each person's use of the church. Parishioners received emotive letters, slightly differently angled to reflect the recipients' interests and values, but all with the reminder that 'St James Norlands is as much a part of this neighbourhood as the squirrels in the park or the shops on Holland Park Avenue.'

Each recipient's point of leverage was carefully judged. To those living in the square, in houses valued at over £1 million, the fundraisers wrote: 'How sad would be the prospect if St James's were forced to close, if its White Suffolk bricks were scrawled with graffiti and its 22 stained-glass windows were all boarded up. Or if it were redeveloped as a block of flats.'

Parents of children baptized there received letters beginning: 'If you remember that very special day when Francesca was baptized at St James's . . .'

Celebrities were approached individually: Elton John, for instance, received a letter from the organist, rhapsodizing about the organ's sound ('riproaring good fun'), and inviting him to 'sneak away one summer's evening and come and put the organ through its paces'. (But Elton John gives only to Aids charities, he says.)

The Vicar, the Revd Hugh Rayment-Pickard, said that the parish was thrilled by the awards. 'We didn't realize we were direct marketing: we were just trying to save the church.'

Plans for its future include a nursery centre for small children, and the use of the church for concerts and opera in the evenings.[13]

---

[13] From the *Church Times*.

Working together as a group, brainstorm the many ways that local people identify with the church and so might hold it valuable. Later all this information will be used to ensure that the church can reach out comprehensively to engage people's interest and contributions. Identify local beneficiaries, including church members.

Consider:

- Whose house value is enhanced by being in a conservation area that includes the church? – Name the streets.
- Which groups use the church or the church hall as a meeting place? For children's groups, how many parents might be contacted as the church's provision helps their offspring?
- Do the local school or schools use the church as a meeting place, as a local history source or for other purposes such as occasional services?
- How many people look to this church for baptisms, weddings and funerals and would be disappointed if it were gone?

If the church is fundraising to launch a new community project this will appeal to local people's community spirit in a new way. Most would recognize the value of a healthy-living centre for the elderly (a youth club for pensioners) or an after-school club for children, or an opportunity to work for people with mental health problems. Local participation for these purposes may be quicker and easier to engage than for a building project, so if the church already houses local groups, neighbours and residents will identify this in the church communications and will want to help keep a worthwhile cause going. After all, many of them will actually know the beneficiaries.

Team-building

There are often local people with organizing skills who would be willing to join a church fundraising team. It is very unlikely that the church will have all the skills and resources it needs even if it has great ideas. Remember that local people who are centres of local networks themselves will communicate a sense of the church's credibility to their network. Invite the organizer of the village fête, a local Scout or Brownies leader, a youth worker, or organizer of a local pensioner project. Consider groups that benefit from the church's presence or facilities and leaders who might make good team members. As we target *local ownership* of the church project it does not matter that these are not church members: you are engaging their partnership, their resources and their energy around a project that will ultimately be guided by the church council. Ensure you include an overall

group that has social, financial and administrative skills. When you have identified key people inside and outside the church who will join your local fundraising team, organize the team-building day.

> On a major street in London many local businesses are waiting for a request and an
> opportunity to contribute to the repair of *their historic church*. How do we know?
> They have already said so to a local music producer, and the church has only to
> ask. You can be sure the church will now ask and do so graciously and in a
> language that the businesses understand.

Have a planning day

Although those gathered may all be acquaintances, spend the first period (45
minutes) getting to know each other in the context of the fundraising challenge.
Go round the group giving each person time to tell about what they have organ-
ized in the past, and what training and skills they have that might help the
project.

• Agree together on the fundraising target and how long the church estimates it
  will take to achieve it. And decide whether to stop when the sum has been
  raised or whether to continue with planned events for the whole year even if
  this raises more money.

• Agree that if the group's best efforts have not reached the target in one year,
  there will be a pause and review of progress. (If outside people have committed
  a year to the project, it is unfair to assume they will go on. Churchgoers will
  probably know that they will continue regardless. If you stop and review, *and
  if you have all enjoyed your year's work*, the outside people may continue with
  you.)

> The local fundraising group in a south London church decided that with their best
> efforts they would raise £10,000 for the restoration of the church spire. After a year
> they had raised more that twice the sum, and since the spire was still incomplete
> they continued. When they finished after two years, they had raised more than
> £80,000.

Especially with local fundraising it is important to know who is the 'champion'
of the project. The champion of the group will be the person that the group all
agrees is going to help them maintain their commitment. This person will follow
up if members stop doing what they agreed to do. The champion will not do the

work themselves in this case but may bring it back to the group to re-allocate if a person is really unable or unwilling to continue their commitment. The champion is there to ensure that through thick and thin the team will attain its objectives. For those who are football-minded, a key gift that Sven Goran Eriksson brought to the England team training was his ability to identify leaders who would find ways to keep the team focused and engaged despite the odds against them. He identified both David Beckham and Michael Owen.

- Choose your David Beckham.

- Produce minutes of this part of the meeting that identify clearly who has committed themselves to a task by the time of the next meeting.

- Plan a calendar of events that is taxing but not overwhelming. Do not expect every one of you to do everything, and especially do not assume that your vicar or minister can or will do everything!

- Brainstorm first, collecting every kind of idea, then highlight several that the group believes it may have, or can find, the resources to complete.

- Allocate *responsibility* for organizing and arranging, to one or two people for each event. Ask those people to bring outline plans and arrangements to the next meeting so the group can all be confident that their 'event' is going well.

Lay leadership

Lay leadership is really important to local fundraising. Often lay people have skills and networks the vicar cannot have. Often they have skills and training that are more appropriate. They may also have credibility that the vicar cannot have: in the pub a local builder will gain attention in setting up a darts or pool challenge that few vicars can match.

Additionally, there will be local residents who have come to the clergy at a point of personal vulnerability, for assistance, for counselling, for confession, and for other reasons that may create a vulnerability or a sense of gratitude. For the vicar to ask for a contribution could result in a conflict of interests or the abuse of relationship with a vulnerable person. When another church member or fundraising group member asks for time or money the emotional and psychological pressure is not there. This is why local fundraising must belong to everyone and be championed by lay people; clergy either cannot or should not be creating undue pressure towards contributing.

Networks and contacts

The wise church builds its house on the rock. Through comprehensive local fundraising the church will develop a network of local contacts and level of good-will. The local profile will be raised. This goodwill and common purpose can be drawn into the ongoing life of the church. Don't keep the sacred and secular apart! Plan to invite all those who have contributed during fundraising to a cele-bratory event at the end. Invite the bishop and have a roll of honour so that each of the major contributors is invited up to be thanked, and to shake hands with the bishop. They may receive a token gift, flowers or card. Put on a photo exhibition of the variety of events so that everyone can find themselves and feel recognized.

Have another event to launch the church's new community programme or to re-open the repaired building. This can be a church service followed by a social event with refreshments. Non-churchgoers who have helped raise money will now have friends in the church and will know you well enough to follow your lead through the liturgy and will enjoy the prayers of thanksgiving that name the events they have worked on or in which they have participated.

The fundraising group must keep lists of people who have contributed, who have enjoyed the events and with whom the church can maintain some kind of contact – maybe a card to each of them at Christmas, acknowledging them per-sonally. Perhaps the card should come from the fundraising team member with whom they worked most often. Once made, friendships and partnerships are too valuable to lose.

Fundraising networks and contacts positively raise the church's profile in its neighbourhood.

Branding

There are many considerations that feed into creating a set of messages that appeal to local residents and businesses to gain their support and engagement in the project of raising funds. Partnership with people involves being able to find the ground on which we are united, having a common purpose over what is ours. The church's branding will have a logo or title that becomes a familiar sight to everyone. Then there will be a strapline that explains in a few words what the fundraising is all about. Both of these may be developed through consultation with local people.

Brainstorm to identify positive themes and values, from which the group can identify positive phrases that encapsulate an objective that both church members, and other local people who may never attend church, can espouse. Have two or three people go through all the ideas and find the phrases, themes and values that are *interesting*, eye-catching and appealing to outside people. Avoid the 'Save our church' kind of theme: it says nothing of values or aspiration or the future.

Once the church captures local imagination, there are endless resources of goodwill and collective determination that can be tapped. It is common in our society today to pull together a programme of fun events and challenges for a good cause in which we all believe. All kinds of charitable causes are supported by local community endeavours, from jumble sales and coffee mornings to abseiling and bunjee jumping.

One church was able to pick up on its history and identified one unusual phrase:

It's been called the craziest church in Christendom, let's keep it that way.

It catches attention; it doesn't have a forward-looking theme, but we can work on that. We stop and look because we wonder who or what is crazy. (In this case it was the Victorian design.)

Another church has explored its role and identity for local people:

St James's Church, the Heart of Piccadilly

Or St Jude's Centre programme of events:

Imagine the possibilities

What could you do and what will you do?

Of all the myriad ideas for events, challenges and donation schemes, only some will fit the church's situation. So how do you choose? If all of you hate jumble sales, then don't do jumble sales!

Above all, if the church has a major fundraising challenge in front of them, there is no point committing everyone to activities they hate. Local fundraising activities need to be at least interesting and preferably enjoyable. Make the programme enjoyable to various kinds of people, by dividing up tasks and running a variety of events:

- Those who like face-to-face work
- Those who like to be behind the scenes
- Those who like buying and selling

- Those who look for bargains
- Those who like the lucky chance
- Those who like personal challenges
- Those who are too busy and would rather give money than time
- Those who like a team challenge
- Those who like a quiet life

The fundraising committee may be filled with active people, and their first ideas may correspond to their personal interests. But the congregation and the local supporters may be interested in other activities. Using the list above, consider people you know and your impressions of what they might enjoy. Then make enquiries, suggesting ideas and getting responses through a questionnaire.

> St Jude's Church, a tiny back-street church, decided to hold a jumble sale on a Friday evening. Despite the advertisement in the local paper and some very good quality goods, very few people turned up. However, a year and ten jumble sales later (now on Saturday afternoons) the returns were continuing to rise. From only £100 on the first event the income rose to an average of £500 per sale over the year. This enabled the church to go from an annual deficit to a small surplus and to pay its contribution to the Diocesan Common Fund in full for the first time.

Assessing your resources

People

With the fundraising committee make a 'map', to see what connections can be identified that might be fruitful. What friends, spouses, voluntary groups do the congregation and local people have that could be productive? A spouse who organizes events for a school or concerts for an old people's home, an organizer on the village fête committee, someone who paints and might do an exhibition or offer a picture for auction. Map them and review the map regularly so the group does not miss chances now or later in the programme of events. A local choir that rehearses in the church just might run a concert to raise money. The church might take a table at a local market to sell its raffle tickets.

Skills

Run through the list of potential volunteers and see who might be able to offer the following skills, which will be invaluable:

- *Computer and word processing skills*, for reports, planning, record-keeping, mailing lists, searching the internet for useful information.

- *Building social contacts*, as some people are great at getting others to volunteer, and making new friends, and enjoy going out to local groups and will be able to explain what the church wants to do and how it would enjoy having this particular group working with them. Contacting the local swimming club to work on a sponsored event, and so on.

- *Local council skills*, as some people will already have contacts in the local council that will prove useful in gaining helpful information – everything from local council plans to when the council is going to make Community Chest grants.

- *Telephone skills*. Most people can use a phone, but some people have a talent for gaining information, organizing and gaining support over the phone. Ensure the person is working to the fundraising group's agenda and then use their skill.

- *Communication skills*. The fundraising group will quickly lose the support of the congregation and local groups if it fails to keep everyone informed of what's happening. As a subgroup of the church council, the group should send notes and reports on all the fundraising group's meetings and plans to the church council.

- *Leaflet and newsletter skills*. For a diverse congregation and with local community supporters, is there anyone who could produce a fundraising newsletter? This will enable the group to quickly communicate news of sums raised, say thankyou to all contributors and give plans of events in the future. The more fun, enjoyment and success that the group communicates the more that people will want to help.

Set up a clear and comprehensive agreement with the church treasurer about processes for handling money, especially cash, to ensure that there is no possibility of money going astray or becoming confused. The treasurer will be key to producing regular updates on the total raised to date.

Resources to get you started and keep you running

Find a corner in the church office where the fundraising committee can keep its papers, files and materials. This will enable volunteers to plan and produce materials, leaflets and letters. Desk space, phone access, stationery and stamps will all be needed.

Prepare a budget for the costs of fundraising so the church council can allocate this sum to the fundraising committee. It is the responsibility of the church to enter the *cost* of fundraising in the annual accounts not just the *profit*. So charge all the costs, then deposit all the income. Never use cash from an event to pay volunteers back for expenses; get the church treasurer to set a good and workable system.

Assessing your neighbourhood

Having looked at the immediate people and resources, now take a broad look at the wider community.

Consider local residents, estates and communities within the neighbourhood. Make a list of assumptions about how you might engage the interest of the whole variety of local people in the church's events programme. Are there certain kinds of events or challenges your neighbours would enjoy? Does the programme of events appeal to all kinds of people in the area? Do you need to adjust your ideas a little to broaden the appeal and fundraise among the widest possible audience locally?

Remember there will be local people who would rather do nothing but might make a donation out of self-interest. This could include using the church very occasionally for a baptism, wedding or funeral. Or the value attributable to homes in local streets or even a conservation area may be enhanced by the quality of the church in that environment.

Because of the value of local churches in the environment councils are able to contribute to repair funds on historic churches (see Chapter 12).

Local businesses may already expect to give to good causes. They may be tired of being asked to contribute items for raffles but may contribute by advertising in the fundraising newsletter, especially if the church is circulating it widely. (Do the sums and ensure that the income from advertising justifies putting a newsletter through doors on the whole catchment area.)

Be imaginative.

> Pizza Express in Bloomsbury, London, sells Pizza San Giorgio, with a few pence from the proceeds from every San Giorgio pizza it sells going to the fundraising project at St George's Church. Several hundred pounds have been raised so far.

If you have major businesses in your area investigate whether they support their employees in volunteering or will support fundraising in which they get involved.

A major accountancy firm in the City of London matches pound for pound up to £300 whatever any of their employees raise for charity. Do any of your supporters work with companies that might do this?

Finally, plan your events programme

What could we all do?
What could we redo?
What would we like to do?
What would our fellow church members like to do?
What would our neighbours like to do?

Either use the list of activities below or make your own shortlist. The potential is an almost endless list.

Indirect fundraising

Raffles

Sales
  Jumble, Christmas fair, bring and buy, table sale, auction of time/skills, cake and jam stall, charity Christmas cards

Social events
  Barn dance, ball, dinner party, coffee morning, square dancing, Morris dancing, multicultural meal, treasure hunt

Challenges
  Abseiling, bunjee jumping, parachuting, and any other challenge sport

Competition
  Darts, football, quizzes, netball, table games

Sponsored events
  Marathons, walks, swims
and so on

One church manages to raise several thousand pounds each year from one raffle. Tickets are printed (remember to get the licence to do this) and prizes are bought. Starting with the church council and electoral roll then other contacts, each person is sent several books of tickets and asked to send back either the £5 and the stubs from selling the tickets or the unused tickets. Very few unsold tickets are returned, and many people ask for extra books so they can sell more to friends, relatives and work acquaintances. It's amazingly effective with prizes such as a holiday and a DVD player.

Many ideas the fundraising group develops are quite effective as social events for the congregation and local people. Think through ways to combine several activities into one event and engage more people. For example, organize the challenge event for abseiling down the tower with a bring and buy sale, where raffle tickets are also sold. Round off a summer fête with a barn dance, so that people come to both events. If the church has had few social events or activities in the past, recognize that it will take some time for people locally to realize that something good is happening and that the church runs successful events that they will enjoy.

Set a programme of activities for the year, checking that the work is spread around the group, finding a variety of organizers so that no-one is overloaded.

An idea that is worth trying: the Thermometer is 'old fashioned' but good. It shows the value of work done and publicizes what is still to be done. It can result in a lucky break.

As the scaffolding went up for a major repair programme on a church in London, one of the trustees received a phone call from an occasional acquaintance. 'I see the scaffolding is going up for work on St Jude's Church. Aren't you involved with that project? Do they have all the money they need, or can I help with a donation?'

The thankyou programme

Everyone who contributes in whatever way must receive thanks from the church (or watch local credibility plummet!).

Get one or two systematic volunteers to work with the treasurer to ensure everyone gets thanked. There are different kinds of thanking that reach different people. Your extroverts may expect public thanks; your introverts may not. Your feeling people want warmth and the more effusive thanks. Your thinking people want to know how their contribution is valued in the big picture.

- After each event, put the amount in the notice sheet/board and thank everyone (don't pick out a few).
- Ensure every individual who contributes personally gets a thankyou note or letter.
- Try to identify those who might feel their gift and contribution has gone unacknowledged, and make sure communication happens.
- The task is easier if the *thanks* are always expressed by the church, not just the clergy. Get some backroom people to do this piece of work; they may be the elderly or more fragile members who cannot make other contributions but will write a card or letter.

Saying 'thank you' means you can ask again.

Key points

- Form the local fundraising working group.
- Assess your area, your contacts, your supporters, stakeholders and what works in your area.
- Brainstorm ideas.
- Plan your programme, cutting your coat according to your cloth – look at volunteers, interests and resources.
- Make it enjoyable.
- Run your programme.

Have a thank you programme.

11

Fundraising from Trusts for Church Buildings

When a grantmaking trust is thinking of investing hundreds or thousands of pounds in any project (or business) they will require a thorough examination to be made to ensure money is not going to be 'thrown away'. Your church will need to have prepared so that your project will function and serve people well to justify the investment. Preparation includes ensuring that the church has addressed all the issues that will concern the funder. The material will, in the church's case, be focused around a specific project and therefore may not include every element described in this chapter, but your preparation will need to be seen to be thorough. As the church applies to trusts and major grantmakers, it will be competing for money against all the other applications that are presented, and it is essential to aim to produce the best presentation of a project that will deliver the objectives of the funder.

When the church applies to the local authority or funders of local regeneration, it is competing with all the voluntary sector projects in the area. If the regeneration money is tied to education and training, the church will be competing against education providers, schools and colleges. If the church is providing a social welfare programme, the provision will have to be seen to be as professional, and as efficient and effective as other organizations, statutory and voluntary, in the area. If the church project has something unique to offer in this field it will have to appeal to outside funders as being as effective and efficient as other welfare projects.

The greater the sum the church wishes to raise, the more preparation it must do. Use this as an opportunity to review the quality of all your internal procedures and practices in running yourselves, your buildings and your project. In being transparent to potential funders, the church itself will first need to be assured that it is well run, realistic in its expectations and thoroughly preparing itself for what it is undertaking and has dealt with all the issues and practicalities that are involved. Later, in Chapter 20, these threads are drawn into a Business Plan, which is a major document about the project that will explain how the church is going to achieve its goals. A Business Plan is increasingly being requested by funders of major grants.

Collecting together the material that this chapter outlines will enable the church to have in one place all the source material needed for fundraising for larger amounts from funders outside the organization. If you thoroughly review your organization with a view to improving how you run yourselves, you will find that people inside the church, who understand organizations, will be more inclined to invest in you also. Remember to consider why people give – and that includes those who care whether the charity is efficient in its giving – and if the review shows that the church is an effective channel for delivering help to beneficiaries that will affect both internal and external giving.

As you work through this chapter you may think the results show the church in a bad light. This is an opportunity to put together an action plan to change the situation. For example, people from ethnic minorities may be under-represented in the committee but a majority of the congregation. Set up a programme to get a wider cross-section of people into positions of responsibility. Similarly, the church may have no young people on its committees . . . plan for change. In the competition for money, if the church down the road has found a way to get all its members, young and old, black and white, active in management, many trusts will prefer that church down the road. If you don't know how to change, go down the road and ask the other group how they managed their change and see if you can copy their method.

Fundraising for church repairs

No-one outside will readily invest in a church that is slowly declining and shrinking. Nor should its members unless they can see a brighter future is on the cards. Now is the time to decide what you want to be in the long term and to consider planning for the long-term future of a heritage building.

How can a church assess whether it is in decline? If a church is setting out on major building repairs to a heritage building, consider why it is in the state it is at present. Perhaps the building has become dilapidated, cold and leaky as a result of considerable neglect – by its own people over several decades. On the other hand, even well maintained old churches need major repairs eventually. The symptoms of decline are:

- declining congregation with decreasing ministry
- declining attention to and funding for maintenance and repair programmes
- declining income.

Decline can be identified quite readily.

Task

Compare the church's activities now with those ten years ago. Is it doing more or less? Check in the annual reports and Annual General Meeting reports.

Has the church kept up with a good minor repairs programme or is the building getting shabbier and less well cared for? Look over the stewards' or churchwardens' reports to the annual meeting and in the accounts.

Compare how much the church spent on maintenance and repair ten years ago with this year. Is it more or less? It should be more.

Compare the church's income and expenditure ten years ago, last year and this year. Has income gone up by more than expenditure or vice versa? Has the church depleted its reserves?

Churches fail over any of these three items. The congregations that decline to below fifteen people find it impossible to maintain mission and new growth. Failure of finances and failure of church repairs will happen at the same time as the congregation declines.

If the church has now reached the 'bottom' where the building is at the point of urgent major repair or abandonment, justifying the repair means getting out of the overall malaise in which the church functions, or at the very least being able to make very clear and convincing the plans to turn the tide on all three of these elements of decline. Even if an outside funder helped repair the structure, the church will still need to address how it is going to pay to run and maintain it. How is the church going to restore the mission and congregation of the church? How will it address the issue of failed maintenance, that is the result of the failure of income on a week-by-week basis?

The general sense of failing that goes with such a scenario of decline is almost always pervasive, swamping individuals and the church collectively. Almost without fail the church will need to address its faith journey individually and collectively. Without a clear and effective mission a church will find it hard to justify fundraising! Outside support may be required to help in addressing the issues of the culture of decline, which are so obvious that members don't even talk about them any more. Thinking and operating in its present way has brought the church to its present state. So significant change is needed to turn the slide into deterioration into an upturn.

If the church works at the following section together over a period of time, it will be hard work, but the process will get members into a new mode of operation that is sustainable and will justify major investment in the church.

The long-term view

Work through the questions below and draft out statements for your church. Develop a mission statement that sets out what the church believes will be the way to achieve its aims. Look again at Chapter 2, as it is possible that local research will indicate a new focus for the church's aims and activities.

When applying for funding to repair a listed building, the church will have to show that it is a good custodian of the building and that investing more money in it is going to lead to greater access and greater use and have public value, as most heritage money is from the public sector.

Down to detail

Churches have Quinquennial, five-yearly, inspections of the building and its curtilage, undertaken by a suitably qualified architect or surveyor. The resultant report informs the church of the state of the building and any causes for concern. In particular, the Quinquennial Report will highlight areas for repair. Normally these are sectioned into repairs needing immediate attention, those to be addressed in the next 1.5 to 2 years and those to be addressed within the quinquennium. Some architects will highlight major issues that will be addressed in say seven to ten years, such as renewing a roof; this gives you time to save up.

The first step on receiving the report is to consider how practically you can address anything that is immediate, using the church's own funds, or items that will cost nothing to address. Pay special attention to items that recur, maintenance, and if you do not have one consider how to put an annual maintenance programme in place to address these items. Outside funders who might help you when the big projects arise will be favourably impressed by a well-maintained church.

The major items are the ones which will immediately be of concern. If yours is a listed church, there are several very considerable sources of help. If your church is unlisted there are fewer options but the National Churches Trust, one of the major funders of church repairs, will consider grants to unlisted churches for structural repair.

THE major funder for structural repairs to churches is the Joint Repair Scheme for Listed Places of Worship, financed by English Heritage and the Heritage Lottery Fund, which offers millions of pounds annually to places of worship, the majority of which are mainstream churches. While there are annual updates and modifications to the Repair Scheme, its major format has been in place for nearly ten years.

The funds of the Repair Scheme are directed at major structural and high-level repairs that keep the building wind- and watertight. So, for example, tower, spire and roof repairs are eligible, and so are all aspects of getting water away from the building: gutters, downpipes and drains.

Because there is an extremely high demand from places of worship there are several fundamental criteria to meet before grants are awarded.

Is the work urgent? Back to the Quinquennial Report; items that are identified as required repairs within two years (or sooner) are eligible.

Identify a single major project. The Scheme will tackle a single repair project not several projects pushed together for convenience (even if the combination saves on scaffolding, for example). So a project may include re-roofing, gutters and downpipes, but not the spire or the windows, even though both the latter items are structural and need work. The Repair Scheme will address the most urgent.

The repair project you identify for work under the Repair Scheme should, on current guidelines, be restricted to less that £250,000 all in; that is including fees and VAT. (There is a stream of the Scheme that will tackle large projects that cannot be reduced to smaller projects, a rickety, dangerous spire for example, but this is exceptional and very few of these grants are given each year, maybe three or four nationally.)

The guidelines and application form for the Scheme may be downloaded from English Heritage's website and there is a link from the Heritage Lottery fund website. Basic information is requested, including use of the church and how often it is open to the public outside of service times. It is a condition of grant that the church is open at least 40 days each year to visitors.

The application does require information from the church accounts, with particular reference to reserved funds. The church's unrestricted funds should be less than 80% of the repair project cost for a grant to be considered, that is both designated and unrestricted moneys taken together.

Ask the church architect to prepare a one-page description of the necessary works in a letter format or as a very brief report. Most listed churches will be replacing like with like in repairs, there is nothing hugely contentious, so Diocesan Advisory Council approval is not needed before a grant is considered and from the church's point of view may be wasteful if more limited repairs are undertaken. Accompany the architect's letter with a quantity surveyor's indicative budget for repair project. The quantity surveyor should normally be independent, not a member of the architect's practice or a subsidiary.

Under European Union procurement rules, for publicly funded projects, the architect and other professional advisers must be appointed by competitive tender, that is advertised openly and the Scheme requires this. If you have a church architect of long standing, with the obvious advantage of knowing the building well and having prepared the repair project, you will have opportunity to explain to the Scheme how your architect has been appointed and the added value inherent in keeping the same architect. Do not agree a level of fees with the architect and members of the design team before your application, as the Scheme will itself make a recommendation on all fee levels as part of its grant offer and you are best led by its advice.

Collect several photographs of the building inside and out, showing its key features and a few additional photos of the specific repair works. Prepare a set for each application identified below.

Expect a visit from an English Heritage inspecting architect after your application. Their report will be added to your application, and any questions or issues clarified before the application goes to the grant-making board. Grade I and II* church applications may be made between April and June each year and Grade II applications between April and September. Decisions may take as long as six months. It's a rather good Christmas present to Grade I and II* churches when they receive a positive response late in December with Grade II churches hearing around Easter.

There are two common reasons for churches not receiving a grant from the Scheme. First, the church has enough money (or almost enough) without help from the Scheme. Detailed questions about accounts are common during the consideration process as church endowment funds must be proven to be just that, restricted so that capital cannot be spent; many churches confuse this with designated funds.

Second, the works on your repair project may be less urgent than the others that applied to the Scheme this year. In this case it is worth reviewing your paperwork, considering with the architect whether you had suitably highlighted the urgency of the works in question, and re-applying in the following year. I have been turned down once on church projects, but all have received grants in the subsequent years.

Grant offers within the Joint Repair Scheme for Places of Worship come in two stages. The Stage One grant, lasting only one year, covers the detailed preparation of the project including:

- fundraising for the remainder of the money required for the whole project

- specialist reports, for example on roof timbers, drains or windows

---

How does the Scheme calculate the level of grant offered?

Consider a grant application for £250,000.

VAT will be reclaimed from the Listed Places of Worship Grant Scheme.[14] At 17.5% that contributes about £37,234 towards your target.

The money in the church building fund will be considered part of the project. The fact that that the Church Council have designated this towards another piece of work will not avert this conclusion by the Scheme. The logic is obvious: it's no good fixing the heating if the integrity of the building itself is at risk through a faulty structure.

The surplus in the general fund will be considered, if it is above what is needed for average running costs.

It is considered that the average church will gain trust grants of an average of £4,000 for the project.

Then the potential contribution of regular church members is calculated at £1 per member each week for a year.

The balance of the £250,000 is the resultant grant offer.

- faculty application and tendering
- preparing an ongoing maintenance plan and access audit.

The Stage Two grant is confirmed when Stage One is acceptably completed and covers the construction works.

During Stage One the church will undertake its other fundraising for the repair project and the sources may include: other charitable trusts, the Landfill Tax scheme and local fundraising. For charitable trusts the material prepared for the Joint Repair Scheme will provide most of the information required. In particular, look at county trusts for historic churches, National Churches Trust, Garfield Weston Foundation and various others. Chapter 13 tells you how to undertake a search for suitable trusts.

---

[14] See the website at www.lpwscheme.org.uk

Funding for features

Many elements of church repair may be tackled as a series of projects with each one taking on manageable proportions. For example, windows may be tackled in phases, the west window, then the east window then successive projects for others in order of the urgency of the repair needed.

There are several sources of outside funds, to add to your local efforts, for such features.

Small local trusts in many areas of the country may make grants because they can see that their grant will make a difference in a way that it would not on a major project (see Chapter 13).

Local fundraising is often most effective on fundraising for features as people can see the project and identify with it as heritage in a way that they can't when it is a roof.

Then you can consider applying to the "Your Heritage" stream of the Heritage Lottery Fund. This scheme specializes in supporting efforts to conserve features, fixtures and fittings in heritage buildings. It is not completely straightforward as the scheme expects heritage activities to accompany the conservation work. This could involve setting up a webcam so that people can monitor the ongoing conservation online; it could involve bringing in schoolchildren for education projects based on the conservation work or activities to engage local people and build their interest in the work.

Features such as war memorials should look at the Wolfson Foundation and English Heritage's war memorials grant scheme. The Glaziers Company (a livery company in the City of London) has an obvious and generous interest in windows. Look out for other small specialist trusts when you undertake your trust search.

There is an element of the Joint Repair Scheme (above) that can grant-aid projects that address Heritage Fabric at risk of imminent loss. If you have a feature such as an extensive wall painting that has deteriorated to the point of imminent loss then it could be worth phoning English Heritage to find out if a grant might be considered. Consider this route if the work could be outside the scope of the "Your Heritage Scheme" which has a maximum project cost of £50,000.

Church alterations and adaptations

Increasingly churches are considering alterations and adaptations to their buildings. Very often, in this time of increasing financial pressure on churches, opening up the church to use by more people is seen as a way of making the whole thing more sustainable, that is financially viable for the long term. There are significant mission imperatives for being inclusive rather than cultic in our approach to and use of our buildings, for in the Church of England the church belongs to the parish not the churchgoers and the vicar is appointed to serve the parishioners – all of them – not only the churchgoers. But here we will address the fact that it makes sense in most neighbourhoods, villages and urban areas, to use their best building for the benefit of everyone by making adaptations that make it usable. It is not always easy.

Major changes in historic buildings take time, appropriate consideration and extreme care. For unlisted churches there is less that might get in the way, but care will still need to be taken as the church will be inherited by a new generation for whom the essential qualities of sacred space must prevail.

The task of fundraising for church alterations, while having the potential of far more sources of funds than working on church repairs, does require a far more detailed and considered and different preparation. The list of preparatory work given here is almost all going to be included or summarized in the material sent to potential outside funders to assure them of just these considerations, that the project is definitely needed in the local neighbourhood, that intrusions and alterations to the historic fabric are only adopted when unavoidable, that once the work is completed the church has a healthy financial plan for the long-term future that makes the investment in change worthwhile.

Liturgical re-ordering

If your plan is to change, for example, the layout of the chancel and perhaps the front of the nave to facilitate new ways of worship, that is liturgically led re-ordering, there are few sources of funding available outside of the church. As the beneficiaries are mostly church members, most of the money will come from their efforts. Do undertake a trust search (see Chapter 13) to make sure, as you may find a local trust or even a national one that might assist.

Do consider all the people who use the church regularly, as potential donors or fundraisers, but also consider all the people who benefit from the occasional services of the church (or even have in the past) such as baptisms, weddings and funerals. An alteration that would make their special day more special could attract their support. Remember that local people may like to give their support through events and sales rather than through direct donations.

Fundraising for added facilities in church for local people and churchgoers

The church would be well advised to go through a fairly comprehensive set of studies that will inform how the adaptation of the building can be undertaken. These are set out briefly here with notes on how to find more information on such reports. While actually forming the basic elements of a well-rounded and well-founded development, they will become the appended materials to fundraising bids. In essence these key reports show the potential funder the appropriateness, viability and actual need for the development of the church.

1. Statement of Significance

The faculty jurisdiction rules in 2000 require a Statement of Significance if a church is applying for faculty to make significant changes to a listed church.

The Statement of Significance[15] includes two main parts, the first is a holistic view of the church in its setting. Describe its role in the local area and its significance to local life and streetscape. Then describe the church itself (and churchyard where appropriate), systematically working from the west toward the east, describing notable features as well as overall aspects of size and style. Individual items such as a font or windows may be graded from 'exceptional' to 'local' or even negative or intrusive, such as the concrete boiler house adjoining a medieval church. This first part of the Statement may be used time and again with faculty applications but the second part will change as it relates to the very specific item/s that will be changed after the faculty permission is granted.

Write this second part of the Statement of Significance only in the light of the local audit of need, the feasibility work, the option appraisal of how the benefits may be delivered and how the architectural solution has been selected.

Detail the actual impact of the changes, such as what will be impacted by the insertion of drains and cables or masked by added walls and so on. So the significance of the change may be assessed alongside the overall significance of the church.

2. Local audit of need and demand

Added facilities in churches in order to facilitiate use by local people for a variety of activities must be based on actual needs and demands of local people if a

---

[15] See www.churchcare.co.uk for a fuller explanation of what is expected in a Statement of Significance

church wishes to raise funds from outside sources, especially from trusts. And the extent to which they meet local needs, in terms of quantity and quality of provision, determines how much money may be raised.

Local demographics which lead to understanding the broadest parameters of local need can be obtained from www.neighbourhood.statistics.gov.uk. By entering the church's postcode into the box presented, you can gain access to breakdowns of demographic information, information on relative multiple deprivation and many aspects of local need. You may find a larger than average local population of children or elderly people, ethnic minorities, people of minority faiths and so on. Much information was gleaned by the last census but pages are being updated with new research all the time.

Once informed of the overall demographic shape of the church's neighbourhood, then it is time to find out which of the needs suggested by the statistics is either met or unmet in your neighbourhood. This is to ensure that you are not unnecessarily duplicating provision. You may have lots of children in your area but you may also be overloaded with nursery provision. There may not be a shortage of performance space but there may be a shortage of event space. You find out the answers to these questions by asking local voluntary and statutory providers, from council departments to arts centres:

- What do you see as the gaps in provision/services for local people that might be met by facilities in our church?

- Do you know of community/business/arts groups who would like to book meeting space on a regular or occasional basis? List them.

- If you are a local service provider what would you expect of our church facilities?

- If you consider that your group/service might wish to use the space approximately when and how often would that be?

- Are you aware of needs in the local area for which a community space might be created in our church?

- Do you have further suggestions and comments to make on our development that might be helpful to our planning team?

- Are there other local facilities and groups to whom we should talk?

Contact local residents and through small meetings or an open day ask for comments and ideas on what might be developed in the church. Ask particularly what facilities individuals know they would use or events and programmes they would attend. Get the numbers down through using questionnaires and other methods of recording.

You can now write up a fair summary of the needs and demands of local people showing that when you prepare your new facilities in your church people will actually turn up and use them, and, as appropriate, pay to use them.

3. Feasibility

The feasibility of your potential project may be considered from several points of view. After ensuring local need these include financial feasibility and architectural feasibility.

You can only have the changes that you can pay for. So feasibility begins with setting some financial parameters. At the time of writing, 2009, it is possible to build a complete modest but very serviceable community hall for £500,000. So it is hard to convince funders to add very expensive adaptations to a church when it would either cost far more than £500,000 or serve far fewer people than a community centre. Here are some suggestions:

- A toilet that will add quality for the visitors already using the building should be less that £50,000 preferably more like £25,000
- A servery that will help add a few social and cultural events each year, such as summer concerts, should cost again in the region of £25,000.
- Adding a meeting room for church and occasional use would not attract outside funding
- Adding a meeting room that will be used daily by 30 or 40 people might raise £75,000 to £100,000 from outside trusts in some areas.
- Adding a lift for disabled access to a crypt at the cost of £100,000 is unlikely to attract outside funding unless hundreds of people each week will use the newly available space

The key factor here is to decide what is absolutely necessary, not just desirable, in your church in order for it to be used by people who are waiting to use it.

Once you know what is realistic financially for your adaptation alongside the functional requirements that are essential, it is time to consider architectural feasibility. That is *how can your architect provide an outline design that meets the functional requirements within your financial limitations?* It is vitally important that you develop your project in this way, or you may, as I have discovered with many churches, have an idea on which the architect designs a flight of fancy which you cannot afford and which is not wanted by local people.

Expect to engage in a dialogue with your architect about how your building will be used and the many practical aspects of the project to get the outline design to an acceptable standard. For example, if you put a new toilet in the vestry which is next to the chancel will people a) be embarassed to be seen trouping up during the service or b) be equally embarassed by the sound of flushing during a quiet moment of prayer; if the vestry is at the back that may not be an issue! If you use the back half of the nave as a hall and meeting room except on Sundays, how will you have access to mid-week services or conduct funerals on weekdays or weddings on weekends?

Look at any suggested architectural solutions in the context of the Statement of Significance and consider their impact on the historic features of the building, aesthetically and physically. Once you have opted for a particular solution you are ready to write the second part of your Statement of Significance (1. above).

4. Options considered

Write a summary of the options you have considered, and how each met or didn't meet your criteria; that is the options of what support you might provide for local people and the path you have chosen. Summarize the facilities you see to be ultimately essential for this increased use of your church. Finally, summarize the options you have considered with your architect and how each fitted or didn't fit with your aspirations.

Preferred option. Now summarize what the adapted church will provide for local people, the facilities, when they will be available, who will use them and how many people will use them, daily, weekly and annually.

Summarize your preferred architectural solution: the one that meets the most of your needs and relates best to the significance of your building.

It can be advisable at this stage in your development to have a preliminary visit from your Diocesan Advisory Committee to look in principle at the changes you wish to make as you can now give them a reasoned approach to the needs you will meet and the impact of changes. Do not go as far as getting faculty permission as the final outcome of your fundraising may limit the work you can actually do and you would have wasted money since a second application would be needed.

5. Benefits that will be delivered

For the kinds of significant sums most churches need to raise for building works, there are other descriptive reports to prepare for outside funders.

• Outcomes: these are the qualitative changes that will happen in people's lives as a result of their use of your facilities. These may be educational, social, health or welfare, and stretch from community cohesion to reducing anti-social behaviour, improved relations between ethnic and religious groups, opportunities for volunteering and many more. When you put these together, consider at the same time how you will measure or record the delivery of these benefits to people who will use your church, by using questions, targeted conversations or worker reports. Some funders will ask you how you will monitor the results of your development and this is it. State it in your bid, but also make sure that the work is done when you are under way.[16]

- Beneficiaries: describe the people who will actually benefit from the church's new facilities. This will be couched in the language of the demographics you researched (above). You can list the groups that will use the finished space, and how they will use it. Appendix 4 on pages 217 and 218 gives an example of how you can describe the groups, the age groups or needs groups, and the numbers, counted on a footfall per annum basis, who will use the building.

6. Description of the construction required

For fundraising purposes, you require very little descriptive material from your architect; this is one advantage of leaving detailed design till after you have raised the money required. It's like being given the possible outline design of a good coat and then when you have the necessary money the design can be made to fit your resources, appropriate in material and detailing.

So ask your architect for a brief one or two page description with an outline drawing of the footprint of the building with the new facilities in situ. This in fact will be a representation of the functions of the new facilities not a design, which comes later.

Make a clear distinction in the architect's description of the work and in the quantity surveyor's budget between several aspects of the work. This will be important as different funders are interested in specific and different aspects of work. For example:

- Actual new facilities: toilets, servery, meeting rooms
- Re-ordering: removing pews, moving altars, changing chancels
- Upgrading: renewing heating, lighting and other existing facilities

[16] The best description and summary of *outcomes* is on the Big Lottery website, as they have initiated and established this aspect of developing provision and services to groups and communities. Lots of funders now use the same language and structure.

If repairs are identified at this stage they should be addressed as in the first part of this chapter and kept separate.

7. Quantity surveyor's indicative budget for construction, fees and including VAT

Most important to the fundraiser is an indicative budget from a quantity surveyor and the bigger the project the more advisable it is that the quantity surveyor is independent of the architect's practice. What you need is an *indicative* budget. The quantity surveyor will sit down with the architect and talk through the outline design and its implications and give you a calculation of what it might cost. Do plan a dialogue with the quantity surveyor so that you can understand the costs and whether they could be lower or should be higher. For example, the cheapest finishes in the toilets will soon be damaged by stiletto heels and stubbed-out cigarettes. The extension designed in structural glass and granite will have been estimated at a far higher projected cost than a more modest but acceptable extension in brick and traditional local materials. See page 219 and pages 242–3 for examples of indicative budgets.

This is a vital step of coming to agreement on projected cost, remembering, from above, that potential funders will compare the numbers of people and the cost of provision in your project with that in the community centre or village hall down the road, as they may have sufficient money for only one such project.

8. Revenue budget and cashflow projection

Since there is no point in a funder investing good money in a capital project if that project may fail in a few years it is incredibly helpful to include a projection for your revenue showing you can afford to run the new facilities and how you will do so. For really major projects, such as the wholesale regeneration of a building, you may need to prepare a business plan, which, in addition to showing how you will run and manage the building, will show how the income and expenditure will work out taking maintenance and repair, staff costs, utilities and everything else into account.

9. Statement of Need

Now you are ready to prepare a Statement of Need for the process of gaining permission for the works that will make your project possible. You will not normally need this Statement for outside funders but this is the point in the development process at which you have sufficient information to write it. In this document you will explain, justify and rationalize your project.[17]

Section A will describe the context of the church, giving information about the social and cultural context of the church, the current use of the church and describing the needs of the neighbourhood for change in the church.

Section B will explain the needed changes in the church in functional terms: including, for example, a toilet, a meeting room for up to 40 people, storage for equipment for childcare, access to various parts of the building for people with mobility problems.

Section C will describe the difficulties you have in meeting those needs, for example, a specific group who cannot use the space without heating and a toilet.

Section D will describe the proposed change to the building that can meet that need. Where more than one option has existed, mention these and why you have chosen your preferred one. For larger projects it will be necessary to explain how several new rooms will be used simultaneously, with the necessary added facilities, to show that the needs cannot be met with one new room. Where the project impacts on the way the liturgy is conducted explain the effects, desired or not.

Section E describes how you have audited the local area and neighbourhood to identify the needs of local people and how you will meet them. This in effect uses your report from Step 2 above.

Section F will indicate how key historic elements of the building will be affected by your proposal; for example, a window masked in the construction of the toilet or servery or moving the font to make way for a narthex meeting room.

10. Evidence of local support, letters, questionnaire results

Of all the churches I have worked with in the last 20 years not all have gained all the money they wanted, or in some cases needed. But remarkably all the churches who went out and got letters of support from a wide cross-section of local people

---

[17] A much fuller explanation of how to write your Statement of Need can be found at www.churchcare.co.uk.

did succeed in raising the money for their projects. I believe that this is no coincidence. Letters and reports on questionnaires and even photos of people discussing the project are direct evidence of local engagement for which there is no comparable substitute.

11. Church accounts

Church accounts will always be needed in the current format and of the standard required by the Charity Commissioners. Always send signed copies of the accounts with your trust applications, not photocopied signatures. Within three months of your accounting year end, the trusts will expect to see last year's accounts, that is by April 2009 they will expect you to send the approved accounts from 2008.

12. For larger projects and for some funders:

Expect to include the following elements which are described in the Business Plan in Chapter 20:

- Option Appraisal
- SWOT analysis
- Risk analysis for construction, ongoing revenue, maintenance and long-term repair
- Business plan including aims, outcomes, beneficiaries, strategic plan, management and staffing, financial management, marketing, monitoring and review.

12

Funding from Outside Sources for Church Halls and Community Projects

While trusts abound that fund church halls run as community halls, and community projects, to win the competition for such funding, churches have to produce fundraising materials to at least the standard of everyone else.

Do note that if the activity happening in the hall or the beneficiaries of the community activity are all church members or are required to attend a religious event in order to benefit, most of what is said in this chapter does not apply. Short circuit this process and go straight to the trust search in Chapter 13. You will find a handful of small trusts who support religious activities and that may support your project.

Before writing to trusts that might support you, prepare the following materials. Each of the items should probably have been part of your project preparation in any case, though churches are notorious for cutting corners on some items, such as options appraisals! Be thorough – your project will be stronger for it.

Repairing and refurbishing church and community halls

1. Local audit of need and demand

Provision of community space for meetings and events for local people must be based on actual needs and demands of local people if a church wishes to raise funds for repair and refurbishment from outside sources, especially from trusts. And the extent to which the hall meets local needs, in terms of quantity and quality of provision, determines how much money may be raised.

Local demographics which lead to understanding the broadest parameters of local need can be obtained from www.neighbourhood.statistics.gov.uk. By entering the hall's postcode into the box presented, you can gain access to breakdowns of demographic information, information on relative multiple deprivation and many aspects of local need. You may find a larger than average local population of children or elderly people, ethnic minorities, people of minority faiths and so on. Much information was gleaned by the last census but pages are being updated with new research all the time.

Once informed of the overall demographic shape of the church's neighbourhood, then it is time to find out which of the needs suggested by the statistics is either met or unmet in your neighbourhood. This is to ensure that you are not unnecessarily duplicating provision. You may have lots of children in your area but you may also be overloaded with nursery provision. There may not be a shortage of performance space but there may be a shortage of event space. You find out the answers to these questions by asking local voluntary and statutory providers, from council departments to arts centres, ensuring you approach a good cross-section:

- What do you see as the gaps in provision/services for local people that might be met by facilities in our hall?
- Do you know of community/business/arts groups who would like to book meeting space on a regular or occasional basis? List them.
- If you are a local service provider what would you expect of our church hall facilities?
- If you consider that your group/service might wish to use the space, approximately when and how often would that be?
- Are you aware of needs in the local area for which a community space might be created in our church hall?
- Do you have further suggestions and comments to make on our development that might be helpful to our planning team?
- Are there other local facilities and groups to whom we should talk?

Contact local residents and through small meetings or an open day ask for comments and ideas on what activities they would like to attend at the hall. Ask particularly what facilities individuals know they would use or events and programmes they would attend. Get the numbers down through using questionnaires and other methods of recording. A questionnaire common to all responders would facilitate tabulating responses for your report.

You can now write up a fair summary of the needs and demands of local people showing that when you prepare your new facilities in your church people will actually turn up and use them, and, as appropriate, pay to use them.

2. For all local people?

In many urban areas the neighbourhood has high numbers of people from minority ethnicities and other faiths. If your hall is truly a community facility and available to all local people it is important to gain, and show how you have gained, the input of these groups and individuals. Don't, as many churches do, assume that people of other faiths and backgrounds will not want to use church-owned facilities; most of them will use any kind of facilities that suit their need for community space. Sometimes church members are fearful that people of other faiths will worship in their church or hall, so discuss this among church members and decide how much you are open to everyone and additionally find out how people who are different from you might want to use your space before making judgements or rules. Remember to be honest when trusts ask about access to tell them if you have limitations on use. Most churches strike a pragmatic compromise and say activities which are 'legal and not inimical to the Christian faith'.

Since most outside funders will be aware of or look up the demographics of your neighbourhood, it is important to address the common prejudice that most mainstream churches are peopled by the white middle class. Prepare simple graphs from the statistics on the government website showing the breakdown of ethnic groups in your neighbourhood. Alongside this include graphs showing the ethnic breakdown of the users of your hall and the hall committee. (If you find you are not representative of the area, you may wish to find ways to address this issue.)

3. Evidence of accountability

What is the legal status of your hall? Many church halls are run by formal subcommittees of the PCC and this is perfectly acceptable. Make sure you have written terms of reference for the committee that can be included with your funding bids. Terms of reference should show how the committee is appointed and how it is accountable to the PCC especially over its focus of activity and its finances. In this case when asked on form for the legal status of the hall the answer is 'an excepted charity, that is registered with the Charity Commission but with no individual number'. Most recently, larger churches are being asked to register fully with the Charity Commission, so will have a number.

As church halls get busier, it can be hard for PCCs to cover all their interests as well as those of the church itself, and more independence is created. This can be one of two straightforward formats.

The PCC can create a limited company totally owned by the PCC and then lease the hall to the company. The hall committee members become the directors. The advantage from the church's point of view is that as the shareholder, the PCC not only receives a detailed annual report, it leaves the committee fully responsible for the finances and if something goes sadly wrong between church and hall the church has power to dismiss the directors and do something else.

The second option, registering the hall as a trust in its own right, creates greater independence between the church and hall, as any charitable trust has to be independent and cannot be run indirectly by another. Therefore the PCC will not have indirect control. For the first generation this may work well but with passing time, PCC and hall committee may become more distant and the PCC may effectively lose access to and control of and decisions about the hall.

4. Evidence of management

Most larger trusts ask questions about membership of the management committee, who is on it and their background; for example list all members of the committee, sex, ethnicity, disability, and work experience. The trust will want to know that any money invested in refurbishing a hall will be well managed during the building stage and the hall will be well managed – and well used after works are complete. A simple phrase 'retired station manager' (or 'teacher') shows someone who has management skills and experience in a way that 'retired' would not. Including information on ethnicity shows in multi-cultural neighbourhoods that the committee reflects both the neighbourhood and users of the hall. Having a company structure, even more than being a formal sub-committee of the PCC, means that the committee can co-opt people of other faiths and backgrounds onto the committee.

The minutes of the committee will show how the committee addresses the fundamentals of good management:

- Income and expenditure, cashflow, financial management, long-term financial strategies.
- Staff appointments and appraisals, staffing adequacy
- Marketing and the effectiveness of various types of communication, programming.
- Efficacy of communication structures with key targets: church, local people and organizations, community projects, church users and potential users.
- Long-term strategy and annual objectives.

- Health and Safety, Children's Act compliance, staff safety.
- Volunteers, management committee, church council.
- Maintenance and repair records and programmes.

5. Prepare a schedule of use

Appendix 4 shows a timetable, like that in school, that identifies all the user groups and activities running in the hall and can also show activities that will be in the hall once it is refurbished. It is possible to use colours to identify, for example, particular types of user groups in which a funder might be interested, such as children, youth, elderly, family, all ages and so on. Numbers commonly present at each session can also be added so giving the total number of users each week and each year. When asked for on an application form, this information has been calculated on a footfall basis. This approach of using a timetable of activities is a great tool for management, to ensure that the hall is well used. Additionally it is possible to calculate the annual income in advance by using the hours booked each week, multiplied by the letting rate. This can be used in budgeting to ensure that the finances of the hall balance in coming years (see budget and cashflow below).

6. Beneficiaries and outcomes

People give to People. No-one would fund your church hall if people were not going to benefit. Use your schedule of use to identify numbers and groups of people who benefit from the hall. Much funding is geared towards people who are disadvantaged or have special needs, so identify them clearly. Include information that shows that the ethnic mix of users of your hall is similar to your neighbourhood and so on. Comparing your records and counts of user groups with information you gathered in your report on needs and demands will give the evidence.

In addition funders nowadays want to identify outcomes; these are the ways in which those who use the hall actually benefit. For example, children in playgroup gain creative and educational skills, parents gain support from meeting with other parents, elderly people suffer less isolation and improved health from their programmes. Social groups offer improved social or community cohesion through working together on common activities. Much greater detail on outcomes and how to describe them (and measure the results) is on the website of the Big Lottery.

Many trusts ask how you involve your beneficiaries in decision-making. Describe what the hall committee does and especially how the beneficiaries of your work have input to your decisions or can get onto your committee. For hall management, it is not normally advisable to have a users' group as managers, but have a management committee that cares for the overall running of the hall and a consultative process so that user-groups can have input.

7. Option appraisal

Here is an option analysis that does a good job of answering internal questions for the church and management committee when addressing issues that relate to buildings, assessing them in the light of the church's own needs.

Another version of the Option Analysis, found more fully in Appendix 10, is a version of the analysis produced by a regeneration board. In this case the options are considered in the light of the targets of those serving wider community needs.

Each alternative route to achieving the overall objective is listed. Option one will assess doing nothing; then options shown that are not adopted and the reasons given; lastly the preferred option is given along with the reasons for adopting it. The categories of assessment of each option are: *Cost*, the full cost of this choice, including for example if a particular adaptation of the building would have higher ongoing staffing costs; *Impact*, considered in relation to the hall itself, its local neighbourhood, and the needs of local people and groups; *Strategic Fit*, this is primarily a consideration of how the particular approach to refurbishing the hall to meet local needs fits in with the neighbourhood and town-wide strategies of other agencies and organizations, such as regeneration bodies and councils; *Risk*, primarily concerns itself here with the ongoing risk, for example of the hall really being able to be self-financing and continuing in good repair, or whether its income is dependent on one key user who may suddenly decide to go elsewhere; *Deliverability*, what makes this option the most deliverable of the options you considered, giving a full explanation of your reasons. This outline for options is appropriate to application forms for outside funders especially those working in regeneration and similar local initiatives.

8. Risk analysis

A risk analysis considers everything that might or could go wrong with your project, financial and practical, sometimes unavoidable, and makes contingency plans for how to deal with the ensuing problems. Start with a list of the things that could go wrong (see Appendix 15 for an example with a tabular layout for your considerations). Next to each possible problem/risk consider the impact of that problem on the overall project. Next consider the likelihood of that problem arising. After this note the Mitigating Action, or what you will do to a) avoid the problem, b) build in safeguards c) take remedial action. So for example, if you fail to raise enough funds you might a) not plan the building works in detail until finance is in place, b) ensure that budgetary control is in place at all stages of the project and spending can never go over budget, so have good project management in place, and c) do the highest priority works first so that if the project is foreshortened it is aesthetic rather than functional work that is omitted.

9. Budget and cashflow projection

Many church halls do function on a financial shoestring, but often too that is part of the problem: no reserves have been built up to cover proper maintenance and future repair. An example of a simple cashflow projection is on page 251. This shows that with annual expenditure on administration, maintenance and minor repairs, money is accrued in a separate fund for larger repair and upgrading as these become necessary. As the hall is fully used by all sorts of people the church should receive a reasonable annual rent from the hall committee/trustees. (This should be at least as much as if the church sold the hall, put the money in the bank and collected the interest as income.) A good cashflow projection, to be updated regularly, gives assurance to outside funders that the future of the hall and the funder's investment has been well thought-out.

10. A description of the works to be done

A one- to two-page description from the architect or surveyor is sufficient for fundraising. If you have a floorplan showing, for example, where a new toilet will go, that can be included. But it is unnecessary and unwise to pay for detailed drawings before you know how much work you can afford! A good feasibility study by an architect shows how much you can have done for what you can afford.

11. Works budget

Using your consideration of options for your work and an outline of works from the architect, work with a quanity surveyor to make a list of actual works and their projected costs. Make sure that the eventual budget includes contingency, fees and VAT. A builder's estimate is seldom adequate unless the company is responding to an architect's specification with a full Bill of Quantities. Additionally, the builder will quote at today's prices and you may take more than a year to raise the money, by which time the price will have changed. A contingency sum allowing for projected inflation over the fundraising period can be included in the budget (see Appendix 5).

Building refurbishment should have longevity as one of its values. As the church plans a long-term strategy for the hall development it will be better to not adapt too closely to the needs of one community project that may not have a long life. It is better to plan for a long life for the facilities and be able to show that the likely long-term needs of the neighbourhood are in keeping with the long-term future of the hall. For example, floor finishes should be resilient, otherwise more money will be needed in two or three years to replace vinyl that is pocked from shoe heels and various activities.

Funders may not be interested in funding the church project if the cost per square metre for refurbishment is greater than it would be to build a new hall from scratch.

Consider the cost of building works set against the potential lifetime of the project. For example, the church would like to repair its hall and adapt it for a daytime project for the elderly, with continued use by all sorts of local groups on evenings and weekends. If the hall repair and adaptation is £200,000 but the project has a likely life of ten years then you can consider that it is going to cost £20,000 per year. Is that a worthwhile investment of money from an outside trust? If they find it is possible to make the same provision in a different building nearby for less money, why would the funder invest in the church's building? Why would you, after all? So in conversation with the quantity surveyor and architect be prepared to ask for a more modest package of works that will still fulfil the necessary functions, a package that is priced more comparably with other community centres and facilities in your area.

For funders use a one-page summary of the quantity surveyor's indicative budget, with as much break-down of the total cost as can be fitted onto one page. An example is on page 219.

12. Description of the project

About two-thirds of outside funders ask for a project description of up to 2 pages of A4, plus a copy of the accounts and any other essential information.

All the research and preparation done above is now précis-ed into this description. First describe the hall, explain the needs and demands in the neighbourhood; summarize the committee and the legal structure. Explain how the building will be refurbished to meet the needs, the cost of works and the amount of money already raised. Fit in as much as you can, but don't reduce the font size or margins to fit more, or crowd the page in any way.

13. Letters of support

Current users of the hall and would-be users can give you letters of support, as well as other agencies and individuals, such as councillors, who see your new provision as important to the neighbourhood. Along with a good assessment of the needs and demands of local people, letters of support make almost more difference than anything else to your ability to raise funds.

14. Accounts

Ensure you have a signed copy of the most recent church accounts, that is within 3 months of the end of the accounting year.

Welfare, education, arts and social projects serving local people

For general community projects, welfare, arts, education and social, the fundraising material is in many ways similar to that prepared for community buildings, with a few differences in emphasis.

1. Local audit of needs and demands

Follow the guidance above (p. 105) for developing your local audit. However, this time you will identify from the demographics the needs and demands of your particular target group. So what is the identiable need for provision for, say, people with mental health issues and what is the demand?

Collect letters of support from potential users, current users, health providers and others who recognize your project will meet a pressing need.

2. Committee details

Your management committee should complete a summary of brief information about each committee member, identifying the skills and experience of the members in managing a project that addresses the need. You may have teachers on an education project, health visitors on a health project and so on, along with people skilled in aspects such as finance in the voluntary sector.

3. Track record

Keep records that allow you to give statistical information on your success in dealing with your target users. For education that may mean people who have moved on to a college course, for mental health that may mean people who are enabled to stay in their own homes. Also collect, in a schedule or programme of activities, a numerical record of programme times and average attendees at each session. This will indicate not only that you are enabling people to develop but that you are attracting enough clients to make the project justifiable. Compare yourselves with other similar projects and their outputs if you are unsure.

4. Beneficiaries

Identify in general terms the backgrounds of those who use your project, or will use it, and show how it fits local needs and demands.

Identify, asking your clients to help you, the direct benefits of the project. To help you explain your outcomes, there is good descriptive material on outcomes and benefits on the Big Lottery website.

5. Budget and cashflow

Prepare detailed, thorough and realistic cashflow projection for your project, using an appropriate rate for salaries, running costs, utilities, rent and other costs. Church projects have been turned down for grants because their budgets were unrealistically low! Again check your budget against similar projects.

6. Job descriptions

For any fundraising for salaries, include a job description for your workers, exist-ing or planned, and ensure your employment practice is up to scratch. The Church Urban Fund have in the past produced excellent material on being a good employer.

7. Equal opportunities

Churches are often considered by outsiders to be sexist, racist and homophobic. Do prepare an Equal Opportunities Policy and Practice Statement. It is not advis-able to state the church is an Equal Opportunities Employer or service provider if there are areas of church life where this is not the case; you should prepare such statements for the project making it clear that it is the project Policy and Practice.

8. Two-page project description

Much of the information you have prepared will be used for application forms. But about two-thirds of trusts ask for a description of the project along with essential additional material, such as accounts and budgets, job descriptions and track records.

In your two-page description include summaries of all the material above. The final paragraph should summarize the funds needed and funds already raised.

9. Annual accounts

Collect a signed copy of the annual accounts for the most recent year, within three months of the year end.

10. How will you monitor progress?

Lots of church projects are monitored and reviewed rather haphazardly, if at all. This is an important area to grasp, as more funders are keen to see good moni-toring, review and action-planning in place.

If the hall or project committee has not operated this way in the past, consider each of the major areas of the project's agenda and consider each fully at monthly meetings, that is one month the year's finances and at another developments in good practice and at another how the project brings in new clients/users. Decide initially who will produce the various monitoring reports that are needed and the date of the committee meeting at which each will be discussed, after which an action plan can be drawn up identifying who will do what and by when.

11. Other questions you may be asked

How does your project relate to the work of other organizations? No community project is an island. There is always a local network of voluntary projects which will be of benefit to your project. This can identify support and share good practice. It is most helpful to extend beyond church networks into your neighbourhood rather than just going to church networks.

How does your project meet our funding priorities? Read the funder's guidelines and relate to them specifically, indicating clearly in an accompanying letter or as part of your project description how your project specifically fits the guidelines and objectives.

What are the overall aims of your organization? A general answer is needed such as meeting the pastoral and religious needs of local people. Do not use a long religiously phrased mission statement, you are almost bound to be misunderstood.

If the project is to continue, how will it be funded? The revenue budget for a hall may indicate self-sufficiency and savings for the future. But community projects should be able to show that there is a comprehensive fundraising programme in place with regular applications going to all the sources that may help them as funding from any one source dries up – as it always will! Many church projects build themselves around Church Urban Fund finance but fail to prepare themselves for the end of the funding after 3 or 5 years. A regular cycle of fundraising applications each year is the answer.

Key points

- Gather information on all aspects of trusts' interests and use this as the pool of information to be drawn on as trust applications are prepared.
- Gather the related material together, such as signed copies of annual reports and accounts.
- Gather several letters from local agencies and individuals supporting your project development.
- Then begin trust fundraising.

13

Trusts and Foundations

Despite the production of books full of lists of trusts and foundations that will make donations to church projects, any one church is likely to find just a handful applicable for their building project and maybe as many as thirty for social welfare, children and youth, or community projects. Many trusts are tightly tied to particular geographical areas; many others based on ancient endowments have failed to upgrade their capital value and now give away a few pounds or a few hundred pounds each year. Such trusts may be useful and helpful when a church seeks funds for its annual children's outing but not significant when the church is seeking funding for a new full-time community project or for a major building repair. Research for the few that really will count is simplified by several key trust guidebooks.

Finding trusts that may fund your project

The research process

Most commonly, these days, research is undertaken through dedicated websites. Dioceses, churches or individuals may subscribe and log on. The search is narrowed down through information on geographical area, type of project and age group and other categories that the data provider has provided.

Consider both national and local charities and most searches will give all potential trusts, local and national. Enter the kind of work you wish to undertake in your project, for example, buildings works, heritage, children, elderly, disadvantaged, health and so on. Do enter your project in more than one way if you can. Search under children, then under disability if this is relevant; or search under heritage, buildings and volunteers, taking a variety of approaches to a project that is going to do more than one activity. Remember that building works are never an end in themselves, so consider the beneficiaries of the building and the ongoing activities and benefits when working on a building project.

- Directory of Social Change at www.dsc.org.uk or Funderfinder are commonly used.
- A good summary of sources is given at www.churchcare.co.uk.

To gather information about grants from Landfill Operators, go to the website of Entrust and click the section on finding funding. This allows you to enter your postcode and then a search results in a list of landfill operators who may make grants in your area. Sift through the list, visiting the various website links and discover who will actually be interested in your location and your project. About 20% are normally possible, maybe two or three operators. The same website will also allow you to enter your postcode and discover landfill sites that are local to you, as landfill operators require information about geographical location before considering a grant.

Many people, especially those new to using internet searches and fundraising, may prefer to use books giving trust information. A wide variety of books are listed in the catalogue of the Directory of Social Change.

Sources of Grants for Building Conservation[18] is a useful summary of trusts that will fund church building works especially for the conservation of heritage material.

Funds for Historic Buildings[19] is produced with annual updates by the Architectural Heritage Fund, who also have a website: www.ffhb.org.uk. The trust specializes in grant-aiding work to save buildings at risk, often being reclaimed and found new use by small voluntary groups. While not a key target for a funding application, their funding guide (free to access online) does include trusts that will fund churches.

Most useful for the beginner at fundraising, the regional guides, such as A Guide to Local Trusts in London, from the Directory of Social Change[20] are a must-have for community projects and church hall funding. Each of these guides lists major trusts funding in the region and then particular trusts within limited geographical areas such as boroughs or counties. It includes major church charities.

The Charities Aid Foundation FOCUS Series: Religion selected all the religious trusts from their comprehensive Guide to Charitable Trusts and put them in one smaller handbook. It is now out of print so ask around other local churches to see

---

[18] *Sources of Grants for Building Conservation*, Cathedral Communications Ltd, The Tisbury Brewery, Church Street, Tisbury, Wilts SP3 6NH.

[19] *Funds for Historic Buildings*, Architectural Heritage Fund, Clareville House, 26–27 Oxenden Street, London SW1Y 4EL.

[20] Directory of Social Change, see 'Resources and Connections'.

if one can be borrowed. The larger comprehensive Charities Aid Foundation guide to charitable trusts is available but expensive and will be in the local reference library.

For those prepared to read more extensively for an out-of-the-ordinary trust, many other major guides are also available from the Directory of Social Change and include a further few major trusts who will fund work on church buildings (though none that are not listed on the Council for the Care of Churches website on fundraising) and many for other charitable causes. *A Guide to the Major Trusts*, volume 1 and *A Guide to the Major Trusts*, volume 2 speak for themselves, but the catalogue from the Directory of Social Change includes many other titles that may prove useful for particular projects and information on training programmes and their annual Charity Fair.

These books are all expensive, so it is worth visiting the local library and checking that these guides are really necessary before buying them. To the beginner, only the first three are really of help for straightforward trust applications and are good to keep on the bookshelf.

Collating the information

Build up a file of all your selected trusts, gathering the contact details and application procedures, and double-check their exclusions sections. Under exclusions, many trusts who will not fund religious causes will fund religious buildings or church-based activities that benefit everyone in the local community.

A minority of trusts will provide application forms of their own. These request particular information some of which is unique to that trust, but most of the information is covered by the preparation outlined in Chapters 11 and 12.

Prepare your material

Using the explanations in Chapters 11 and 12 collect the information that will be appended to each application, copy and collate. When a trust asks for a letter of application, I use a letter to explain how my project fits their criteria and then still include a two-page description.

Church buildings

Prepare:

- Description of project
- Legal status of applicant (such as Parochial Church Council)
- Cheque payment details (name as on bank account)
- Information on who uses the church, how many and how often
- Information about money already raised for the project and money the church will raise itself locally
- List of trusts to whom you are applying
- Description of the church and its setting, its Grade and any notable or at-risk features. Explain the need for and urgency of the project.
- Photographs, inside and out
- Contact details, name, address, phone and email

Church adaptations and alterations

Prepare:

- Statement of Significance
- Local audit of need and demand
- Feasibility study, that is an assessment of what can be provided to meet the need at a realistic cost
- Option appraisal
- Benefits of the project, benficiaries and outcomes
- Outline description of the works from the architect
- Quantity surveyor's indicative budget including fees and VAT
- Revenue budget and cashflow projection for the altered building
- Statement of Need
- Evidence of local support, mainly letters along with questionnaire results
- Church accounts, some trusts ask for two or more years' accounts
- Summary description of the project on 2 sides of A4

Church halls

Prepare:

- Local audit of need and demand
- Equal opportunity policy or equivalent
- Legal status and evidence of accountability
- Evidence of good management
- Schedule of use, showing times, numbers of users and types of groups
- Beneficiaries and outcomes
- Option appraisal
- Risk analysis
- Revenue budget and cashflow projection
- Brief description of work to be done (from architect)
- Quantity surveyor's indicative budget including fees and VAT
- Summary description of the project (2 sides A4)
- Letters of support
- Annual report and accounts

Community projects

Prepare:

- Local audit of need and demand
- Committee details
- Legal status
- Track record
- Beneficiaries
- Budget and cashflow projection
- Job descriptions
- Equal Opportunities policy
- Two-page summary description
- Annual accounts

- How monitoring is done
- How funding will continue at the end of the grant
- How the project meets the particular funder's guidelines

Some Dos and Don'ts

1. Name and contact details

Ensure that the description you provide to trusts has the name of the organization at the top, followed by the details of the contact person with address, phone and email and finally the name of the particular project

2. Name of trust and their correspondent

Address the trust correctly; they do change their names from time to time and often change the name of the correspondent. Check in a current funding guide and do not use old information.

3. Spelling

Presentation needs to be extremely good. Spelling should be British English not Spellcheck's American versions. So after completing each set of bid documents and forms re-read everything and take time to do all corrections. If you are unsure on any element of spelling or grammar (or perhaps should be) get someone else to check the material.

4. Project name and organization name

These may be provided on the heading of the description but make sure they are also on each page of the appendix and any accompanying letters. Trustees reviewing bids have so many bids to look through, including constant reminders of who you are is important.

5. Layout

Make the layout spacious and easy to read. One trust now asks for print of at least 12-point to make applications legible. Leave space between shortish paragraphs, and if the content doesn't easily fit the page précis the text, do not reduce the print size.

6. Paper quality

Use good quality paper and avoid recycled or photocopier paper.

7. Phone use

Use the phone only if the guidelines invite you to and do not try to get a hint of whether you might get a grant from the person who speaks to you. Only the trustees can make that decision; the correspondent on the phone may only offer guidance.

8. Leaflets

If you have a fundraising leaflet do enclose it with your bids, but do not make one specially, certainly not an expensive glossy one. The leaflet will really be evidence that you are fundraising locally and that local people are committed to the project.

9. Keeping copies

Trusts to whom you apply will contact you. So keep a clear copy of every bid in its own folder so you can lay your hands on it when a phone call comes in and can then answer any particular questions.

10. Letters should be on the church's headed notepaper

Use the church's headed notepaper and include a reference to the church's charitable status. Most trusts only give to registered charities. The Church of England

and each of its churches is a registered charity, but without the requirement of having a registration number from the Charity Commissioners. As appropriate you may wish to state that your church is an Excepted Charity, to reassure potential funders of your status under charity law. Under the heading state clearly the name of the contact person, with their role in the church in brackets. Try not to use paper that gives a list of various church personnel, it is confusing.

11. Thankyou programme

Pre-designate someone to send thankyou letters to all trusts that make contributions. Shamefully, a number of churches forget!

Key points

- Be concise and be precise, using a major application as a model.
- Be interesting as well as informative; avoid the trustees getting bored.
- Make the application look and feel good.
- Use the church's name often enough in the text for it to be remembered.
- Never use any abbreviations for any reason.

The materials prepared should be in the language of the funder and the sector in which they operate. While church language is understood by the Church Urban Fund, most other funders of halls and community projects will not understand words like parish, vicar and churchwarden or even nave, chancel and narthex!

14

Major Individual and Corporate Donors

Being able to engage with major individual donors and companies requires several new facets to your fundraising. The professional fundraiser working with major national campaigns will work on major individual donor strategies all the time. Many of the principles are transferable, but, in total, their strategies would be more applicable to the national church than the local one. A nationally recognized church that can employ professional fundraisers may successfully choose that route. If the church is setting out on a fundraising programme for a building of international significance or even a cathedral this is a 'must-include' aspect of fundraising. Many local churches with no existing potential Big Name donors should consider this a very long-term approach or give it a miss altogether. Here in this chapter we only tackle an adaptation of that method as it might apply to the local church.

There are many church locations that exclude those churches from big-donor fundraising. Many village churches have no connections that will bring them introductions to wealthy individuals or businesses. Many churches in areas of urban deprivation have no residents or contacts that will introduce them to wealthy individuals either, but churches in these more disadvantaged locations may have access to government regeneration and other funds not available to churches in areas of comparative wealth. This reinforces the value of assessing your potential fundraising opportunities (see Chapter 6).

The first considerations are internal. The church needs enough self-understanding that it can allow others to 'own' the project, although these outsiders are not members. Outside donors will want to be proud of their project, may want to show it off to others, and to say, 'Here's where we decided to place the new toilets, because . . .' The relationship will require hospitality, and when such a donor is present they will expect to be treated as they are treated in their own social and business circles; the church and its key staff will need to give this person lots of attention. This may go against the grain of the church culture but talk among members about the implications thoroughly beforehand and enjoy the occasion.

Then the church needs enough self-understanding to present their project in terms understandable to the potential donors, without violating their own mission and integrity. The language is crucial for communication that will reach outside donors, but it will not happen without the inner security that allows the church to look at and describe itself through outside eyes. Many of the little things that are important to our church life have been parodied by a relatively cynical culture in which we live and work. But there is a great deal of goodwill among people outside the church who, given the opportunity, are prepared to engage with the church's values and activity. Also, many wealthy individuals are already church members who are open to making contributions to further the work of other local churches.

If your sense of Christian identity cannot encompass the spirituality and good-will of people who are quite different from you, then it is unwise to get them involved in your project. One church received a major contribution from a patron. After her death, the husband wished to place a commemorative plaque – which was acceptable to the Diocesan Advisory Committee – in the church. The Parochial Church Council refused, questioning the Christian credentials of the donor and not wanting to commemorate someone who 'was not a Christian'. The *first* donation should not have been accepted. Review the church's ethical policy and avoid such situations before they happen, as they bring discredit on more than just that particular church.

'Getting your ducks in a row'

Major donor fundraising involves considerable time.

About 10 per cent of the time will be spent initially on thorough preparation. About 80 per cent of the time is then spent on building relationships, listening to and understanding the key outside people. The final 10 per cent is asking for money.

Preparing the background material

What is the church's rationale for its future, its building project and its relationships with outside people? Review the church's values and ensure that there 'is room in your heart' for the donors that are drawn in.

Consider again a series of concentric circles used in Chapter 6 (Figures 6.1 to 6.3). The inner circle is the church members – those who are already committed. The next circle is made up of people for whom the church is some kind of home – the youth club and others who use the space regularly. The outer circle and the space beyond are the areas with which this chapter is concerned.

Most of the prime major donors will be contacts that already have some value, such as local residents and local businesses. Some will already have been aware of the church, through occasional church services, baptisms, weddings, funerals, or social events in the area or through business involvement. Of the latter the interest may be that businesses have employees in the church and its neighbourhood.

To consider this development, explore each of the following categories and decide together what the scope is for people who are not church members to be taken to its heart. People who become the church's major donors do so in a significant relationship of friendship and mutual commitment.

Spiritual and religious

What respect and friendship is the church prepared to develop and sustain with people of other faiths or none? How about Jewish, Muslim or Hindu contributors? How important is it that potential donors agree with the church's Christian beliefs, doctrine and churchmanship? Decide before seeking donors.

Heritage

When an outside donor offers a huge donation to restore the church organ, will the desire for heritage integrity be allowed to control the work if it is a condition of the gift? Do you know beforehand what the church wants so that the church does not have to turn down a considerable donation? Will there be room for negotiation? In receiving a grant from English Heritage the same dilemma arises, of course, as they make their grant conditional on the quality of future works to the heritage building for some years. Most churches cope with this condition. Is a restored organ that is not quite what the church thought it wanted better than an organ that doesn't work at all? Could the church enjoy the restored instrument along with the donor?

Architecture

The National Gallery has a new Sainsbury Wing, providing the extra facilities the gallery was seeking. How much influence can a wealthy benefactor, providing new facilities, have over style, design, location and even maybe which architect works on the scheme? What if the donor contributes to one part of the works only, the part that matters most to them and perhaps less to the church? Such a gift is essentially restricted and can only be spent on that piece of work; does the church want the work?

History

Many outsiders, including tourists, see churches as museums, places to visit as a means of recollection of the past. They visit at times when there is very little evidence of the living church visible and relate to the 'quaintness' and aura of things past. How can the church build a relationship with such people, find common interest and build that interest into a financial commitment?

The commitment to history and heritage has provided a large proportion of the finance for the restoration of Christ Church, Spitalfields, in London, and much time has been spent on negotiating a working balance between restoring original materials and designs from the eighteenth century and the needs of the contemporary church. There will almost always be a workable compromise that can be found through negotiation.

Neighbourhood and community

Local residents have a huge vested interest in the quality of their environment and its assets, from historic buildings to community services and facilities. In wealthy areas local residents are willing to join and contribute to church initiatives as long as they can see that the project has relevance to their lives, their aims and their values. As a church, explore your own values for the environment and seek for potential common ground.

As the church works to draw major donors from the area outside the circles and into the first circle of commitment, it is these areas of common interest and mutual respect that will feature highly.

Reasons for outsiders making donations

This list cannot be comprehensive, but each represents a contact point.

- Heritage
- Civic pride
- Social responsibility
- Philanthropy

- Tradition
- Social welfare
- Architecture
- Education
- Faith
- Music and other arts
- A good funeral, baptism or wedding
- Friendship
- Environment of their property

Using a chart such as the one below, consider who in the context of your church would be the beneficiaries that could be identified if such a donation were made. This will form an important and specific element in the approach prepared for each individual donor.

Interest	Beneficiaries
Heritage and history	Tourists, school visitors, historians, local people developing a pride in their own area and its history
Civic pride	Local town or village's sense of pride; a business area's sense of pride and well-being
Social responsibility	All who may benefit from the overall welfare of the community
Tradition	People of the area whose extended families have long-term connections with the community and church, some from far afield
Social welfare	Children, young people, disabled or other groups among the congregation and others who use the building regularly
Education	Local schools who use the church as a meeting place, as a history project and as a religious education project
Faith	The church and its members, those who benefit from pastoral care in the area
Good funeral	The memory of a loved one preserved for the family

The most difficult step is perhaps the next one. When the church has identified the potential areas of interest and the identifiable beneficiaries, then begin the process of identifying specific donors by name. Start with no more than twelve. If the list results in more names, put some into a second round.

Sphere of interest	Potential donor names
Heritage and history	*Local resident interested in heritage*
Neighbourhood and community	*Key local residents*
	Local resident and benefactor of education projects
Civic pride	*Local business leader*
	Local chamber of commerce member
	Trading association members

A church may find that some of their own members fit these categories. In this case the church has someone who has already moved into one of the inner circles of Figure 6.2 (p. 42). That person may not only make a large donation, if approached with the same care as anyone else on this list, but may also act as advocate in contacting others. Wealthy people in positions of power respond well to being approached by people that they consider their peers. Most donors will not be famous but enjoy being approached or later recognized and thanked by a more famous patron (see Appendix 1).

The target donors are approached individually; the approach is personally tailored and appropriately made.

Consider each target person or group. Consider a key objective the church may have in common with them. Decide on a clear message. The message will tie in with the messages on the church's fundraising brochure. (Brochures are mentioned below and covered more fully in Chapter 17.)

Work out where and when to have a meeting with the target person and which one or two people will go to the meeting. Those people must represent the heart of the church, its leadership and sense of direction, *but must* be comfortable with the language, atmosphere, and culture of the person being approached. Peer to peer is best. If you are meeting a titled person send a titled person or the nearest the church has, along with a senior member of the church or staff.

Plan every detail possible. Your manner must be personable, friendly and relaxed. You must appreciate and affirm their values, even if only being happy for *them* to hold those values. Their gift of whatever size must be openly valued against the fundraising target. And do not gush over the person, unless you are normally a gushy person; it will become an embarrassment to everyone including the donor, who may be put off.

Make the meeting sociable but purposeful. Let the person talk, let them ask about your concerns, and tell your story (that is the church's fundraising story) when invited to, and invite them to become involved. Tell them you are asking for financial contributions. Tell them of other contributions you have received from similar contributors. Regardless of the level of response or rebuttal, invite the person to a reception or event at the church where they can meet people involved (the patron will be helpful here, but if you have no patron many mayors have proved very willing to act as the dignitary for churches).

Sometimes the initial approach may be to a group, for example the chairperson of a local business association may invite you to address the group. At such a session there are two possible approaches that you can discuss with the chairperson: *either* it is an invitation to ask for money – this is applicable if the chairperson has already donated or promised a donation – *or* it is a preliminary to meeting each of them individually.

Often the more the potential donor gets involved, the more they subsequently give, but not always. A gift well received and openly appreciated and acknowledged may also result in further gifts. It has happened at times that a donor has made a small gift to see how the organization reacts before making a bigger donation.

Take the process carefully and seriously. The church will end up with lots of new friends who share in the responsibility for the future. The church will also eventually end up with the money. This kind of fundraising is more like setting a ball rolling and staying with it than putting a toe in the water and pulling it out.

If the approaches seem to produce nothing – collectively, that is, as any individual may prove to be uninterested – look again at the process. Go back to lining up your ducks more effectively, prepare the information more carefully and give particular attention to the message and the story for each individual. The story may have changed because someone late on the list has made a donation, and those earlier may now be interested because a peer of theirs has shown generosity they are prepared to match. But you may have to improve the list of friends and rebuild the relationship stage.

If the church is approaching members of the congregation for larger donations, keep several issues in mind. The member concerned will, within the life of the church, have focused concerns and objectives that reflect their particular interests. Their interest may be churchmanship, heritage, mission, welfare, parish life and ministry, values or lifestyle issues. The issue has the potential to become contentious, and in this case it may be better to not ask for a specific donation, as it is more important to have the person's continued membership than have an upset over money. They may instead be a good person to have involved in a patron's role, inviting donations from their peers outside the church's circle. Such potential donors will, if the congregation is well informed, know all about the fundraising and will be part of stewardship and legacy programmes.

Finding advocates

Progressing from the original set of target donors is a significant step. You may of course have had more than twelve on your original list and can now move to the secondary list. It is more likely that in order to develop further a major fundraising campaign you will wish to draw on people with whom you have had no contact previously in the circle of donors. The most direct way to do this is to look at the original twelve targets and identify who among them has got significantly involved with the project. These are the people to invite to become advocates for the fundraising scheme. The people who are now committed members of the fundraising circle can assess who among those they know might become a donor, for all the same reasons the church used to identify the original set of target donors.

The next step will be to go through the message and story preparing the stages and agreeing how the approach to new people will be made by the donor-become-advocate. Some flexibility will be needed, but the offer may be as simple

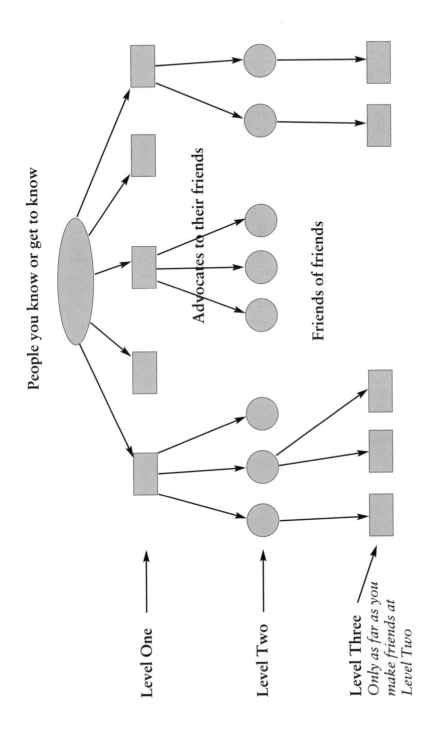

People you know or get to know

Advocates to their friends

Friends of friends

Level One →

Level Two →

Level Three →
Only as far as you make friends at Level Two

Figure 14.1 Finding further donors

as an opportunity at a specially arranged dinner party for a couple of church people to speak about the project and ask for help to arrange a church visit.

Progress can only be made from one stage of friendship to the next when people in the most recent target level have become involved enough both to give and to become advocates. In effect only when a donor has become a real friend at the heart of the church can they become an advocate. The church may find itself with quite a circle of new friends, most of whom are happy to give without interfering in the processes of church life. The church may find new skills are also offered.

Most importantly, having taken people to heart and built good friendships, look after these donors. They and the church may be able to help each other in the future.

Key points

- Big donor fundraising does not happen quickly.
- Build the relationship while being open about your fundraising story.
- Ask for money when the time is right and full appreciation can be given.

Note. Many major fundraising agencies make major donors one of their main streams of work. It is not an easy route for local churches, although churches with a national and international profile will use such a process with the professional fundraiser.

15

Securing Grants from Public Sources

Probably the largest grants for local projects, church and community, are from the public sector. Several major funding streams are provided directly from local or national government, from quangoes and from the National Lottery. Most recent additions include grants to offset Value Added Tax, by the Listed Places of Worship Grant Scheme, and Landfill Tax grants.

Regeneration of areas of deprivation

Over the past decade successive governments have attacked the blight of urban and rural deprivation through a series of targeted initiatives. Starting with City Challenge and moving forward through New Deal for Communities, Health Action Zones and Education Action Zones, the initiatives are now progressing into more specialized projects tackling environment and leisure as well.

Vast sums of money are being targeted into creating change in small geographical areas. On the whole the resultant strategies in these locations are led by local government or health authority managers. All are aimed at enabling local communities to become active in changing their own environment.

The theory is excellent. Initiatives that tackle deprivation and social exclusion are most effective when they engage local people in formulating and leading the development of solutions. This involves finding means for 'capacity building' that involve training and developing skills among local people in leading and managing projects. In practice many senior workers in the strategic partnerships that develop are still professionals from the regeneration sector. But many small local groups and businesses benefit, and where latent skills and talents are uncovered, there is considerable success.

Any church that is located in the target area of one of these initiatives may become a partner in the regeneration initiative. The regeneration grants will target specific areas of community development, and the church, in becoming a partner, is delivering the targeted benefits to the local community.

For the church that is struggling to survive and to maintain its buildings, seeking a new identity as a weekday-as-well-as-Sunday church, this may be a direction to take up. It is not a quick fix and will not work if the church is seeking to use the regeneration strategy as a fast way of getting money. The regeneration partnerships and agreements will tie the church into delivering targets for at least several years. Fundamentally, the church will identify itself with a network of partners who will work together with the benefit of central government grants to fund their initiatives. Faith groups are increasingly becoming accepted as effective agents in delivering change in regeneration areas. It is accepted that their focus may benefit more members of their particular faith than other people, but since their people are also local residents this is not a major problem, as long as facilities are provided that are open to all without the beneficiaries being required to join a religious activity.

One note of warning in following this route is that while many urban and rural churches have made enormous contributions to regeneration projects with mutual benefit, this is not everyone's experience. At the senior and government levels there has been considerable discussion and affirmation of the role that faith groups are able to take up in regeneration, but there is a problem at the grass roots of some regeneration projects. From the experience of a number of churches it is, in some projects, very difficult for mainstream churches to be acceptable to the officers at grass-roots level and on regeneration boards. It is almost as if 'faith groups' has been taken to mean minority faith groups and not Christian groups, just as ethnic groups has been taken to mean *minority* ethnic groups. In other words, this approach is a bit of a lottery, and it is worth preparatory investigation before putting a great deal of energy into this form of fundraising, or having an immense amount of determination to appeal against prejudice that does not accept majority faith groups as acceptable agents to deliver community change.

The direct and indirect benefits of getting engaged in regeneration partnerships are several. Ministry finds new dimensions as new contacts and networks are established. Very often the presence of church leaders among local consultative groups and on local forums generates new interest and respect among local community leaders. Money does become available for building and community projects, the former where there is a clearly identifiable benefit to many local people and the latter when the project is within the targets the regeneration board wishes to see delivered. Many new and valuable contacts will be made through the partnerships that develop, and it may well be that the greatest benefit to the church will come through a peripheral relationship for which the regeneration initiative makes an opportunity. In parallel to this, regeneration strategies become extremely time-consuming, and many people fall by the wayside. The most persistent at staying with the process are the most likely to receive support and grants. The application processes are often pressurized by very short deadlines, the language and structure are tortuous and long-winded, and the accountability after grants are awarded is equally consuming. It is worth it for big wins.

Regeneration boards and consultative groups vary greatly from one another. For this reason, the suggestions given here for developing partnerships with the regeneration board are quite general; the specifics of who to contact and how to contact them will vary from area to area. The local Council for the Voluntary Sector or the Voluntary Action Council are very good first contact points, if the church does not receive information delivered to every resident and local group.

Local conservation and community development by local authorities

With the regeneration strategies of central government taking centre stage in many areas of deprivation and social exclusion, both the conservation and community development departments have in recent years taken a much lower profile in most boroughs. Some boroughs do still continue to allocate funding to these departments that can be given in grants, and using the approaches given below it can be well worth contacting them. If the church is located in an area with no regeneration initiatives, these local authority departments may well prove able to provide considerable support and, at times, grants. Since every borough is different, the church should at least meet up with officers in these departments to explore possibilities.

Developing partnership in council and government schemes

Unlike trust fundraising, developing partnerships always begins with face-to-face contact. Phone calls and meetings can be set up with local council and voluntary sector workers who will be pleased to advise on what they are aware is happening in the area. If a major regeneration initiative is planned or under way they will know ways for contacting its officers and managers. In the conservation department, ask additionally if the council makes grants to your type of project and how to apply. Also, ask the community development department about the council's current strategy and future possibilities: Are they making grants? In some boroughs other departments are seeking partnerships and looking to invest in local building facilities in order to engage in project partnerships.

> The Social Services department in one borough has rebuilt a three-storey church hall in return for a long lease on two floors, in order to have facilities for a town centre drug and alcohol dependency centre.

Nothing will come of one meeting. The onus is on the church to take initiatives to develop the relationships with departments that seem promising. Sometimes referrals have to go through several departments before you find the people who are the right ones with whom to work.

If no progress is being made and you seem to be going round in circles, invite the local councillors to a meeting at church, talk to them about your interests and seek their advice on who to contact next. You may get a meeting with the council's chief executive or a deputy. Many borough-wide councils of churches have regular high-level meetings with council leaders or officers, and the hierarchy of your church, such as area deans or archdeacons, may know about such connections that will bring more potential contacts.

Most of all, the fruitful relationships will be developed face to face.

What might the departments be doing that would help the church?

Conservation and listed buildings departments

All boroughs have a department that deals with planning issues and listed building consent. In addition to policing the buildings in their area, these departments also have a role in designating listed building grades. They review the area and designate conservation areas where the overall environment is worthy of protection, not just individual buildings.

The Local Authority (Historic Buildings) Act of 1962 and the Planning (Listed Buildings and Conservation Areas) Act 1990 permit a local authority (whether at county, district or parish council level) to contribute grants or loans towards the maintenance or repair of historic buildings in its area, including churches.

For some boroughs this department also leads on initiatives that target local heritage. The borough may have Department of the Environment Funding, Heritage Lottery Funding and/or support from agencies such as Civic Trust, to undertake major projects to protect and enhance heritage and conservation areas. A church located within such a zone may benefit from the investment of grants that are distributed via the council. Follow the leads given – there is some money in this department that you may be able to access.

> A church in Brixton, south London, applied for a small grant from its local council to contribute towards the match-funding needed before major external refurbishment of their heritage building could begin. They received a large grant that provided all the remaining match-funding, as the borough was working to regenerate the town centre from years of dilapidation and neglect.

Community development

This department, which may not have much money, does often know who is doing what and where, and how to make contact with the appropriate departments. They may play an active role in regeneration strategies, but in recent years have had little money to contribute through the department itself.

In some boroughs the community development department administers Community Chest grants. These are small grants for which any local group may apply, usually up to £1,000 or sometimes £3–5,000 for one-off projects. Such sums can be a great help in developing feasibility reports or running a brief pilot project with a community group. Town halls often have Community Chest leaflets available at reception for the general public to pick up. Recently, Community Chest in some boroughs has offered match-funding when an organization has been offered a Lottery grant; this is how the Brixton church above received help.

Regeneration initiatives (listed more fully below)

The City Challenge schemes of the 1990s were replaced by Single Regeneration Budget grants. These tended to make significant capital grants and less revenue, until it was discovered that although such change might brighten up the looks of an area, significant community development and business regeneration was needed for change in the lives of people who are socially excluded. Strategies for change must be multi-faceted and long-term; there are no quick fixes.

Recent initiatives of interest have included Healthy Living Action Zones, Education Action Zones, Neighbourhood Renewal Schemes and New Deal for Communities. The National Lottery has also provided grants that are designated to similar geographical areas and have included work with children, leisure, dependent elderly people and the environment. Current and upcoming schemes are announced regularly. Gaining information through the local council and the voluntary sector is the key.

As central government increasingly works through regional structures, the actual grant streams and methods of application are likely to become increasingly varied. Again borough officers should be aware of what is happening and should know how to make contact. In their early days, regional government offices are proving only as strong as their officers and managers. At this regional level, churches may find a greater level of misunderstanding and prejudice, or new opportunities. While agencies such as English Heritage are aware of the significant role churches are fulfilling in maintaining listed buildings, officers in regional government may be unaware of the place of churches' work in heritage and community sectors and dismiss them too readily. It is probably advisable for churches collectively to find ways to ensure that regional government develops the kind of understanding of faith groups in heritage and community that central government and its departments have acquired as a result of past church initiatives at a national level. Anglican dioceses along with senior free church partners would be advised to set up high-level initiatives to undertake appropriate lobbying to ensure that in the various regions of the country their constituents are not unreasonably or unfairly disadvantaged.

Find a forum

All government initiatives in regeneration are conditional on many levels of consultation, so after phoning around and meeting council and voluntary sector officers, the next step is to find the Consultative Forum. Consultation processes have no power; all the bright ideas and responses are collected up by the relevant officers and result in influencing rather than directing decisions. However, the by-products of such consultation meetings are several:

- Knowledge of what *may* be or *is* planned, with circulation of reports and other documents that explain the purposes and strategies of the regeneration board.
- Relationships that may be initiated with leading players from all sectors, who come along to the meeting.
- Access to key people who do have power, that you may identify in the meeting and with whom you can at least get an introduction and probably agree a future face-to-face meeting.

Who to talk to

Powerful people

Council officers, especially department heads and directors, have power. Low-level officers do not always have the power they would like you to think they have. But affirm them and use the opportunity to get a meeting with their boss.

Voluntary Action Council senior officers often have the ear of key council leaders. Cultivate this relationship and even use their mailing networks and membership to get your message out.

If the borough has town centre managers, the most effective ones carry significant power and lots of influence. They have a good overview of integrated solutions to multifaceted problems.

Influential and sometimes powerful people

Councillors are influential, depending on the committees of which they are members. Chairs of committees are particularly good to know. Review the local councillors in your wards and find out their committee connections; they will always want to help – votes depend on it.

Members of Parliament

Good constituency MPs take an interest in all kinds of local organizations. Their influence may help a church to find access to local organizations, as well as council officers and department strategies. It is most helpful when the MP and the local council are of the same party.

Business partners

Businesses in a local area have a great deal of influence on strategic development. If it is possible and if it will help the cause, it may be worth meeting the local Chamber of Commerce members and enabling them to understand what the church is seeking to achieve.

Occasionally larger corporations can act as excellent advocates. In the Brixton church (above), the local regeneration board had great respect for a business plan prepared by a church with the help of business partners. Later in the process of the building development, the managing director of a multinational corporation wrote a letter of support that succeeded in reversing a decision against awarding a grant. The result was a grant of over £700,000.

Local networks

When regeneration money was to be pumped into a south London housing estate for an Estates Renewal programme, local churches and voluntary sector groups worked together to gain funding for a community worker who would relate to the whole patch, not just one parish or one project's catchment area. Every church benefited.

Talking the talk

Keeping the church's project alive in the minds of the people making decisions is the key to the ongoing process. Keep talking and updating people already met and who have expressed interest. Keep informing decision-making groups about the church's progress and developing plans. Keep inviting people from the places of power and decision-making to events or annual meetings, Christmas parties and community open days to keep the relationship friendly. And if possible hold public launches of stages of the church's project, as long as you can get along a good crowd of people to celebrate progress, and invite outside contacts in the council, regeneration, and the voluntary sector.

The buzzwords that are current in this arena are ones that church members should get used to using about themselves and others, especially before filling in an application form in this sector.

Use words like 'charity' and 'faith group' rather than church. Use 'charity' and 'voluntary sector' as the church is a charity in the voluntary sector. Use 'community group', 'local initiative' (not 'church initiative'). Understand that church projects are nearly always user-led, and that 'user' is not a pejorative word any more than 'client' is in a social work project context. Use 'neighbourhood' rather than parish. Identify all the church's partnerships with other agencies and begin to use terms like 'black-majority' and 'black-led' where these are relevant.

Avoid such words as 'Anglican', 'White', 'Church of England', 'parish', 'vicar', 'tradition', and 'mission'. Chapter 7 includes more work on language. Remember that what you mean to say with your words is not always what is heard by others, because they have their own set of understandings that works like an interpretative shield. It is best for the church to learn the language of this sector and describe themselves and their work with that language; there will be a reduced chance of misunderstanding.

This sector may not be easy or straightforward, but it can be very lucrative.

Summary

1. Assess the time that's needed.
2. Review your priorities in the urgent/important debate. See Chapter 4.
3. Decide who among the church has the skills and connections.
4. Research where to gather additional information.

5. Read between the lines: understand the objectives of the outside funder.

6. Look at the assessment criteria and be completely realistic.

7. Stop now if your accounts are not 'externally examined' up to date. Why are funders wary? (25 per cent of fraudulent applications to the Lottery Community Fund are churches – is this just an urban myth, or might it be true? How can you show that this is not true in your case?)

8. How does anyone outside know that your house is in order? Look at your trustees, the make-up and skills of the group, your financial reporting, your maintenance reporting and your fulfilment of your objectives.

9. Read the local community agendas and be on the networks for integrated solutions in deprived communities. Know your role in the local web. Get yourself built into it.

10. The Equal Opportunities debate. PC or not-PC. Know the practice and follow it faithfully.

11. Read the material from the funders again before filling in forms.

The Lottery funds

After its introductory three years, the government has diversified the streams of funding, replacing the Millennium stream with several new funds targeted at particular areas of need.

Active Communities Development Fund aims to encourage people with disabilities, people from ethnic minorities, women and girls, and those on low incomes, to participate in sports. Community groups can apply but must be in partnerships with at least one other organization that is from the not-for-profit sector. It has lots of money, a rolling programme and no deadlines.

Contact details: Sport England 0845 7649649; email info@sportengland.org; website www.sportengland.org.

Awards for All is another rolling programme that offers small grants of between £500 and £10,000 for local community groups. At present only available in England, the programme is designed for community groups with small incomes. Almost any need can be eligible from any theme – heritage, arts, sport or community activities.

Contact details: www.awardsforall.org.uk.

Community Capital Programme Funding is targeting *bona fide* community organizations that are unable to raise funds elsewhere and represent a sport that is recognized by Sport England. Your project must cost more that £5,000 and be able the raise 35 per cent match-funding to make up the total needed. Some projects in priority areas in the poorest 20 per cent of wards in England can get up to 90 per cent. Projects in the School Community Sports Initiative, building or upgrading school facilities to be used by the wider community, can get up to 80 per cent grant aid. This is another rolling programme with no deadlines.

Contact details: Sport England as above.

Big Lottery is the big funding stream for community projects. The fund supports charities and voluntary groups that work for disadvantaged communities and individuals to prevent or reduce disadvantage. Charitable groups who are not necessarily registered charities can apply. Again, this is a rolling programme without deadlines. One grant stream at present ranges from £500 to £60,000. If you need a greater sum there is another grant stream for larger projects with a maximum grant level that varies according to region.

Bear in mind that this programme changes from time to time without warning. A CD for application forms is promised. It's a rather slow process to download forms from the website and you still have to work on and send in a paper copy.

Contact: www.biglotteryfund.org.uk.

Task

When planning to apply to the Big Lottery ensure that, overall, the way you answer questions will give a strong picture answering the following fields of concern:

The organization is well managed and financially sound
Identify the committee, and its make up, skills and structures of accountability; the current staff, and their skills and accountability.

The organization reflects the diversity of the community it serves and takes account of the community's needs in all its work
Illustrate through user management, user consultation and local area statistics.
Indicate consultation outside the project and review processes that take the local area into account.

Beneficiaries are involved in all aspects of the project and have full access to it

Consultation with user-groups; users are on the management committee and present at the annual general meeting.

If awarded the grant, will the organization be able to manage the project well?
Plans for development, projections about programmes, projected costs and cashflow.
History of competence and continuing high standards.

The project responds to a clearly defined need
Assessment of the area, local information, consultation.

The project is not replacing statutory services
Show this is not a replacement service.

The project has clearly defined and achievable objectives based on a reasonable project development plan
Include the purpose, objectives, development strategy and action plans.

The project budget is accurate and reasonable and is matched by realistic income projections
The project will be monitored and evaluated against its objectives; and show how it will continue to review its purpose, strategies, values and quality of service.
Indicate how monitoring, review and action-planning are built into the committee's programme.

If awarded the grant the organization will be able to manage the project
Income and expenditure projections given for the first year with estimates for several years following, listing assumptions on which these are made. Statements to be included on pricing policy for building users and evidence of management understanding given through cash flow forecasts and strategic development plans.

The Heritage Lottery Fund is a major stream of funding with a wide spectrum of beneficiaries. The main fund grant-aids a wide variety of conservation and heritage schemes. Of particular interest for churches are the following:

The Repair Scheme for Places of Worship is run jointly with English Heritage and spends £25 million nationally per annum.[21] The scheme has run in

---

[21] Figure for 2003.

three-year programmes with only limited periods each year during which applications can be made. Parallel schemes run in Wales, Scotland and Northern Ireland.

Your Heritage makes grants up to £50,000 for smaller non-structural conservation of features but not furniture.

The Main Grants Programme (greater than £50,000) will fund church projects other than building repairs; but projects must include heritage benefit to wider communities, such as greater access to the public and education. At present the latest Programme is focusing on conservation and heritage activities.

Contact: Heritage Lottery Fund 020 7591 6000; or website www.hlf.org.uk.

The Lottery Arts Fund is administered by the Arts Council. It may offer grants towards arts facilities and arts projects in churches. There is a possibility that it may help with work on organs for concert use while the Heritage Lottery Fund may help with conservation of significant heritage organs.

More central government funds

Government schemes have previously been focused through the Single Regeneration Budget, which has now been discontinued as a means of delivering help to deprived areas. Some areas will still be paying out grants for a while, but essentially the whole scheme turns into the new *Regional Development Agency*. This will be a fund spending more than a £1 billion annually. Funds come from the Department of Trade and Industry, the Department for Transport, Local Government and the Regions, the Department for Education and Skills and the Department for the Environment, Food and Rural Affairs. As a single pot covering a number of aspects, it is hoping to provide 'joined up' solutions in tackling social exclusion and deprivation.

Each Regional Development Agency will determine its own priorities, ways of distributing funds and timescales. Look out for local news in your regions and you will find ways to benefit in partnership with community and neighbourhood partners.

English Heritage is the main source of government funding for heritage church buildings in England. *CADW* (Welsh Historic Monuments), *Historic Scotland*,

and the *Northern Ireland Office Historic Monuments and Buildings Branch* do similar kinds of work in their areas. The majority of English Heritage's grant funding for places of worship (Grade I and II*) is focused in the Joint Repair Scheme with the Heritage Lottery Fund. Present priorities are the structural repairs that are essential to keeping buildings wind and watertight.

While the application process is relatively straightforward, to ensure success in the process, prepare thoroughly. If possible, produce statements of significance and need (see Appendix 7), and produce a report on public access and on disabled access. In addition, give a good report on how the church has undertaken maintenance in recent years. A condition of grant includes the production of a ten-year maintenance plan. The church's architect will be able to assist in drawing this up.

The Landfill Tax Scheme will benefit some churches, especially those embarking on community development programmes. Under a government scheme landfill operators may divert tax to environmental causes. One of the allowable target recipient groups of such money is heritage churches. The recipient must be located within ten miles of a landfill site, not necessarily the operator from which a grant is received. For more information the main administrative agency involved is called *Entrust*. Some boroughs have worked together to ensure maximum take-up of these grants and can give information. Groundwork UK have been very successful in getting such environmental grants and are worth contacting for projects of mutual interest.

Listed Places of Worship Grant Scheme may be contacted: tel 0845 601 5945; email: nptcallcontreuk@cslplc.com; www.lpwscheme.org.uk. It functions to make grants equivalent to reducing VAT expended in the repair works on listed places of worship. This is a relatively pain-free way of getting a rebate on money spent.

The European Union does make grants. However, only the most persistent or experienced are advised to apply. The objectives and conditions are rather convoluted and change annually. In partnership with other agencies and local government, this might become a profitable option.

Key points

- Research potential funding in your area and make connections.
- Keep using local forums for information and developments.
- Get members of the congregation researching through their networks.

16

Public Appeals and Internet Fundraising

Public appeals

Just occasionally I hear of a church whose public noticeboard promoting fundraising has actually resulted in a large donation. It is gratifying, but the best use of the public notice or the local communication is to raise the level of local knowledge and involvement and lead to more specific and personal ways of asking for support.

The noticeboard, with or without the ubiquitous Thermometer, goes public about your intentions. It is backed up by articles in the local newspaper, by leaflets through the door and opportunity to get involved in a fundraising activity.

The public appeal can only really reach the church's natural audience. For most churches this is essentially local. Some major heritage churches over a number of years develop a worldwide list of interested friends, and in this case contacting them through an appeal letter from a major patron is important.

Whether the potential supporters are in a local neighbourhood or spread around the world, find an opportunity to tell them about success. At least the Thermometer tells people that the target is close.

A public appeal should only be undertaken when more than 50 per cent of the money is raised; no-one likes to donate to something that might never meet its target. If the church has raised £50,000 out of its £2,000,000 target, turn that into successfully raising 60 per cent of a first phase of repairs.

Internet fundraising

The question being asked in the voluntary sector is whether Internet fundraising is ever going to be profitable. This is an indicator that for local churches, and even for major ones, this is not yet going to be a major financial source. That does not mean we should not use it.

A Friends network, local and worldwide, can be sustained through email.

Progress can be updated, requests for donations made and even thankyou letters sent. While 'cold-calling' through email is not acceptable or profitable, you can ask each of your contacts to send the message on to a friend who might be interested. But do not add to the 'spam' of large numbers of unsolicited mail that pollutes the email networks.

Webpages are great for carrying information about a church and what it does and are therefore useful for updated communications on the fundraising programme. But ensure that you are able to keep updating and that the page and its contents do not grow tired. Include the web address in all the church's communications and people may begin to look it up. In terms of fundraising, the only people who currently seem to give through church webpages are those who already know the church and are comfortable with credit card donations over the Internet. Secure giving through the Internet with a credit card can be arranged through the Charities Aid Foundation and other providers.

For webpage donations, those who wish to donate are happy to have a direct request. So make your donations page easy for busy people to gain access and use.

Key points

- Use clear and immediate donation information on the webpage.
- Watch for news of innovative ways of fundraising on the Internet that can really result in funds.

17

Publicity, Public Relations, Marketing and Newsletters

The first concern in the creation of publicity material for fundraising must be the variety of audiences to be targeted, the response the church wants from each of them, and what is the best way to ask for it. Often it is possible to encompass these various audiences in one leaflet. The following example carefully indicates to outsiders and newcomers the value of the church to a variety of interests that will meet in the church and it is clearly couched from their viewpoint.[22]

> The church (not just the building) is always open in some way for your requirements and to give counsel. We are not here just for Baptisms, Confirmations, Weddings and Funerals, but to worship God as a community and share his bounteous gifts to us.
>
> We are not exclusive and are always pleased to welcome newcomers. Everyone is welcome to all or any of our services – to just visit is wonderful, but to take part as a lay reader, steward or member of the Parish Church Council is a worthwhile tribute to God.
>
> Some of our number are devoted to the maintenance and decoration of our fine 900-year-old church and its surroundings.
>
> Others are dedicated to spreading the faith by education of our children at Junior Church, and at adult house groups organized throughout the year.
>
> We have an excellent organist and strong choir of a very high standard who contribute to our worship whether at a regular Sunday service or at your wedding or other major festival.

In the commercial sector, and increasingly in the charity sector, questions are asked such as 'How do people see you?' 'What do people see?' 'Do outsiders understand what you want them to understand?' 'Is your message clear to

---

[22] From the stewardship leaflet of St Giles Church, Bredon.

others?' It is common in both the church and charitable sectors to be extremely muddled, with resultant mixed messages to hearers. What we ought to do, what we might do, what we actually do, what the church authorities think we should do, all get mixed up into our description of our church.

The purpose and values of the church

Before preparing fundraising messages, for written and verbal presentation, it is extremely important to go through a process of writing down a simple purpose and set of values statements. The purpose should be a one-sentence statement; it is not readily usable if more. Keep the one-page mission statement for internal consumption.

Purpose

Our purpose is to serve the people who live, work, visit or worship in Camden Town, through the regeneration of St Michael's Church.

We will provide a sustainable future for St Michael's Church in its liturgical and pastoral ministry, its service to its parish and in the opening of the building to use by a wider public.

The values statements suggested throughout our previous chapters cover aspects that are of interest to outside people for whom one particular value may be more important than others; and their 'highest' value may not be the same as the church's. The variety of stated values may enable outsiders to appreciate the balance in what the church does.

Prepare simple values statements that reflect the overall balance of your church. Include worship and pastoral care; heritage, building care and main-tenance; local community welfare, education and well-being; finance.

Values

Worship heritage:

We will support additional uses which respect and relate to the building's Christian heritage.

We believe that every individual has a spiritual dimension and churches can make a place for its development.

Architectural heritage:

We appreciate the inspirational qualities of the building's architectural heritage and believe they speak to the present day.

We value the way in which the building's present condition is attractive to those who visit and we seek an appropriate approach to its restoration.

Community use:
We believe the building belongs to all who wish to use it.
We recognize our responsibility as a church to provide a place of welcome and hospitality to people of other faiths and none.
We believe Camden Town needs places which can contribute to the community development of the area.

Event use:
We believe the church can encourage and support the arts, cherish the story of the local community and enhance the quality of life and personal development of individuals.
We believe in making the arts available to all, especially to provide an opportunity for those who do not have ready access to the arts.

Finance:
We believe that the combination of users in the church buildings should pay for its upkeep and maintenance.
We welcome the opportunity to make a financial contribution to the life of the local community.
We recognize that we cannot fund the project alone.
We believe that the church and the buildings will become sustainable financially.

Think about your image

It is increasingly common to address the *image* of an organization. Everything from the style of logo, the way pages are laid out, writing style, the paper used, the colours or lack of colours all speak of the image. Far more is involved than just what photo is used! In Chapter 13 on trust fundraising it was advised that a church applying to trusts should purchase some high quality writing paper, not just grab a handful of photocopier paper. Why? Cheap paper can imply that the church is cheapskate in its approach to outsiders or even that low quality paper is fine for these people, so suggesting how the church really values the trusts. A wide variety of factors, visual and tactile, project image even before words are used. Then the actual words and phrases may be upbeat, depressing, succinct, rambling, focused, interesting, deadpan, boring, attractive and more. An exercise in looking at how you see yourselves is a good prelude.

Ask a group in the church to meet and write in answers to the questionnaire at Appendix 8 and then share the results.

The questionnaire is an adaptation of a commonly used form. It will draw out lots of positive statements from church members. This is an important process particularly if there is an air of confusion or despondency about the challenge of the church's finance or fundraising. Such a mood must not creep into fundraising communications. When individuals join a fundraising project by making a donation they will only be generous towards something positive and forward-looking. The church's messages must have at least those qualities.

'When does a product become a brand? When it acquires personality.'

A strapline, or it may be called a by-line by some people, may be helpful where a variety of publications are going to be used. This will be a simple response-provoking, often emotive, short phrase that 'fits' the church's image of itself and its aspirations. It reveals a quality of the 'personality' of the church that people outside may find attractive. Some of the most famous promotional phrases are worth a look. Nike says 'Just do it' and appeals to the aspirational, the pragmatic and the self-belief of its target audience. The phrase implies that 'you can if you try'. Of course, they would like the reader to wear Nike trainers and kit when they do it and we all know that. 'The listening bank' would have us appreciate that they specialize in giving focused attention and flexibility to the needs of the customers.

Often a phrase will have meaning at a variety of levels. One church is considering 'St James's Church, the heart of Piccadilly' and a Benedictine-style religious community that runs creative workshops is using 'Imagine the possibilities'. From the branding exercise above, review ideas on the sections about animals, cars, famous people and Bible stories as these images (and the reasons for them) will help inform phrases. The 'heart of Piccadilly' example reflects a church that has a strong ministry in meeting people at the fringes of society in welfare work and in spiritual development; it is a base for many fringe groups who are marginalized in society – the phrase fits. The community referred to above is running programmes that encourage people to develop themselves, to explore personal and spiritual possibilities. The first catchy phrase they came up with was 'Just be it', which might have been fun but did not include the inspirational quality they were seeking. The phrases appeal to the heart and the imagination rather than the descriptive and rational.

Find the line that fits your church and use your questionnaire for bright ideas. Brainstorm among church members and the church council for possibilities.

Preparing written material

As you have worked through potential target donors in the preceding chapters you will have identified areas of work in which they might be interested. Now for each of those interests you should write a simple and positive message that shows your intentions and the directions you intend to travel in the future. Be clear and succinct as you will draw on these messages when you prepare articles, brochures or meetings about your project and its funding.

Identify a message to engage the interest of each of your target audiences.

Brochures

A brochure is always back-up; it will never on its own elicit donations. Once those fundraising have met someone, explained the project and asked for help, the brochure will be left with the potential donor as reinforcement and reminder of what has been said. In some settings brochures will be left out on seats during events or for drop-in visitors, and in this case considerably more effort will be needed to create a brochure that looks different and grabs more attention than all the other paper and posters in the church.

Use a logo and the strapline from your questionnaire. Do not clutter the brochure with unnecessary or clichéd material. Only astonishingly beautiful churches should put a picture of the church on the front cover – that's what everyone does. Can you be different and use a photo that causes people to focus in, and try to include people's faces? Ask your brochure designer to help.

The very first statement, either a strapline or a key sentence flagged across the page, must be an attention-grabber.

Following the first attention-grabbing statement come *several points of interesting information*, contextualizing the fundraising project and its significance. But remember the messages for target audiences from your questionnaire; use nothing that does not have to be said for these audiences. Church members will not be the primary target of the brochure; although they will each want to receive one, outsiders are the primary targets.

St Jude's Church welcomes many local people for baptisms and weddings, and many families have loved ones buried in our churchyard.

Our church is packed with local residents for festivals and special occasions.

The choir and organist bring beautiful and uplifting music and the schoolchildren fill the church for their concerts and presentations.

St Jude's runs a busy programme of activities for local people, including Brownies, Scouts, yoga and dancing.

The people of St Jude's care for this ancient building on behalf of all local people to ensure it is here to serve many generations of local people in the future.

Then give information on the project you are targeting and include the fundraising success to date. Include several simple and informative points about the church and project.

Over the next two years we are planning the following repairs and improvements:

Roof and drainage repairs	£120,000
Improvements at the main entrance and new toilet that is disabled-accessible	£23,000
Renewed electrical wiring and security system	£27,000
Redecoration	£47,000

Most members of the general public assume that churches are centrally funded. Today members of the public will raise sceptical questions, ask about rumours, urban myths or even about the bad press that the church has received. To get beyond this effectively include a few statements that answer the most frequently asked questions. Just make the statements; you don't need to put in the questions themselves.

[Isn't the Church really rich?]
St Jude's Church is funded by the contributions of members of the congregation and those who use the church for occasional events such as weddings and baptisms.

[Isn't the church sexist and racist and run by middle-class people?]
St Jude's Church welcomes everyone who would like to join with us, we exclude no one and are inclusive in our work, our employment and in the use of our building. Our church is reflective of the rainbow, all colours and kinds.

[Hasn't the church got a terrible reputation for child abuse?]
St Jude's Church knows that our children are our future. We provide a welcoming, safe and exciting programme of activities for children and young people.

[Doesn't the church push religion at everyone?]
St Jude's Church is a welcoming building that has meeting space used by all sorts of groups, from Alcoholics Anonymous to Indian Women's Dance, from Brownies to the Pensioner Club.

> *[I thought the church was closed.]*
> St Jude's Church is open every Sunday and is being used more and more by local groups on weekdays. We always welcome visitors and enquirers . . . and are open every Saturday morning – drop in to see us.

The church's fundraising group may realize there are other frequently raised issues that should be addressed. But don't try to fit in everything, so include three or four such upbeat statements that will move the reader out of a sceptical mind-set and encourage them to ask other questions when you meet face to face.

Everything will lead the reader to the section on how to donate. This must be straightforward, logical, simple and cover all possibilities (see Appendix 9). Churches have many committed donors who are happy to use traditional banking and cash methods. But increasingly there are people who will want to use more direct and instant methods of giving.

'Would you enjoy the challenge and excitement of engaging in this major [*heritage* or *community* word] project that will establish . . .?' is an enticing question that encourages the reader to follow further through and get ready to help. 'There are many ways to donate money to the scheme and in addition we will invite you to fundraising events.'

State how much you have to raise, ask people to give generously and tell them how to give.

- Cheques are made payable to St ———
- Credit card details (if the church can access a credit card facility[23])
- Banker's order information so people can give over a period of, say, a year
- Gift Aid form so the church can regain the tax
- Name/s to contact with enquiries
- Address for sending donations

See Appendix 9 for more detail.

Within a few years the systems now being developed for email fundraising and Internet donations will find their way into a form that can easily be used by churches, but this is not yet realistic for smaller local churches. Some larger nationally identified churches and cathedrals could be using these methods and will help hone up the workable processes for the rest of us.[24]

---

[23] Credit card donations may be processed through the Charities Aid Foundation and other agencies serving the charity sector.

[24] If your church is in a position to raise money through email and webpage, an agency such as Charities Aid Foundation will provide access to secure systems.

Brochures do not have to be comprehensive, complex and sophisticated unless they are designed for a special event for complex and sophisticated people. Above all avoid retelling the church's history or its architectural significance at length in the brochure; at most allow half a sentence on significance unless you are fundraising among a group of historians or heritage architects, which is unlikely. If someone were to ask for such information at a face-to-face meeting, tell them you will get the information and send it to them. This you will be able to do, having done the preparation in Chapters 11 and 12. Do not start writing the brochure at the beginning of your preparation; do it at the end when all the information is readily available.

Newsletters

Keeping donors, supporters, advocates, church members, friends and neighbours updated is important to avoid staleness in the campaign. Momentum builds up and then grows or flops. A newsletter helps sustain the effort.

Telling stories is the best way to celebrate successes, in newsy snippets. Get personal stories from individuals and include thanks to all donors. Use photos as much as possible. Digital photos may easily be inserted into the text and are simply reproduced, even on a photocopier.

Remain positive and highlight achievements, not disappointments.

Public presentations, interviews and meetings

Use the content of your brochure as your speaking notes. That is, stick to material which the church has agreed presents the image they want to project, the information that is useful and the messages that are appealing. This makes most sense since you have the brochure for backup.

Interviews

When being interviewed on television or radio Prime Minister Maggie Thatcher had an approach that despite infuriating some interviewers did ensure she got across her message. It appeared that having prepared her message earlier, regardless of the question she was asked she presented something from her own agenda. It was a fascinating way to avoid awkward questions or hostile interviewers and take advantage of the opportunity. Interviewers on local radio will seldom be that difficult or hostile, but their questions on a short interview may all come from the 'frequently asked questions' above which tend to focus on negative or cynical images of the church rather than the positive message of a progressive church that you want to communicate. Prepare yourself well, practising with sample answers so that you can communicate all your positive brochure-based information while the questions you are asked may not be as friendly as you might wish.

Key points

- Be clear and succinct.
- Write your promotional material in the language of the listener not the church member.
- Write your messages for the interests and questions of those outside the church.
- Choose photos that are full of energy.
- Do not write a brochure about the church's history but about the present and the future. The history can be offered through a historical guidebook.

18

Out-of-the-Box Ideas

There are always new, innovative and slightly crazy ideas that happen in the world of fundraising.

Several London churches have been and are benefiting from advertising banners on their scaffolded buildings. This can be a good plan for city centre churches on busy streets whose scaffolding comes right out to the pavement. It is lucrative.

Radio aerials may yet prove to hold a positive contribution, as church spires often still dwarf other buildings.

A vicar in the east end of London was sponsored, along with her churchwarden, to camp out on the church roof overnight. The venture raised lots of publicity and some money.

Brave vicars, nuns, churchmembers and friends jump from aeroplanes, take very long walks and undergo all such challenge events.

St George's Church, Bloomsbury, received a donation from every Pizza San Giorgio that the local Pizza Express sold.

Innovation and novelty will get the local news and public interest. Accompany this with a winning message, and progress will be made.

If your church tries some new and different approach, please contact me via the publisher and I will include as many good stories as I can in the next edition! Or send me an e-mail to maggie.durran@virgin.net.

With some regularity solicitors drawing up wills for their clients are told, 'and some other local charity should be added'. Circulate local solicitors with information about your church so they may think to suggest it to their clients as that other local charity.

19

Some Legal Issues

This chapter will raise several legal issues and suggest some solutions. However, these come with a warning. The author is not a lawyer but is quoting from the experiences of other churches. *Any advice given in this chapter should be worked out in detail with your own legal adviser. Answers found here can only be general not specific.*

The legal structure

When the church considers extending the ways in which it works as a means of making the church sustainable in mission and finance, the legal structure in which it operates should be an element of the review.

Two key aspects of what a charity may do should concern the trustees and church council members. Each charity has an *object* or purpose. It is the responsibility of the trustees to ensure that the charity spends its resources, its activities and its finances to fulfil this purpose. The annual report and accounts are designed to show how this has been done.

The second aspect is the *powers* of the charity. The *powers* are the means by which the charity is allowed to do its work. These powers are in the opening statements of a charity's constitution and cover the means by which the charity can achieve its purpose, whether running welfare projects, owning or purchasing property or promoting religion.

A *charitable trust* is registered with the Charity Commissioners and has a specific charitable *purpose* or *object*, such as preserving the heritage, education, social welfare, promoting the arts *for those who are not its members*. The charitable trust is controlled by lots of rules, such as trustees not being beneficiaries or being employed by the charity. It has a set of *powers* built into its constitution that define the ways in which it can achieve its object.

A *charitable company* is registered with the Charity Commissioners and with Companies House. It is a not-for-profit trading company. Besides having the status and object of a charity, it is controlled by company law.

A *Parochial Church Council* is an excepted charity; that is, it does not need to register with the Charity Commissioners *but* is controlled by the Charity Commission's rules – for example, in the ways it does its accounts and the ways in which it can fulfil its mission. The *object* of a church is the promotion of religion and related religious activities.

A *company limited by guarantee* is a trading company owned by the parent organization that holds the shares. It can be used as an 'owned' trading company to benefit the charity that owns it.

So you look at your project and choose the right horse for the course.

The charitable trust

If the church's endeavour is a community project – a centre or service project (the poor, education), it may be best to establish a separate charitable trust. Then the structure it operates protects those it serves as well as the trustees. The community project will be able to find trustees who are skilled in the field and will help to manage it to a high standard. The church will be able to attract trustees who will work as its partners in this 'good work' but would not sign up to the religious activities of the church council's purpose in promoting religion.

A few of the charities who will fund community projects will not fund religious organizations, though most will fund their non-religious charity work. A separate charitable structure from that of the church can therefore be a financial advantage to the project.

It is possible to set up the community project as a permanent sub-committee of the church council with outside members co-opted and its own particular purpose, and for many outside funders this is acceptable, the Big Lottery being one.

The church may wish to receive money such as legacies or major grants that are only for the church building and its continuing repair and maintenance. Setting up a building preservation trust may for some churches be the best route. This is a registered charity with the specific purpose of preserving the church building.

The church may wish to have a service agreement for working with local unemployed people or a youth club, and the local authority may not pay a grant to an organization whose purpose is promoting religion although they would for social welfare.

But remember, it is the primary task of the trustees to ensure that the activities and the money involved are used on the new charity's stated object and nothing else. The responsibility is not transferable. The charity cannot and must not be directed, controlled or manipulated by the church council. It may have trustees and officers in common but they have separate responsibilities.

The charitable company

This is designed for trading. However, many mainstream large charities register this way for the protection it gives to trustees. The trustees/directors are protected by company law from financial liability as long as they run the company responsibly. There are people with skills who will be trustees/directors in this way as the structure protects them from liability that would damage their own professional practice or put their own assets at risk.

The church or charity that wishes to trade in order to fundraise will probably need to set up a separate trading company. Most church and charity powers do not include trading as part of the allowable activity of the charity. For example, running a shop or market is not a listed power for the charity, but a company running a shop can give all its profit to charity. Calling the activity fundraising does not change its legal status as it is not a legally allowed activity. Fundraising through collecting donations *is* legally allowed. Occasional sales, raffles and similar activities are normally ignored by those authorities who audit charities as long as their income does not exceed 10 per cent of the charity's income. Remember, letting surplus building space, whether church, halls or parking space, is counted as investment, not trading, so is outside this 10 per cent.

Trading is subject to Value Added Tax, and keeping trading activity separate from the activity of the church, in a separate company, saves the balance of the church's activity from becoming liable for VAT. Rent is not subject to VAT in the normal run of affairs, but other kinds of trading are, including taking on a service contract in the supply of social welfare or youth provision. Get professional VAT advice if you are setting up a new project so that you are paying appropriate VAT from the beginning.

Over the years, I have seen that it is far easier for a company to be businesslike rather than 'too kind' in letting the church hall. Clergy and church officers often feel obliged to 'give in' to bad tenants when criticized for asking for money that is due!

The Church Council

This is designed for maintaining and promoting the Christian religion, and as such is controlled by myriad rules.

The church council undertakes some income-generating activities and church council members are protected from liability. Renting out space to provide church income is acceptable. *But* because members of the church council are not personally liable, commercial interests such as banks are very wary of making loans to churches. They can't easily (or without major scandal) confiscate a church if the church council has run up a major debt or failed in its business; so they won't deal with the church council in the first place. Two or three banks will now make loans to charities and will consider churches. They expect to see a very robust Business Plan to assure them that repayment will be made.

The members are elected annually for responsibilities related to the promotion of religion and running the church; they are not there for their business or social-work acumen.

Some community projects are set up as permanent subcommittees of the church council and have 'terms of reference' equivalent to a constitution. This form allows for continuity in the subcommittee without change of personnel annually. Some outside people with skills will join such a management committee for a community project. However, the finances are still within the church council umbrella, so the financial ups and downs of the community project should be considered, and whether the structure gives sufficient protection to trustees – both the church council and the project. Could one of these groups spend the money of the others? How can you safeguard against this? Does the finance of the community project distort the overall picture in the annual accounts, making the church look more or less viable? If it makes the church look more wealthy this can be a disadvantage when fundraising for building repair grants.

Insurance

Whichever umbrella or combination of umbrella legal structures is employed, go through the whole thing with the church's insurance company so that everything is thoroughly covered!

Licensing

Look through the list below, and the local authority licensing department will be able to give you more information on what is applicable to your situation.

If you are selling food from a stall at your own or someone else's events, check that you are covered for the following.

Basic food hygiene certificate – Food labelling is required to show all contents and a use-by date.

Public entertainment licence – Contact the licensing section of the local authority, and the forms make it clear what to do next.

Music and dancing licence – Check with the local authority about their requirements. Remember that public use of music, live or canned, is covered by copyright, and a royalty payment may be required.

Liquor licence – Apply through the local Magistrates' Court. Or negotiate with a local pub licensee to see if they will run a bar for the church and split the profits. As a church, you may not supply alcohol or sell alcohol (it is not a charitable act to give people alcohol or sell it to them). The cost of alcohol cannot go through the church accounts, even for the sherry with Christmas carols.

Street collection permit – Get permission from the local authority if you are going to collect on public space (not needed on private property).

Lottery/raffle permit – For selling tickets over a period of time, over £250 or including cash prizes.

Health and safety at work – For all events and for volunteers and paid workers.

Bouncy castles – No licence is needed, but check health and safety as there are many associated accidents and injuries.

Trading activities – All need permission, usually planning permission, as well as faculty for Church of England churches.

Planning permission, listed building consent, faculty and building regulations.

'Fit person' checks on staff and volunteers.

Playgroup registration.

Data protection registration.

Minibus registration – Insurance may be invalidated if personal cars are used as 'minibuses'.

Fire inspection and fire precautions.

Gaming and amusement machines.

Phonographic performance licence.

Performing Rights Society.

Copyright and royalty permission.

Film and video licence.

Theatre licence.

The law and fundraisers

There are significant laws controlling the work of fundraisers, reflecting the government's concern that in some cases too small a proportion of money raised was actually being passed on to the charity concerned.

The rules apply to businesses or people who are not salaried employees or volunteers of the charity in question.

No professional fundraiser is allowed to go out to raise money for a charity unless it has a written agreement with that charity.

The regulations require the fundraiser to include certain information about the charity concerned and about how they are being paid by the charity. This is to ensure the charity has agreed to the fundraiser's work and that the members of the public have enough information to allow them to make a proper choice about whether to donate.

There are similar rules when commercial firms advertise or promote themselves by promising to give to charity. If the condition of a donation is that the charity display a logo or promote the donor, this is trading not fundraising; effectively the donor is buying advertising space.

Further information is available from the Charity Commissioners, and information booklets can be obtained free of charge.

Key point

Check with church authorities, a solicitor or a charity sector specialist when you need legal clarification. Check twice, act once.

20

Preparing a Business Plan

A business plan is the method an organization uses to set out a coherent strategy for the future. It is a tool for managers but also includes clear statements on where the organization is heading, why it is going that way and what it hopes to achieve by going there. The core of the material is the purpose and aims, the result of vision and leadership. The bulk of the content is the manner of organizing the church's resources so that the purpose is achieved, and this is accompanied by enough practical and financial evidence to indicate the basis for the management decisions.

Many churches have in recent years developed a written Mission Statement or a Mission Action Plan. Since many of these have been fairly theological/theoretical, albeit inspiring, the challenge now is to take the Mission Statement and *build a strategy for achieving it*. The strategy is pragmatic; it is based on what we can actually do with the resources we have. The management element of the plan indicates the detail of how we organize our work, our staff, our buildings and our finances to fulfil our strategy.

It is not rocket science, but it can be disorienting because it is a new way of approaching an old problem. Jesus told his disciples to go into towns and villages to preach the gospel without packing spare clothes, and to depend on the goodwill of local people for sustenance. He even told them what to do if they were not well received. Having been the leader and taught them the vision, he was enacting his strategy for getting the word out to as many people as he could, using his resources to the best effect. We are doing the same even though maybe our world is more complicated.

The Business Plan is a means of review and action planning by which a church may review all its activities and see that each and every key activity is actually fulfilling *what that church is setting out to achieve*. The first review is of the Mission Statement or purpose. It does not need to be long but it does need to be specific: *things which that particular church actually does or can do*. For a local church this will be geographically specific. The same is true for a diocese. Missionary Societies may have a world agenda, but most include only part of the world. Similarly the church in its purpose statement will say something about its vision of itself in relationship to its neighbours and catchment area, its own smaller world, Christian and non-Christian, rich and poor.

During the past 15 years the use of the Business Plan has become an element of fundraising. First the Heritage Lottery Fund and the Lottery Millennium Fund and then others began to ask to see an organization's Business Plan before considering a major grant. Many charities, especially the smaller ones, had never drawn up a Business Plan. The funders began to issue guidelines of what they would like to see presented as a Business Plan to help the application process. Therefore what was essentially an internal document producing clarity and specific plans for action has become an external document as well, one by which we may be judged.

Every church would be advised to set out in words what they are going to do and achieve and the manner in which they will organize their resources to ensure that they deliver according to plan. But there are additional elements that are required when the Business Plan is for outside perusal. Never lose sight of the fact that the Business Plan is essentially and primarily the church's self-determined pathway to achieving its purpose. The secret is in setting out that internal strategy in such a way that the outside funder can see that the church is well managed and effective in what it is doing, and well worth backing. The form allows the major funder not only to identify the realities of how you run your project (your church and your community project) but also to have a clear format that enables comparison with other applications for their money. The world of funding is competitive. The Heritage Lottery Fund regularly updates its expectations for the plans it wishes to receive – get the latest guidelines that will help you supplement the format given in this chapter.[25]

Life is made a little more complicated by the fact that different funders of large grants propose different formats. Their formats are suggestions only, and to present a really well-prepared plan in a slightly different format is not a problem as long as it is self-explanatory and covers the essential points. What is covered in this chapter is a combination – it includes everything for which *several* major funders currently ask. It may also require you to consider issues and aspects of running your church or project that you have not formally considered before – in that way it may be excellent preparation for better management.

In the course of this chapter the principles explained will be set in parallel with examples that have been produced by a variety of churches. All the examples used have been taken from churches who have effectively raised very large sums of money. Additionally, they are inner city churches with very limited resources of finances, clergy hours and lay people hours. Each has found that the invest-

---

[32] Look online at Esmee Fairbairn Foundation, Heritage Lottery Fund and The Big Lottery for their latest guidelines.

ment in preparing a thorough Business Plan has proved worthwhile internally in their own management of mission, ministry and church life. As a presentation of themselves, their strategies for the future and how they will achieve their aims, it has been effective in raising grants.

For struggling churches with financial and building problems this business planning process facilitates a clear and achievable pathway from the current struggle for survival towards effective and sustainable ministry. For more thriving churches it will provide a clear accountability for the effective and efficient use of resources in achieving mission targets. A well-prepared Business Plan will enable church councils to consider new ventures in mission and service with clarity and reason. For example, it is straightforward to project into the costs and budgets the cost of a new community project serving local people. The church council will be able to see the full cost and its effect on their finances, not take a stab in the dark.

The outside funder as well as the shrewd church council member will ask several questions as you begin major fundraising. Will your project continue to be well maintained in the future? Will it be well run? Will it continue along the lines you are proposing for years to come – the lifetime of their investment? The Business Plan will show them how you intend to deal with these questions.

So the challenge is to present for yourselves and outside bodies a clear picture of what the church has planned for the future, how it will work out in detail over the next five years and how the church will ensure its continuing delivery. The church will show that their project is needed, it is justified and financially realistic and viable. It will show that the church is effective in its work, in doing what it says it aims to do. The plan will show that you are efficient, doing your work in a cost-effective way. It will show, for example, how many activities have been provided and at what cost, and that the church's delivery of a service is of the highest professional standard, whether building works, church services or advice to homeless people.

Finance is a key element that indicates that the project is sustainable, that it is well planned financially to continue into the future. (Too many churches spend huge sums of money on items like heating systems without considering whether they can afford to run them; *or* seek grants for repairs to water damage but have no annual programme for clearing the gutters that would have prevented the water ingress in the first place.) The financial projections will show good stewardship of resources such as the church building.

Overall the Business Plan will show that the project is a good model of delivery, it is well managed, it fits well into the premises and the location and it suits the local neighbourhood and the skills and interests of members and volunteers.

Review the language used and translate it as necessary. If the Business Plan is for internal use then 'churchiness' in the language is not a problem. But outside the church those needing to understand the plan may not know what PCC means or what a parish actually is. Look again at Chapter 7 and review your language. Remember too that statistics that apply to a parish might be more readily understood if taken from local council wards; that's the form generally understood in the world of the funders. Try www.neighbourhood.statistices.gov.uk.

Setting out the plan

The Business Plan will contain three main elements, namely the long-term strategy, the business plan (how that strategy will be delivered year on year) and the marketing plan. The latter is a particular form of a communication plan that will highlight how you intend, for example, to encourage more members of the general public to visit your newly restored church. Expect the final Business Plan to have a contents list such as the one opposite, although there will of course be minor differences in your list.

The Executive Summary

The Executive Summary functions as a summary of all else in the plan, telling the reader what they can expect to find. The maximum size is one page and includes an overview of the content and direction of the whole plan. It is designed to enable the reader to know what is unfolding as they read on. It is good to summarize the key activities and developments to which the plan will refer. It is advisable to write the executive summary after the rest has been developed and written.

In a Business Plan for fundraising, the page will include a description of the project for which funding will be sought, its significance to the local community, the historic significance of the building and key issues about public benefit.

A simple executive summary:

All Saints Community Hall is located in an area of urban deprivation. It serves a wide spectrum of local people from all ethnic groups.

A major programme of repairs is needed to bring the Hall up to current requirements for disabled access and health and safety. The programme will include works that will make the facilities available to up to twice as many as the current 200 users.

The works will cost £111,000, of which we have raised £84,000. We are seeking a grant of £10,000 towards this total.

Contents

Executive Summary

Key People

Brief History of the Project and Organization

Current Activities

Option Analysis

The Strategy

Purpose

Values

Context

SWOT Analysis

Aims

Outputs, Outcomes, Inputs, Activities

Objectives

The Pathway

Delivery

    Buildings and facilities

    Capital works

    Staff and management structure

    Community project partnership proposals

    Risk assessment for project strategy

    Risk assessment for ongoing activity

    Risk assessment for construction

    Monitoring and review

    Critical path

    Critical success factors

    Revenue development

    Sinking fund projection

    Lettings income

    Marketing

    Fundraising

Appendices (including accounts, annual report, specialist reports)

A more complex executive summary for fundraising, *or* a summary for internal use:

The Guild Church Council

St Andrew's Church is built on sacred ground. It has been a place of Christian worship for at least a thousand years. Recent excavations revealed Roman pottery around the spring under the west end of the crypt. St Andrew's benefits from the endowments of wealthy benefactors dating back to the Middle Ages. The Church Foundation, which maintains the buildings and churchyard and pays for additional staff, dates to the fourteenth century. The charities that help the poor of south Camden are endowments that have been added by wealthy members in the following centuries. The present church, taking over the medieval church foundations, was designed and built by Sir Christopher Wren.

St Andrew's Church was one of several significant heritage churches that were severely damaged in the bombing of World War II. A significant rationalization post-war resulted in eleven City Churches being designated Guild Church, as opposed to Parish Church, and among these was St Andrew's. The result was the decline of St Andrew's as a worshipping congregation with a mission to its neighbourhood. Housing Archdeacons of Hackney in the vicarage with a non-stipendiary role as vicar further depleted the investment in ministry. More recently the church has been open to the public for drop-in visiting and as a base for the Royal College of Organists.

St Andrew's Guild church council is now re-establishing the worship, mission and ministry of the church.

Key people

List the people who are key to the development and delivery of the Business Plan. For example:

Vicar/minister
Churchwardens/deacons/stewards
Church council members
Treasurer
Independent examiner of accounts
Architect
Quantity surveyor
Legal advisor

Brief history of the project and organization

In a fundraising Business Plan, the Heritage Lottery Fund asks for a brief history of the project. Other funders ask for an introduction to the project (that is, the subject of fundraising rather than the organization as a whole) and the development to the present.

For historic buildings, the Statement of Significance and Statement of Need will form a useful part of the project description, giving both the building's history and the current repair project.

For the church hall or community project this can be a summary from realization of the need for the project, local community audit results, consultation results and determination of the way forward.

See Appendix 7 for statements of significance and need.

Recent history

This may be an unnecessary addition to the church's internal business plan. However, a church that has new people in the key positions on its staff or church council may find it beneficial to reiterate recent project successes. The Heritage Lottery Fund asks for a brief history that outlines recent achievements and recent project details. In approaching such a funder for a major capital grant, many churches will not have had a recent major building works programme to quote. List some achievements over the past five years.

When applying for revenue funding the church will need to give enough financial and management information to show that it is able and experienced in the good delivery of revenue projects. If it is a new venture with no previous effective experience then full details of all aspects of preparation that indicate the foundations for effective management will be advisable. Chapter 11 gives details for preparing for a revenue project and recommends the Purple Packs from the Diocese of Southwark[26] as good preparation. For a church hall it would be advisable to work through all aspects of management in the book *Managing your Community Building* from Community Matters.[27]

[26] Purple Packs from the Diocese of Southwark, Trinity House, 4 Chapel Court, Borough High Street, London SE1 1HW.

[27] Community Matters, 8/9 Upper Street, London N1 0QP.

Current activities

For an outside funder, a summary of activities currently in place gives a better picture of the applicant. A diagram, as for example in Appendix 4, will illustrate much of what happens and give the numbers of people involved. An additional summary paragraph will be useful, as not every reader of your plan will enjoy getting information from charts.

Include information on ethnicity and disadvantage from the neighbourhood as well as the church. Include other information, profiling the users of the buildings and the community projects if it adds useful dimensions to the picture. Chapter 11 has several examples of material being presented in tables and graphs. With a summary in this section, the graphs and tables can be appended.

If there are positive identifiable impacts that the church is making in the neighbourhood, these should also be added – for example, noting the local value of provision for children or the elderly, for roles in supporting schools or other local provision. One church identified all the hours its church council members spent volunteering in the church *and* all the hours they spent volunteering locally. The summary was impressive and clearly identified them as people who engaged constructively in the local neighbourhood.

Option analysis

While this item is requested by the funders, most churches have gone through an implicit option analysis when tackling fundraising for major building works. What were the factors that informed the decision to repair, demolish and rebuild, to partially replace with social housing, or to redevelop in partnership with a developer? There may be fewer options with a listed church but even then with imagination a multi-use option may be the way to a sustainable future. For a hall or community project a similar analysis of options can be undertaken.

The most straightforward way to present the church's option analysis is to create a grid and score the answers out of five. (See Appendix 10.)

A form such as this may be used as an internal way of evaluating preferences – let everyone fill in their preferences with a numerical score and add them up. However, inherent within the preferences are some pragmatic questions. While long-standing members may wish to repair the church and go on as they are, the money for repair may not be available, and certainly will not be for a church that is unsustainable financially. Change the column headings to suit your available options. Use the table and additional text to summarize the options in the Business Plan.

The strategy

Having chosen your option, the *strategy* is the umbrella long-term plan that guides the direction of the day-to-day work and detailed allocation of resources. The responsibility for the strategy belongs with the church council as the trustees of the church.

Step One will identify Purpose, Values and Aims of the project.

Step Two will research information internal and external to the church that is pertinent to the strategy.

Step Three will identify the Inputs, Outcomes, Outputs and Action that are essential or desirable for the delivery of the strategy.
- *Inputs* of time, money, tools and people that will be required.
- *Outputs*: what and how much gets produced or delivered (quantitative).
- *Outcomes*: what differences will be made in the short and long term by the activities, and how these meet both the church's purpose and that of stakeholders and the needs of current and potential users.
- *Actions* are the key things to be done for the strategy to happen and include some clear initial objectives.

Step Four will ensure consultation with relevant key staff on the direction the church council is leading towards. If the work is drafted by a small group, all members of the church council will need to discuss and adapt the draft strategy until they are able to adopt it as the way forward.

Step Five will be writing up the strategy and communicating it to all the staff, volunteers, members, beneficiaries and key outside people so that everyone can own and endorse the strategy.

The resultant strategy will present:
- A clear vision
- A path to follow with SMART objectives (explained below)
- Support for and understanding of the plan throughout the organization
- The capacity for flexibility – of time and of order – in reaching the objectives
- A manageable review process.

Purpose

In a succinct form tell the purpose of all your activity. This will relate to any specific long-term project and show how its purpose fits into the overall purpose of the church.

A purpose statement is not the same as your church's Mission Statement or Mission Action Plan. It is a clear and succinct summary of what the church is setting out to achieve – no whys or wherefores or conditions, they fit elsewhere. And unless limited to an internal audience, it will be written in non-religious language.

Purpose

We will repair and restore St George's Church and provide for a sustainable future in its liturgical and pastoral ministry and its service to the congregation, parish, wider community and visitors.

Values

Stating your values enables the church to include the perspective of its ethical and other values that by their nature limit the kinds of activities you will undertake. But they can also allow you to address potential or perceived prejudices among outside people about churches; with the church's values statement it is able succinctly to state how open it is.

Different churches have added different values statements that are important to their mission.

It is in this section that you may add an equal opportunities statement that will affirm to outsiders that you are not simply self-interested or interested in people of your own kind.

All Saints Hall has an Equal Opportunities Policy

Access to membership of our councils, committees and other groups, and use of the Community Centre, are available to all without unfair discrimination and to ensure that no-one is disadvantaged in any of these matters by conditions or requirements that cannot be shown to be justifiable; and we will work to ensure that there is no discrimination on grounds of race, nationality, religion, ethnic origin, disability, sex, marital status or sexual orientation, where any of these cannot be shown to be a requirement of the job or office concerned.

It is the Committee's intention to ensure this policy is applied in

- Recruitment, selection, training, consideration for promotion and treatment at work for those who are employed in a paid or voluntary capacity within the organization
- Access to the benefits, facilities and services provided by All Saints Community Hall.

All groups and individuals using the Centre are expected to commit themselves to this policy.

The National Lottery includes its own values statement to make its programme clear. The Big Lottery has made the following statement:

> We welcome applications from religious organizations which want to carry out work in the community, but we do not normally fund projects:
>
> That are designed to promote religion itself
>
> OR
>
> Where people must take part in religious services to benefit.
>
> Sometimes projects that benefit particular communities will mainly benefit people from one religion. We will accept this as long as your project plan takes steps to make sure that it will not exclude others for religious reasons.[28]

On this basis, churches may apply for grants from the Big Lottery where the benefit involves activity that is not related to church membership, but to wider community programmes.

Our Values

Church

St George's is the parish church for ———. We wish to build up its provision for local people and visitors through:

- Maintaining the worship and pastoral care
- Increased provision for people of the local community, targeting particularly those in need and deprivation
- Providing access and education to young people, schools, students and other visitors
- Continuing encouragement and welcome to heritage and other visitors.

Heritage

The church will be open to people interested in architecture and history.

We will maintain a permanent presence showing our Christian purpose.

We will include information and educational materials on the local area, its history and present story, on Hawksmoor and the history and restoration of St George's Church.

Community

We will continue to develop our partnerships and friendships with local people, including wherever possible those of various faiths (locally mainly Muslim) and other local groups.

---

[28] Community Fund application pack, 2002.

We seek to increase provision of community meeting space and facilities for long-term projects addressing the needs of local people.

Finance

Our church has been self-financing and will continue to be so through church activities, letting and other activities.

We would like schools, local community and education groups to be encouraged through concessionary rates, to visit and use the facilities of St George's Church.

Repair, restoration and maintenance

We will restore and repair our building in accordance with best current practice and standards of workmanship, to a standard appropriate to a project of world heritage significance and to reflect historical, aesthetic and practical considerations and the aspirations of our funders and ourselves. We will create a Sinking Fund to continue a responsible level of conservation, maintenance and repair in the future.

Welcome to all people

While being a parish church in the Church of England, St George's offers equal opportunity to all, welcoming and working in partnership with people of all races and creeds and is inclusive of people regardless of age, gender, sexual orientation or colour.

Context

Research under the categories illustrated in Appendix 12 will uncover new information about the opportunities and challenges that impact on the church's strategy for the future.

In this Appendix we offer two possible ways to indicate the context in which the church works. Use the most appropriate set of headings for the church's situation.

Strengths, Weaknesses, Opportunities and Threats

The SWOT analysis (Strengths, Weaknesses, Opportunities and Threats) diagram offers another aspect of contextual analysis. It takes the internal and external factors of the organization and evaluates the organization's abilities and activities in that light.

Customarily presented in a box, the Strengths and Weaknesses elements encourage a thorough review of the organization itself, while the Opportunities

Strengths	Opportunities
Weaknesses	Threats

and Threats refer to aspects from the surrounding area that impact on the development but are outside the organization's control.

In preparing such analysis internally or in applying to external funders, do not avoid or cover up weaknesses. Most researchers from outside will be able to see weaknesses even if not told directly; the most constructive presentation identifies weaknesses but states clearly how these weaknesses are being addressed in effective management. For example, the church's inexperience in fundraising may be balanced by the advice that your diocese has to offer through advisers and courses. (See Appendix 13 for a worked example.)

Similarly the Threats from outside can be addressed in mitigating action (see 'Risk Analysis' below), and information can show that the church is taking advantage of local opportunities, not simply observing them.

It is a model that I find more helpful for a church preparing for setting a strategy than as a presentation tool to other people. But funders do like to see such analysis.

Aims

The aims of a church are the major activity areas it is undertaking to fulfil its purpose for the very long term.

Aims

St Jude's Church is the parish church of ——— and will continue to be the centre and focus of mission and ministry of the church.

St Jude's Church will continue to be open daily to visitors.

St Jude's Church will be a meeting place and location for community development initiatives and provision for disadvantaged people from its neighbourhood.

Outputs, Outcomes, Inputs and Activities essential and desirable to achieving the project

Now the strategy becomes specific, dealing with resources and how they will be used.

Outputs: What and how much gets produced or delivered (quantitative)

Outputs are things that can be counted or measured. Here is the point at which the church explains how much service it will provide to how many beneficiaries. Look carefully at the objectives of potential funders so that you understand what the church may need to include in order to have a realistic expectation of gaining their support.

When preparing visitor *numbers* there must be a rationale that indicates realism and that the church will be able to project numbers realistically from existing user and visitor numbers and local experience. Do not overestimate in order to make an impact. Local authority funders may withdraw grants if the organization does not reach the numbers it promised, and others will follow. Of the projects developed by the National Lottery Millennium Commission, most, even with lots of professional number projections, reached only half or less of targeted numbers. By 2003, some had already closed as their financial projections depended on high numbers. Lower numbers and realism would have resulted in different financial projections and fewer project failures.

A restoration and repair programme will deliver a clearly defined *number* of fully usable spaces. High quality suggests good lighting and heating and attractive finishes, proper signage and a place appropriately staffed and cared for.

A community development programme will have a clearly defined target *number* of people who will be served by its groups and programmes.

For a heritage repair and restoration project enumerate the beneficiaries. Existing and continuing beneficiaries are identified, then additional users are listed along with a clear rationale for setting those figures. Figures should not be 'guesstimates' but should be justifiable by reasonable means. If the church expects or wishes to increase visitors by 10 per cent it will have to give pragmatic reasons for the viability of these figures. Go to similar successful churches of similar location, size, age and programmes and see how many people they have using or visiting their church.

The church in the example below has made a particular point of identifying the newly established community facilities in the crypt.

When calculating numbers it may be helpful not to distinguish between regular users who come each week and those who come once. Count the 'footfall' and explain in a footnote that you are doing this. That means that every time a person comes to the building, they are counted.

Outputs

1. High quality accessible public space created. The church seating up to 300 people. The Vestry house has two meeting rooms and offices on two floors.

2. Open to the public 9 to 5 on weekdays, open on Saturdays for several hours. Open on Sundays for public worship.

3. Achievable self-financing strategy using letting income to cover overheads.

4. Up to 12,000 drop-in and daytime visitors. Up to 2,300 from church services. Up to 1,000 from concerts, recitals and poetry readings. Up to 3,500 from arts group lettings. Up to 1,500 from community group meetings.

Note: *these numbers are present levels*. The redevelopment of the Crypt will allow for the addition of a Community Project for up to 50 people each day (12,500) and a meeting room/exhibition space for up to 60 people but estimating 40 per weekday average. (Estimations are taken from existing church and community projects in Camden and similar areas.) New visitors total 22,000.
Overall total per annum: 37,800.

5. Crypt space: fully accessible with all facilities to be established as one large community project space run by a charity partner and with one large meeting and exhibition space for community and church groups of up to 60 people.

Outcomes (qualitative)

What qualitative differences will be made in the short and long term by the activities, and do these meet both the purposes of the church (and its stakeholders) and the needs of its users (and potential users)?

Stakeholders are all the people who have an interest in the project. So for example if the church is seeking a Heritage Lottery grant, then the interest of the Heritage Lottery Fund in people having increased access to heritage and increased education about it will become an essential qualitative outcome.

Outcomes

1. Open for public worship and prayer on Sundays, weekdays and major Christian festivals. Additional provision to care for the community needs of the neighbourhood through increased use of the crypt as community facilities.

2. Long-term maintenance and repair programmes established against the projected income stream, in order to provide for repairs, upgrading and ongoing use.

> 3. A management process that addresses all relevant issues from public safety, protecting the heritage, security, marketing, income and financial management.
>
> 4. A church or public meeting space for up to 300 people made available for use by community and other organizations.
>
> 5. Provision for visitors interested in the Christian faith, heritage, architecture and the arts.
>
> 6. New Parish Room offering educational support exhibitions, materials and 'classroom' facility to visiting school groups.
>
> 7. Disabled access to all areas of the building and appropriate facilities for disabled people.[29]

Inputs

These are time, money, tools and people that will be required for the delivery of the project.

Inputs: the Structure and Resources

Staff
Rector and ancillary clergy
Part-time Administrator: post to be developed in 2003/4
Part-time Verger: post to be developed in 2003/4
Volunteers already assist clergy in opening the church every day and will continue to assist in this work

Finance
To date congregational giving and letting spaces on the site – namely office space in the vestry house, car parking, storage and daily letting of the vestry upper floor – have sustained the church financially.

The increased use of crypt space by community projects and groups will make car-parking income unnecessary in the income targets and financial viability. Wheelchair users will have access to park cars adjacent to the building and will enter through the new lift access.

The future strategy more than adequately covers costs using current figures for lettings and leases. (Commercial letting figures are taken from local letting agents; community project rates are from this and other comparable church and community spaces.)

Lettings and projects
Space available to be let as offices will be equivalent to the present.

---

[29] Fuller information on outcomes as the benefits to people are contained in Chapter 12 and on the Big Lottery website.

> The space for daily lettings (or seasonal, such as the current let to the Royal Academy of Dramatic Art) will be doubled. The same spaces will also be used by the Parochial Church Council and congregation for meetings and social events.
>
> Community project space, totaling 2,000 square feet, will be created in the crypt. It will be fully accessible with good facilities and a combination of large and small spaces.

Activities

These are necessary in order to deliver the project.

List the activities the church is now doing to get the project under way.

Establish a fundraising group.
Finalize the specification of repair and new works and projected costs.
Raise funds for capital works.
Identify sources of start-up funds for community projects.
Identify sponsorship for music and arts programmes.
Identify the key steps in preparing to employ new management staff.
Seek a business partner to develop the café.

Objectives

Objectives are contained, measurable activities. They are achievable targets by which staff can measure their work and know they are productively achieving. Therefore, the church council may only set general objectives around the strategy, with managers, staff and volunteers working together to make SMART objectives for their work.

Specific
Measurable
Attainable
Realistic
Timed

When the church sets objectives as part of its strategy they will be simple and few! They are a way of focusing particular essential activities, on the way to achieving the strategy. They will include everything that has to be done to achieve a particular year's work on the way to delivery.

Simple objectives are essential to an action programme. Often by writing out in detail the items that have to be achieved we find a specific order that has to be followed – a critical path. Therefore some objectives have to be achieved before others can begin. Raising money to pay a community development worker has to happen before such a worker can be recruited.

Year One (2002)
Ensure full support is given to the fundraiser in order to meet the target programme to comply with the requirements of the ——— donation.

Ensure the financial sustainability of the restoration project and beyond, particularly ensuring the viability of the Parochial Church Council during the period of the works when income will be reduced. Identify interim source of income.[30]

Ensure that the development of the specification of works and necessary permissions are all in place to meet the timetable.

Year Two (2003)
Construction programme under way, beginning with structural external and internal works to the church.

Continue church worship and as much community and arts letting as possible using the vestry house.

Engage partnership community work or arts project to take on the crypt.

Year Three (2004)
With the internal area of the church completed, return to worship in the church, while the vestry house is repaired and the crypt completed.

Enter detailed negotiation with community/arts project for the crypt and establish marketing programme for re-opening all facilities in January 2005.

Year Four to Year Five (2005 to 2006)
Relaunch the programmes and projects of the church.

Continue the marketing programme to ensure renewed interest in the restored building, including exhibitions, group visits, school visits.

Establish community projects in the crypt.

Another church had a much more succinct list of Outcomes, Outputs, Inputs and Objectives.

Outcomes

- Revitalized church
- New networks of communication and ministry
- Open access and supportive environment for many people who visit
- Marketing/promotion of worship, pastoral care, mission, major heritage site, café and restaurant

---

[30] Negotiations are in progress with a company who wish to advertise on the scaffolding on Bloomsbury Way. The income will be sufficient to keep the Parochial Church Council viable during closure.

- Partnership in the redeveloped Holborn Circus
- New identity locally in providing refreshment; sacred, meeting and event space; and pastoral care

Outputs

- New restaurant
- New café
- New visitor centre
- New education and information service for visitors to St Andrew's and the City
- New counselling, physiotherapy and other services for City workers
- New events programme for charitable giving
- New housing for clergy

Inputs

- Increased ministry space (office and meeting) as the church re-establishes its identity, mission and ministry
- Ministry, office and meeting space for the new associate vicar in autumn 2002
- Space and strategy for new ministry, such as counselling for City workers
- New staff: clerical and lay, namely associate vicar and business manager
- Increased revenue for the church to cover new commitments, chiefly from leasing out the crypt
- Finance from the Foundation for major refurbishment of the church

Objectives: The path to follow

1. Engage the new church council in the vision and processes to develop support for the plan throughout St Andrew's, i.e. clergy and pastoral staff, volunteers, management team, Foundation and charities.

2. Set out a programme of capital works (which are working towards the overall picture) and proceed both within the finance limitations and in an order that makes sense to the financial development of the overall plan. First comes the creation of a revenue stream for the church council. Then work outwards towards changes that are desirable but less essential to the viability of the church council. Ministry requirements have a high priority alongside those that are financially necessary.[31]

3. Ensure the church council (not just the vicar) has its finger on the pulse of the development, the aims and the means, and is strong enough to steer its way

[31] In the overall strategy the ministry is the only reason for the change and development. The fact that the Guild Church Council does not have the finance to develop its ministry in the ways it wishes to go creates the short-term situation of finance being one of the first priorities. In five years the short-term priorities within the same overall strategy will be very different. Annual reviews of progress that produce new short-term objectives will indicate this fact.

forward through staff and key personnel changes. Achievable through careful development of the Guild Church Council and its subcommittees.

4. Establish a revenue programme and cashflow projections to undergird new developments including increased staffing.

5. Produce a programme for staff changes and project development possibilities to parallel the programmes for capital works and revenue projections.

6. Set a review programme for 11 months' time to report on the achievements to date and set next year's objectives.

Delivery

The main body of the Business Plan now addresses delivery; that is, how the resources of the church will be managed in order to deliver the strategy. On the whole trustees or church council members will be intimately involved with setting out the strategy. The management plan for delivery may be worked out by appropriate staff who have a far more particular understanding of resources, workloads and financial detail. Much cannot be written by committee but will be drafted by those directly concerned and then ratified by the church council.

Most complex developments of buildings and facilities involve decisions that impact on management. Inherent within these are options.

Once the decision has been made to redevelop building facilities in a project that includes residential, community and retail space, how will those facilities be managed? This will be an issue of resources: do we have the time, skills and networks to undertake the work, or should it be done a different way? (See Appendix 11.)

Make out your own form and the possibilities for each aspect of management time and skills and use it as a way to sift possibilities and come up with the most workable plan. What worked with another church may not be the best for you, as your church has different skills and resources available to it. You may include a summary chart in the Business Plan to show that you addressed all issues and then summarize the route you have chosen and the reason you have chosen it.

Buildings and facilities

Include a summary of the development of facilities. Highlight existing and potential new uses of space and facilities. This is not a list of works, but an identification of the changing needs in using the building, such as the need for adequate toilet and kitchen facilities, or the need for accessibility for disabled people.

Highlight all options with regard to facilities and summarize points to address, including financial, maintenance and staffing.

With new requirements for public buildings to make reasonable provision for access by the disabled, it may be advisable to include here a summary of the church's disabled-access features and plans. (It is assumed that 'reasonable' in the Act means both financially and physically; that is, the church may not have finance to pay for all planned works but will do so when it can, and additionally that some accommodation will be made for churches limited by their listed status.) A Disability Audit could be appended.

Church	Continuing use in worship life of the church, private prayer, visitors and tourists
Vestry house ground floor	Continuing use as church, community and letting space until works begin in 2004
Vestry basement	To be used as church office and meeting space from December 2002. With the vestry house becoming the continuing working space until works on the vestry house begin in January 2004 May revert to leased office space from January 2005
Sacristy (new build) with disabled access and rooms	Rector's office Church administration office Sacristy
Crypt community project space	New community project(s) to be established for January 2005
Crypt meeting room	New use as church, community and letting space after works completed in 2004

Capital works

A summary will be needed of the building works required to create, develop, or refurbish facilities. A verbal description of works (see below) and an Indicative Budget from the quantity surveyor (Appendix 14) are the best way to present this.

For very major programmes of works for which a substantial grant will be necessary, a more exhaustive description and budget may be needed from the design team. Preliminary enquiries with the potential funding body will enable the church to provide the required information.

To indicate the church's maintenance programme, a Ten-Year Maintenance Plan is increasingly being required before major works are funded by outside agencies. The Council for the Care of Churches produces a Calendar of Care which outlines the essential maintenance tasks. Necessary information to add related finance to the plan may be gained from recent maintenance invoices or from the church's architect. Aspects of financing such works are already incorporated into a Projected Cashflow (Appendices 18 and 19) as the church will need to show both that such maintenance works are scheduled and that money is set aside in the budget to pay for them.

Estimates for the ongoing upgrading, repair and replacement of utilities such as lighting, wiring and boilers are addressed in the financial strategy below.

Capital Building Works

The following major works are planned. (Further details are appended in the architect's report.)

1. Exterior restoration with major stonework repairs, cleaning, drainage and roof cover renewal.

2. Internal restoration with repair, conservation and redecoration where appropriate.

3. Internal conservation will reinstate some elements of the original design (the church was designed to be oriented East–West but this was changed fifty years later with changing street alignments).

4. Crypt development and rebuilding sacristy to give disabled access at all levels.

5. Vestry house restoration.

6. Reinstatement of lions and unicorns on the spire.

7. Churchyard repairs including reinstatement of railings to street elevations.

Crypt Development

Layout and uses

The crypt is currently entered with difficulty even by the able-bodied. The new development will complete past disinterment of bodies from several 'side-rooms', where they pose a continuing risk to the fabric of the building: the incursion of water cannot be remedied as there is no present access to these vaults. The usable crypt area will then be equivalent to the overall footprint of the building, some 30 per cent larger than it is now.

To make the crypt into usable and attractive community project space the following works will be undertaken: part will be refurbished as a Parish Room with use by the church and community groups and to function as a visitor space with exhibitions and related programmes for local people and visitors.

A new venture, for which this is essential ancillary space, is working with the borough education department in running education programmes for local schools. Local history studies are part of the National Curriculum at key stages 2, 3 and 4. The Parish Room in the crypt with exhibition material of the restoration programme will enable visiting school groups to see both the restored building and the processes involved. The exhibition will be open to the public.

The larger portion of the crypt will become multi-function spaces for a new community project. It will consist of meeting space and several side-rooms for counselling, small groups and offices. (See below for potential partner projects.)

A new lift will be built, giving access to the crypt and ground floor. In addition, the new build will include space for the church offices (rector's office, sacristy and administration office).

Refreshment facilities and toilet facilities are included.

Staff

Make an assessment of staffing requirements, present and future. Outline existing staff and their responsibilities. Add an outline of new staff and their responsibilities and how the accountabilities work between new staff and existing staff. Describe the present and future accountabilities and who reports to whom and how often. How do staff report to the church council or project committee?

Describe how management will be developed. Explain how workers are managed on a regular basis.

Explain what training will be provided and any changes required to produce appropriate levels of professionalism. For outside funders include job descriptions of new members of staff, especially those for whom the funder will pay.

Management Structure

Accountability

The Parochial Church Council is an excepted charity. That is, it is controlled by charity law but is not required to register with a charity number. The members of the Parochial Church Council are functionally equivalent to charity trustees, having all their responsibilities in law.

The Rector is an office holder employed by the Diocese and paid by them. The Rector is also ex-officio Chair of the Parochial Church Council.

At St George's Church all other staff and volunteers are employed by the Parochial Church Council. Paid staff are line-managed by the Rector. The church-wardens meet with the staff on a monthly basis (more often if required) on behalf of the Parochial Church Council.

Staff

The planned staff:

- The rector and other clergy are continuing.
- Part-time administrator.
- Part-time verger.
- Cleaning has been undertaken by volunteers.
- Volunteers have assisted in supervising weekday opening of the church and will continue to do so.

Community project partnership proposals

For many churches planning to develop new work such as community projects within the premises, these are often managed by people and organizations with relevant experience. If your church is working closely with other organizations or the local authority, explain their relationships.

If the project is for the refurbishment of premises such as a church hall that has been and will, in future, be used for lettings to community groups and local residents, this should be explained; and it is useful to include, for outside funders, letters of support expressing interest in continuing to book the hall.

St George's Church has been approached by two major community projects for use of the community project space in the crypt.

1. ——— Charity operates in our area and is seeking community project space within its catchment area, with good transport links. They make grants to individuals and revenue grants for community groups. Their target area includes our church. The target beneficiaries include people (mainly women and children) who are refugees, homeless, victims of domestic violence, the elderly and sufferers from HIV and Aids.

   The Charity is seeking to extend its work into delivering counselling, advice and other support services. Their project would include crèche provision for young children while parents are receiving counselling or advice or participating in group work. The Charity has revenue funds that will constitute the majority of funds needed to establish the project. The potential of establishing this new venture in the crypt of St George's Church will be further explored in the autumn of 2002.

2. *Arts and Community Project*. A national arts charity has opened dialogue about the use of the crypt as a community arts project. After board meetings for trustees to explore possibilities, the director of the arts project may further the exploration in the autumn.

Risk assessment for project strategy

Increasingly charities are being required to develop Risk Assessment programmes as part of the annual reporting programme. Risks are inherent within every type of work; the church's task is to identify such risks and to consider the likelihood of them happening, then to consider the impact of each one happening to the life and viability of the church. Risks that have a high impact even if fairly unlikely should have contingency plans. Thus the fourth column of the Risk Assessment chart (Appendix 15) is Mitigating Planning and Action. That is, what we can do to avoid the risk and what we can do to lessen its impact. Usually mitigating action includes some action the church council should take now in order to avoid the risk ever happening, rather than just mopping up afterwards.

Strategic risks affect whether the project will happen and what will be the effect of a variety of potential problems.

Construction risks will be assessed by the design team on a major works programme.

Management risks that will hamper the ongoing life of the project should be addressed in the same way as the strategic risks, addressing likelihood, impact and mitigating action.

Risk assessment for ongoing activity

The following operational risks should be addressed by the church council and mitigating policies and action established. Use a grid such as the one in Appendix 15 to assess the level of risk. Many dilapidated halls have historically failed to follow policies that reflect good practice. Before reopening the hall, instigate good practice in all aspects into policies regarding use. Create another grid such as in Appendix 15, identify all risks and list the mitigating action that will be taken by when and by whom.

1. *Fire*: electrical, heating, plant and machinery, smoking, combustible waste, flammable liquids, storage, arson, fire-fighting equipment.

2. *Crime*: burglary, theft of money, pilferage, violence to staff and visitors, theft by staff.

3. *Health and safety*: slips, trips and falls; manual handling; machinery and working equipment; electricity; transport; fire safety; hazardous substances; noise; vibration; display screen equipment; young employees; volunteers; maintenance and building work; building users and audiences.

4. General precautions and contingency measures for aspects of *risk to visitors* and other users.

5. *Licensing* as required by the local council.

6. *Food safety.*

7. Essential *routine maintenance and repairs.*

8. *Information and data back-up.*

9. *Accidents*: first aid and liability to be covered by insurance.

10. Insurance to cover all anticipated uses and to protect for loss of business of those leasing or letting facilities in the building.

Risk assessment for construction

When a risk assessment is required for building works then this should be produced by the professional team, to whom the church has given responsibility for delivering the construction project. It should include aspects of health and safety and issues such as completion of works. Each of these issues has an impact on the church business plan, as later completion will impact on the date on which the church can expect to get letting income.

Monitoring and review

Through the meetings of the church council a programme of report-back procedures will enable corrective decisions to be made over:

- Income and expenditure, cashflow, financial management, long-term financial strategies.

- Staff appointments and appraisal, staffing adequacy. Initial appointments will be subject to a six-month probationary period.

- Marketing and its effectiveness, comparative cost and effectiveness of various types of communication, and programming.

- Efficacy of communication structures with key targets: church, local people and organizations, community projects, church users and potential users.

- Long-term strategy will be addressed in three-year business planning and annual objectives.

- Parochial Church Council. To develop procedures for action planning, for developing members' skills, and increasing breadth of expertise.

- Monitoring and reviewing the impact of the events programme on the ongoing life of the congregation and ministry.

Often these items are new to church councils. If this is the case, take one of these items as a main topic on the church council agenda to set up a way of operating with one or more persons designated to bring progress reports at a specific review date in the future. Thus a rolling programme of reviews gets under way.

With the first item, finance, updates should be made monthly to the cashflow projection and brought to each church council meeting. A major budgeting task should be undertaken at the end of each financial year for the one that follows, and if monthly reports have been presented to the church council, producing a new budget should not prove too arduous.

Critical path

A *critical path analysis* is a relatively straightforward way of recognizing the interdependence of various activities and identifying those which are essential before another activity can happen (see Appendix 16). Simply, it tells the church where to expend most energy and in what order. It gives a guideline for timescales but identifies points that must remain flexible so that if the first stage is delayed all dependent future stages are equally delayed. This is especially helpful when fundraising, as there is no way to determine exactly how long a multi-faceted fundraising programme will take.

Critical success factors

Critical success factors are items which have to happen for the development strategy to work. They can be identified from the critical path analysis that integrates all aspects of the development. In the example at Appendix 16, all streams of development are dependent on the fundraising for an administrator and each separate stream has finance as a critical factor, but the different streams are not always dependent on each other.

Revenue development

The church's revenue budget and cashflow projection is probably the key element of the business plan. Some outside funders will ask for a quarterly or even monthly cashflow projection, and these are very important for assessing the viability of a project that will employ paid workers. Even for outside funders of repairs and capital works programmes, the cashflow projection will ensure that the targeted levels of income and expenditure are in line with all the church's aims and objectives as well as balancing during coming years.

Starting from present levels identify the changing incomes and expenditure as the plan progresses. Include budgets and cashflow projections. Identify money in hand and money to be raised.

Two different budgets are included (Appendices 18 and 19). The first, more simple budget, for St Dunstan's, clearly identifies ongoing income of the church and parallel costs that are ongoing from now (Appendix 18). Following this there are the items for which we anticipate expenditure with parallel anticipated income.

Each is clearly outlined and matched up so that it is possible to look at future plans and consider the impact of the success or failure of fundraising on the overall financial picture. For example, if a particular aspect of fundraising fails or a particular stream of income is late in arriving it is possible to assess the impact on the programmes of work the church is running.

The second budget, for St Jude's, is more complicated, as the church's current finances are more complex (Appendix 19). It has had several streams of activity running for a number of years, each contributing to the financial viability of the entire church. With a major capital repair programme about to start, some types of income will be curtailed while only some costs disappear. The cashflow projection indicates the level of deficit that the ordinary cashflow (not building works) will suffer. This information has enabled the church council to seek alternative income while car parking and occasional letting cannot take place. Additionally it has helped them assess what level of additional income the new crypt space will need to produce from lettings, if they are not to put car parking back onto their newly restored courtyard areas.

All budgets should be explained through simple notes attached, and more detailed reports or research should be appended.

If, as in the examples for St Dunstan's and St Jude's, the budget and cashflow projection is prepared on Excel or Lotus 123, those streams of income may be individually identified and test projections printed that show the impact of changes such as income reduced by 10 per cent. The more comprehensive the church's development plans the more likely it is that the potential funder will seek justification for each projected stream of income and expenditure. This may require, for example, asking a chartered surveyor to value leased space or for researching other community letting spaces in your area to ensure that the letting rates and frequency of bookings are realistic and appropriate.

If the church is refurbishing a space that has a full programme of existing uses, a record of all these may validate your projections of user rates, and letters from those groups may assure that groups will be prepared to pay a higher rate for a newly refurbished meeting space.

Sinking fund projection

On each of these budgets above, there is a book-keeping line identified as *sinking fund*. This is a summary of anticipated costs (quantifiable at today's rates) that may be anticipated in a long-term maintenance and repair programme. These are identified in order to determine how money should be accrued annually into the sinking fund in order to properly maintain the building over twenty and more years.

Some items such as upgrading electrical works anticipate that current works will have a long life but require upgrading for increased technical demand over the years. Items such as toilets and kitchen that receive hard wear will need almost complete renovation several times over twenty years.

It will not be possible for the church council to invest in the sinking fund until revenue has covered immediate running costs. However, in the period immediately after opening, there should be relatively few repair costs.

In the example given here, the quinquennial inspection and consultation with the inspecting architect were sources of the projected lifespan and potential cost of equipment, mechanical and electrical, decorative finishes, stone and brick repair and any other major repair that needed to be taken into account. Since churches that had new roof finishes post-World War II are beginning to need replacement slate or copper, fifty years was taken as the line on the chart at Appendix 20, indicating that renewal needs to happen in 50 years. The far right figure gives the cost (at present levels) and the renewal cycle by the number of stars. All are given at today's costs. Inflation will need to be added to the sinking fund target each year.

This gives an indicator – not an absolute figure – of how much a prudent church council will save for rainy days.

The architect provided these figures to enable the church to project its costs forward and make its budget.

Annual charges

1. Boiler/heating system	£1,500 fuel cost and £750 maintenance
2. Electric light/power	£800 fuel cost and £500 maintenance
3. Fire alarm/security	£1,000 maintenance

Replacement costs

1. Boiler/heating plant and equipment	£45,000 (after 20 to 25 years)
2. Ventilation systems	£10,000 (after 15 to 20 years)
3. General electrical system (light/power)	£40,000 (after 25 to 30 years)
4. Fire alarms/security	£15,000 (after 20 to 25 years)

These figures are very approximate and based on the information we have available, our feasibility report and the following assumptions:

Under-floor heating to the church.

Crypt in use but not heavily serviced.

All heating is via 'wet' systems.

The costs are based on today's prices and the major planned refurbishment has been undertaken.

Design life is based on standard life factors published by CIBSE.

No detailed calculations for energy use.

Lettings income

Lettings income is for many churches a key element in their financial viability and appears as a line on the cashflow projection. The justification for what the church projects as letting income will be examined carefully by potential outside grant-makers.

It is common for churches to undercharge user groups, and some realism should be built into the Business Plan. To be sloppy with existing resources does not commend the church to outside funders. Even in very poor inner-city areas of London the charge of £350 to £500 per day is both common and realistic for a fairly ordinary church hall. For high quality spaces, listed churches with good facilities and capacity for large numbers of people, the charge should be higher. Except for regular user-groups who have proven themselves to be well disciplined and careful, the cost should also cover a caretaker on site during the booking to unlock, lock up and generally ensure all is running well. A deposit is normally paid to cover the possibility that the visiting group causes damage or fails to clean up properly.

The Business Plan will need to show several key elements:

- The rate charge is compatible with other community facilities (or commercial if the activity is commercial) of a similar kind in the area. That is, community halls as well as churches. Research the rates at other premises and set your church's rate appropriately. Include information on the research.

- The quantity of bookings is realistic. If your space is already busy before the refurbishment this can be indicated on a chart of existing users. Potential new uses (shown on the same chart) will need some justification to show you are not being over-optimistic, by including, for example, letters from people interested in booking your space in the future. This is especially helpful if you are planning to refurbish the church space with a particular target group in mind, such as under-fives or the elderly.

Most churches will have a fairly simple projection of letting income.

For example, a church may have to justify many millions being spent on its repair. It will be necessary to ensure it is open to the public and staffed to care for visitors, so it has to find a significant income stream.

Having decided in general when the congregation will be using the space, the cost of their use against the overall cost of the building's running costs was calculated. The church is going to contribute the cost of utilities and other direct costs of the congregation's use of the church for the days/hours it uses the building each week. The congregation is a small one with a vast building, so it has to raise income through additional uses.

Local community or charitable user groups, including charitable arts groups, will pay a rate based on the rates of similar premises in similar areas of London (ascertained by phoning around).

Commercial uses, business receptions and banqueting rates are based on the location, size and quality of the facilities and the rates of comparable spaces in London.

Churches who are able or willing to allow bookings for wedding banquets (with suitable supervision and safeguards) should charge a fee similar to hotels and halls who regularly book such events.

Marketing

Outside funders normally ask for a marketing report. This can at times be as large as the Business Plan itself. The principles are what is important.

If the Business Plan indicates an increase in daily visitors, how is the church going to contact the new people and attract them to the building? The numbers the church has suggested might come (with the increased advertising) are based on what reasonable assumptions? This can include similar churches, local authority plans for pedestrianization and other factors.

If the number of new visitors impacts on financial viability (i.e. income from them is essential to the budget), then the assumptions become more critical. Many major millennium projects failed abysmally in being able to predict numbers of paying visitors who would be attracted; and since most were over-optimistic, outside grantmakers will show scepticism over the church's numbers. When finance is involved, include a summary of the effect on finances of less optimistic visitor numbers. For example, what impact would a drop of 10, 30 or 50 per cent have on the church's income?

Where letting income is involved, how will the church actively promote bookings and lettings and ensure that the rates are maintained at a sustainable level? Unless the church is fully booked at present before grants are spent, you should plan to show several active forms of promotion, and for this you can get ideas from other local churches and halls.

Just as with visitor numbers, the letting levels will need to be tested for impact on the overall budget. If the church fails to attract new user groups, what impact will this have on the cashflow? Again use the percentage model of drops of say 10, 30 and 50 per cent. Could the project go bankrupt and all investment be lost? Funders know it can happen and will want to see reasonable and realistic plans to avoid this.

When commercial bookings are essential to viability for the future, then significant engagement in the commercial marketing of facilities and meeting spaces will have to be evident. Whether lettings are for conference space, banquets or local consultation, the projected level of booking will need to be well justified. The funders will want to see that the church is able to maintain itself in the relevant commercial marketplace and able to update itself to continue to have a competitive edge in that market. If commercial bookings are essential to your church's business plan, a report from an appropriate marketing consultant may be advisable.

The structure of a *Marketing Report* as an element of the business plan will include:

The *mission statement* and a summary of what the church is about.

The *objectives* the church wishes to achieve over five years.

A *marketing audit* of the local area, prepared as in the work on context (above, p. 188, and Appendix 12), but in this case focusing on aspects of the area relevant to marketing. For example, are there passers-by who might be attracted into the building, or will the strategy need to draw people off the beaten track? This will include an assessment of people who already use the church and how they are attracted. Assess too whether there is competition from projects like your own or from dissimilar ones.

An *internal audit* will highlight how the church's communication strategy responds to the local audit, and particularly any changes needed.

Have you succeeded in maintaining your market and bringing in new people, and by what methods? What resources of people time and money have been used in marketing?

What are your *marketing objectives*? Do you need to set out in new directions, and how are you going to develop those?

Then there are four Ps to present. What is the *product* you are marketing? For some people this may be heritage, for others it may be community programmes, for all churches it will include worship, mission and rites of passage. What *price*/cost is involved in marketing, including the cost of advertising and other forms of communication? You should also include consideration of the cost of the product you are marketing. Your heritage visitors may come in free – or at a price. Your community space will be paid for by those using it. Assess the *price* for which you are marketing your product against others in the marketplace and justify your levels. (Note that the price here has implications also on the viability of your cashflow projections – can you afford to go as low as your competitors?) Where will you need to *place* your marketing information – whether advertisements or articles and information? Lastly summarize all your *promotional* activity.

Fundraising

Include an outline of the church's fundraising strategy, indicating possible sources of funds and action that is being taken. This enables the church's fundraising committee to have a systematic approach to the tasks and to be able to explain their strategy to the church council and others outside the church such as potential funders. Including this section in material sent to outside funders enables them to understand the overall strategy. Some funders will want to be sure that all sources are being thoroughly covered as they do not wish to make a grant that is not about to be used. So for example when an application will be sent to English Heritage, some funders will want to wait till after English Heritage responds before agreeing their own grant.

Appendix 1: Communicating with potential donors

Churchgoers

Potential donors	messages and mutual objectives	methods of communication
Committed donors		
PCC, staff, electoral roll	church for the future, collective responsibility for vision and ministry	meetings, sermons, legacies, envelopes
Intermittent donors congregation, past members	ongoing church/meet needs; church for the future	meetings, sermons, envelopes
Interest, may not give drop-in visitors	open for prayer & ministry, an open sacred space	events, donor point, envelopes
No interest YET personal contacts	I belong, will you help?	brochure

Concerts and Recitals

Potential donors	messages and mutual objectives	methods of communication
Committed donors		
Intermittent donors concert producers	home for arts/music, it's beautiful but it's peeling	concerts mailing lists, music societies mailings
Interest, may not give concert goers: 90 concerts and 150 recitals	place we like	brochures, volunteers, donor point, envelopes
No interest YET		

Café

Potential donors	messages and mutual objectives	methods of communication
Committed donors		
Intermittent donors company	a good business environment	letter, meeting, brochures
Interest, may not give customers	for your enjoyment	brochures and fundraising events
No interest YET customers	customer interest and satisfaction	brochures, collecting boxes

Market

Potential donors	messages and mutual objectives	methods of communication
Committed donors		
Intermittent donors stall holders	good business environment	letters, personal contact
Interest, may not give	for your enjoyment	brochures and fundraising events
No interest YET customers		posters, brochures

Tourists

	Potential donors	messages and mutual objectives	methods of communication
Committed donors	heritage visitors		brochures, donor point
Intermittent donors	hotels etc	mutual benefit of environment,	brochures, donor point
Interest, may not give	return visitors	while we're in London we'll go to St James's	brochures, donor point, envelopes
No interest YET	drop-ins	architecture, history, style,	brochures, donor point

Letting groups

	Potential donors	messages and mutual objectives	methods of communication
Committed donors	dance, exercise, childcare, Taize group, Zen Buddhist group, churches	mutual commitment	volunteers, brochures, envelopes, donor point
Intermittent donors	meeting room users	place of safety	brochures, volunteers, donor points
Interest, may not give	mailing lists		brochures
No interest YET			

Charitable Trusts

	Potential donors	messages and mutual objectives	methods of communication
Committed donors	past contributors	Sir Christopher Wren, Grinling Gibbons	personal contact with trustees we know OR local business partners know
Intermittent donors	trusts with national heritage agenda	read guidelines	written application
Interest, may not give	trusts with a local connection	read guidelines	contact any trustees we already know and apply in writing
No interest YET	trusts with church repair and conservation agenda	read guidelines	apply in writing

Appendix 2: Fundraising action plan for St Augustine's Church

Key people	Relationship	Meetings and work
1. Project manager	To work on our behalf with the design team (architect etc.) to look after programmes and costs	Meet the project manager and update
2. English Heritage	Make major application in Spring 2001	Phone for application pack
3. Father ———	To update on practical matters To develop 'values'	Fundraising group meet the vicar and update
4. Church council	Update and engage in programme of activities and in building relationships	Meet church council on ———
5. Patrons and friends	Working group to meet with key patrons to develop fundraising events for 2001	Meeting to be set up
6. Friends of St Augustine Newsletter Appeal	To help in fundraising and gaining donations	Working with vicar on next issue
7. Legacies	To enable people to make a legacy to St Augustine as part of their stewardship, should they wish to do so	Attend seminar on legacies, and then working group to suggest how to proceed
8. Single Regeneration Budget in Kilburn	Fundraising group to talk to local workers about help with building this relationship and how to proceed	Meeting to be set up

continued

Key people	Relationship	Meetings and work
9. New Deal for Communities	Father ——— to meet with committee member again to explore the benefit this might bring	Meeting to be set up
10. Schools	Continue to develop relationship and at appropriate times get letters of support sent out	Clergy to follow up
11. General community contacts		Briefing when the capital budget is prepared and church council can discuss how they and the congregation can help in talking to local people, perhaps with a leaflet to help
12. Archdeacon	To keep him up to date	Letter to be sent

Appendix 3: Leaflet for a stewardship programme

CHRISTIAN STEWARDSHIP 2002

claim back the income tax on small or large occasional gifts to the church as provided that we have a record of the amount you have given. **Special *yellow* GIFT AID envelopes are also available for occasional use.**

The basic rate of income tax is 22%. This means that if you give under GIFT AID for every £1 you give the Church is able to claim back from the Inland Revenue 28p income tax.

HOW GIFT AID WORKS

You give		Tax Back	Total to Church
£ 5	*per week* 1.40	6.40	332.80 *pa*
£ 10	2.80	12.80	665.60 *pa*
£ 15	4.20	19.20	998.40 *pa*
£ 20	5.60	25.60	1331.20 *pa*
£ 25	7.00	32.00	1664.00 *pa*
£ 50	14.00	64.00	3328.00 *pa*

Do we give grudgingly?

"All things come from thee, O Lord, and of thine own do we give thee
... 0.7% of income?"

HOW SHOULD I PAY?

Either by

- **BANKER'S ORDER**

or in the

- **WEEKLY STEWARDSHIP ENVELOPES**

Banker's Order forms and packets of Envelopes may be obtained at the Stewardship enquiry desk at the back of church.

IF YOU PAY INCOME TAX

Under what is now called **GIFT AID** the church can recover from the Inland Revenue the tax that you paid on your offering.

Every member of the congregation who is paying tax should fill in a GIFT AID form which can be obtained at the Christian Stewardship enquiry desk.

Make sure that you put your **full name, address and postal code** on the form. You don't have to say how much you intend to give. The form covers what you give through banker's order or in your envelope. We are also able to

Giving is a sign of our love. We give to the church

- not only because the church needs money - and it does!
- but because giving is part of our response to God's generosity

**I NEED TO WORSHIP
I NEED TO PRAY
I NEED TO GIVE**

OUR PARISH NEEDS EVERY WEEK

	£
Common Fund (Diocese)	770
Maintenance of two priests	110
Insurance	220
Fuel & Electricity	39
Altar needs - Bread, wine, candles etc	29
Printing & Stationery	18
Organist & Music	106
Fabric, Cleaning, Repairs etc.	24
Total	**1316**
Missions at 10%	131
TOTAL NEEDS	**£1447**

WE NEED £1447 a week to do God's work at S. Augustine's Kilburn

We cannot do God's work without YOUR regular and generous giving

HOW DO I FIX THE AMOUNT THAT I SHOULD GIVE?

Two Ways of Thinking about your Giving

A. YOUR 'SHARE' of your Church's needs

There are approximately 150 active members of the congregation at Saint Augustine's.

ONE SHARE of £1447 is **£9.60**

We need an *average* **of £9.60 per person PER WEEK.**

Some cannot afford a whole share
Some can afford more than one share.

What about YOU?

B. A PROPORTION OF YOUR INCOME

The Bible suggests **ONE TENTH** *of what YOU receive*

The Church does not tell its members how much each should give, but many Christians do give a tenth as a token of their commitment God's work in the parish. Others are working their way towards the Tenth.

- *Example:* Take home pay **£100** per week; **you give £10** to God. Take home pay **£150** per week; **you give £15** to God etc.

What about YOU?

WHAT ARE WE ASKING?

Only **Three Things**

- That you seek God's guidance in **PRAYER**
- That during the next few weeks you **CONSIDER INCREASING YOUR GIVING**
- That if you are paying tax you fill in a **GIFT AID form.**

Appendix 4: Use on a daily basis of All Saints Community Hall

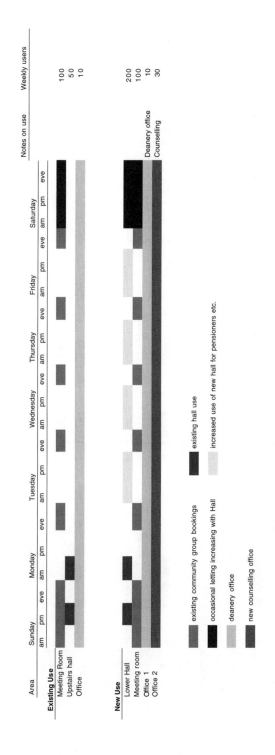

Area	Sunday			Monday			Tuesday			Wednesday			Thursday			Friday			Saturday			Notes on use	Weekly users
	am	pm	eve	am	pm	eve	am	pm	eve	am	pm	eve	am	pm	eve	am	pm	eve	am	pm	eve		
Existing Use																							
Meeting Room																							100
Upstairs hall																							50
Office																							10
New Use																							
Lower Hall																							200
Meeting room																							100
Office 1																						Deanery office	10
Office 2																						Counselling	30

existing community group bookings

occasional letting increasing with Hall

deanery office

new counselling office

existing hall use

increased use of new hall for pensioners etc.

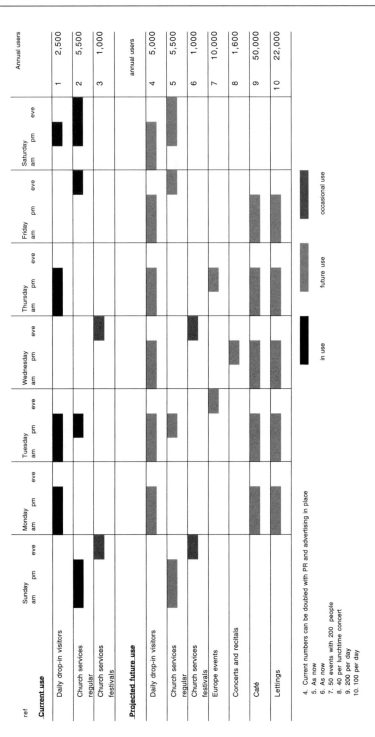

4. Current numbers can be doubled with PR and advertising in place
5. As now
6. As now
7. 50 events with 200 people
8. 40 per lunchtime concert
9. 200 per day
10. 100 per day

Appendix 5: A budget for building works

Sydenham, All Saints Church Hall Refurbishment

revised: 9.1.01

Item		Builder:	A	B
	Prelims section total		6,932.98	27,977.83
1.1	Demolition		835.38	1202
1.2	Parish and Meeting Rooms (G02/G03)		1104	989
1.3	Ground Floor Toilets (G04/G05)		989.88	950
1.4	Entrance Hall (G01)		345	357
1.5	Grounds Store (G06)		17.25	8
1.6	Kitchen (F05)		258.75	179
1.7	First Floor Toilets (F02/F04)		1196.88	186
2	Builders Work			
2.1	New Entrance doors (D1)		1,298.25 incl.	
2.2	Hall (G07)		1544.7	1245.8
2.3	Grounds Store/ Fire Exit (G06/G07)		2118.38	1411.6
2.4	Ground Floor Toilets (G09/G11)		3570.56	2523.7
2.5	Kitchenette (G08)		2737	3861.35
2.6	First Floor Meeting Rooms/ Deanery		5515.8	4986.2
2.7	Kitchen (F05)		2909.5	1959
2.8	First Floor Toilets (F02/F04)		894.6	1825
3	Services: general		2435	1784
3.1	Disabled/ Male Toilets (G10)		1764.96	1610
3.2	Ground Floor Female Toilets (G11)		1070.25	690
3.3	First Floor Female Toilets (F04)		806.25	401
3.4	First Floor Male Toilets (F02)		1128.25	658
4	Finishes		13653.83	12307.52
5	Electrical Works		18301.13	7000
6	Hot and Cold Water		2342.7	6000
7	Mechanical Works		7330.96	6000
8	External Repairs		1311	720
	Tender totals		82413.24	86832
	Fees as Lump Sum		£ 12,000.00	£ 12,000.00
	Sub-total		£94,413.24	£98,832.00
	VAT @ 17.5%		£16,522.32	£17,295.60
	Project Cost		**£110,935.56**	**£116,127.60**

Appendix 6: An application for funding for All Saints Community Hall

All Saints Community Hall

Revd ——, All Saints Vicarage,

Application to Esme Fairbairn Charitable Trust ref. EFCT/G2

Summary

All Saints Community Hall is located in an area of urban deprivation. It serves a wide spectrum of local people from all ethnic groups.

A major programme of repairs is needed to bring the Hall up to current requirements for disabled access and health and safety. The programme will include works that will make the facilities available to up to twice as many as the current 200 users.

The works will cost £111,000 of which we have raised £84,000. We are seeking a grant of £10,000 towards this total.

Applicant

All Saints Community Hall in Sydenham is owned by All Saints Church, which is an excepted charity (The Church of England Measure). It has its own committee and accounts and includes representation from the groups using the Hall.

This application is from the Hall Committee.

The Background

The All Saints Hall in Trewsbury Road, Lower Sydenham, is in an area of multiple deprivation. Locally there are high levels of poverty, lone-parenting, domestic violence, higher than average numbers of pensioners, a high proportion of people from ethnic minorities and large numbers of children whose mother tongue is not English. The need for community hall facilities is greater than current provision.

In the seventeenth century Lower Sydenham was referred to as 'a poor ignorant village in Kent'. Today, in the London Borough of Lewisham, the parish is still an area of multiple deprivation. The Sunday congregation of about 50, drawn from 100 people on the membership roll, is representative of the area. Of that 100, 25 per cent are from ethnic minorities and 12 per cent are lone parents; 74 members are unemployed, including 41 pensioners.

The Committee

The Hall Committee of seven members has two from ethnic minorities, and two are disabled. The Committee meets regularly to consider the use of the Hall, the financial situation, bookings, maintenance and any other issues that arise.

Our Committee meets quarterly and more often if necessary.

The Committee reports to the AGM of the church.

Users with problems or questions contact the Chairperson.

Current and Future Use

Current groups include: a local black-led church, the British Legion, a children's dance group, St John's Ambulance, Weight Watchers, a judo group, a Credit Union and a table tennis club. Those groups needing a small meeting room will be accommodated in the upstairs meeting room or in the hall.

The Parent and Toddler group, at present limited to one session per week, is planning to open more often. Other enquirers for regular space include an Indian dance group. There are constant enquiries for a hall for Saturday events, for children's parties and other community and family events. These can in future be readily accommodated on a regular basis. Groups for the elderly are wishing to book the hall once it is located on the ground floor. We are developing a growing partnership with a nearby hostel for asylum seekers who, with limited finance, need opportunities for activities and friendship; we hope to encourage them to use our facilities more. The Allotment Annual Show, children's parties and other occasional lettings result in many more one-off users.

At present an average of 200 local people use the hall each week, including 45 children, 30 teens, 60 elderly, 35 disabled, 26 lone parents, and of these approximately two-thirds are female. The users are reflective of the ethnic mix of our local community.

We anticipate that the number of users, with increased use for the elderly and children in particular, will be approximately double the present numbers. The project will include works that will make the facilities available to up to twice as many as the current 200 users.

A sign board on the street advertises the Hall, and many others hear by word of mouth.

Outcomes

- Immediate increase in facilities available for booking by local groups and local people.
- Offices for two local organizations.
- Local opportunity for a charity offering counselling to young people in our neighbourhood.
- We have many elderly users for whom our social provision is a key element in countering their isolation.
- We are seeking to offer facilities and social space for asylum seekers for whom we are already providing activities and social contact.

Equal Opportunities

All Saints Hall has an Equal Opportunities policy. All groups and individuals using the centre are expected to commit themselves to this policy.

It is the Committee's intention to ensure this policy is applied in:

- Recruitment, selection, training, consideration for promotion and treatment at work for those who are employed in paid or voluntary capacity within the organization.
- Access to the benefits, facilities and services provided by All Saints Community Hall.

Access to membership of our councils, committees and other groups, and use of the Community Centre, are available to all without unfair discrimination, and we ensure that no-one is disadvantaged in any of these matters by conditions or requirements that cannot be shown to be justifiable. We will work to ensure that there is no discrimination on grounds of race, nationality, ethnic origin, disability, sex, marital status or sexual orientation, where any of these cannot be shown to be a requirement of the job or office concerned.

The Problem, the Project

The All Saints Hall at present has lots of problems. The facilities are run down and do not meet current health and safety or access requirements. The toilets, which are downstairs, are dilapidated and inadequate. The largest space – the hall – is upstairs and inaccessible to the disabled and many pensioners and is therefore unsuitable for many community events. The rooms downstairs are too large for offices but manage to include some small group meetings. The building is in need of refurbishment throughout.

The architect's plans to meet the various current needs and provide for new and extended uses are ideal. The hall will be downstairs with easy access to the toilets and the kitchenette, making its use attractive for many community and family events and for organization and group meetings. Upstairs, with additional toilet facilities, will be small offices and a meeting room. The present uses will be located in one office, and a new user, South London Psychoanalytical Psychotherapists, who specialize in work with young people, will have the other office. The work will take approximately three months to complete.

The Costs and the Funding

The architect has tendered the project, and the refurbishment will cost £111,000 (details attached). We have received grant help of:

Church Urban Fund   £15,000
South East London Healthy Communities Fund   £5,000
Peabody Community Fund   £10,000
Lloyds TSB Foundation   £4,000

From our own funds   £50,000

We are seeking help in raising the balance of £27,000. As continuing provision for 200 people and providing new use by up to 200 more this is a good investment in community provision.

We are also approaching Goldsmiths Company's Charity, Henry Smith Charitable Trust and the Wates Charitable Foundation.

Ongoing Funding

All Saints Community Hall is self-sustaining with regard to revenue and will not require external funding for running costs.

Our ongoing financial procedures include:

- 2 signatories on cheques
- report on finance at every meeting
- treasurer does the banking and receipts are always issued
- payments out are only against invoices
- we produce annual accounts that are examined by the chairperson and by the treasurer of the church.

Appraisal of Options

All Saints Community Hall was extremely dilapidated and had very limited access for disabled facilities as the Hall was upstairs and the meeting room and offices were downstairs.

In consultation with our architect it proved possible to reverse the facilities and provide a downstairs hall with full access. In its current state the upper floor is not usable. In order to extend our facilities to meet the needs of local people we have decided to seek funds to undertake a full repair.

The building works overall are designed to address current standards of disabled access.

Our building work is supervised by our Architect, ——— (RIBA), who has undertaken any necessary building regulation approval. No planning permission is needed as there is no change of use and it is not a listed building.

Key People

The architect is ——— (RIBA) of ——— partnership, address: ———

The Client Representative will be Revd ———, address: ———, phone: ———

(Attached:
Latest accounts
Costs from the architect/builders
Schedule of use
Charts showing demographics)

Appendix 7: A statement of significance and a statement of need

Parish Church of St Martin, Gospel Oak
Diocese of London

Statement of Significance

St Martin's Church, a Grade I Listed building, was built in 1864–5, at the sole cost of the wealthy Worcestershire businessman and philanthropist John Derby Allcroft, partner in the glove-making firm of Dent and Allcroft, and to the design of Edward Buckton Lamb (1805–69).

It is now one of the best known of Lamb's churches, having recently featured in Simon Jenkins, *England's Thousand Best Churches* (1999), p. 430. Pevsner notes it (*Buildings of England: London except the Cities of London and Westminster*, 1952, p. 360) as 'indeed the craziest of London's Victorian churches, inconfutable proof, if proof were needed, that the Victorians were not mere imitators in their ecclesiastical architecture'. He suggests that the mixture of derivative and original elements here, 'results in an unprecedented whole which is both striking and harrowing'. His comments echo those of the *Builder* (1866, p. 781) that the style is that 'in general use at the time of Henry VII; but the building must be considered rather a characteristic expression of that style, than as a reproduction, for it would be difficult to find an absolute precedent for any portion of the work'. Sir John Summerson described St Martin's in the chapter, 'Two London Churches', in *Victorian Architecture: Four Studies in Evaluation* (1970).

From the outside the church's most notable feature is the tall (40m) unusually thin tower (the pinnacles were removed following bomb damage during the Second World War), dominating a complicated patterned tiled roof and the Kentish ragstone exterior walls. 'I know few towers so tormenting as this one in proportion, modelling and silhouette. Most towers answer a question. This one asks' (Summerson, p. 73).

At the foot of the tower, a north porch leads to the interior. Here the most striking feature is the overwhelming, dark timber roof, covering the whole of the nave and the two transepts, and supported by hammer beams springing from the capitals of semi-detached columns at the head of four massive stone piers. Beneath the roof the ragstone walls appear to move off in all directions. An apsidal sanctuary, with its wooden roof now painted in bright colours, and original windows by Clayton and Bell, finishes the nave to the east. Tall plain windows in the transepts and at the west end (the stained-glass here having been lost in the war) now light the church. There are memorial windows to the west of the two transepts by the William Morris London factory.

In 1901 as part of a general restoration of the building, a low alabaster screen was provided at the entry to the chancel, with an alabaster pulpit and reredos and a brass eagle lectern. At the same time an alabaster reredos was placed in front of the lower central stained-glass at the east end.

In the late 1920s a new choir vestry was built (Albert J. Thomas) adjoining the porch and north-west corner of the church. This was converted in 1990 (Triforum) to a small integral church hall, and a certain amount of internal reordering was undertaken at the same time. The font was moved to its present position in the south transept, and the pewing at the west end was removed.

The main impression of the church interior is light and space. As Goodhart-Rendel wrote (*English Architecture since the Regency*, 1953, p. 136), 'something was achieved towards roofing a large preaching space with ingenious carpentry and adapting pseudo-mediaeval forms to structures of a kind unknown in the Middle Ages'. It is 'a completely original, and, I think, almost perfect, solution of what a large auditorium for Protestant services should be' (Goodhart-Rendel, 'Rogue architects of the Victorian era', *Journal of the RIBA*, April 1949, p. 251).

Statement of Need

The church roof, with its heavy timbers and complicated patterned tile covering, has not been thoroughly overhauled since the church was completed in 1865. It has begun to leak badly in several places, and many of the tiles are damaged, broken or dislodged by weather and vandalism. These need to be renewed, the roof timbers thoroughly inspected and refurbished if necessary, and further steps taken to ensure the watertightness of the roof as a whole.

The ragstone walls and tower are eroding and crumbling – there has been no general work on these since the 1930s. Apart from the loss of most of the stained-glass windows and the pinnacles on the tower, the church survived the war relatively unscathed. However, in the last few years there has been subsidence in the south wall of the church (where there was additional underpinning in the 1890s) caused by trees (now removed) growing very near the wall and interfering with the drainage. Movement of the wall is being monitored. As well as repairs to the damaged wall, investigation of the rest of the structure is advisable to ensure that after this length of time the weight of the roof is not placing undue strain on the walls generally.

There have been problems with the carry-away of rainwater from the area of the roof where the late-1920s addition adjoins the original structure, exacerbated by recent more extreme weather, which have led to the kitchen in the new hall being flooded on several occasions. Work needs to be undertaken to remedy the difficulties here.

Appendix 8: Questionnaire for a branding exercise

Branding exercise

Describe in one sentence what the church does.

Describe in one paragraph what the church does.

Where would you like the church to be in five years' time?

Who are the key beneficiaries of the work the church does?

What is unique about the church?

If the church was a car or a businessperson or a famous person or animal or colour or country, which would it be and why?

If the church were a Bible story or character, which would it be?

What are the top 5 values that the church has?

What would be your mission statement for the church?
Okay, not the printed one – what is your version?

What would be your vision statement for the church?

Complete the following sentence: 'I am passionate about the church because . . .'

If there were *one* guiding principle to the church what would it be?

What does the church not do?

Which projects would the church not take on?

Appendix 9: A form for donors

Name:

Address:

A LEGACY

Please tick here ☐ for more information on leaving a legacy for St Jude's Church.

GIFT AID

If you are a UK taxpayer please tick the box so we can claim back 28p for every £1 you give, at no extra cost to you.

☐ Yes. I would like St Jude's Church to treat donations I make from today's date as Gift Aid donations.*

Name of Taxpayer:

Date:

No, as I am not a UK taxpayer I am unable to take part in the Gift Aid Scheme.

* The amount of tax reclaimed by St Jude's Church must not exceed the amount of income and/or capital gains tax you pay in any tax year. Please advise us if your donations no longer qualify for Gift Aid.

To make an instant donation please call with your credit card details. Lines open during office hours.
020 ——— ———

I would like to give £ _____
(I enclose my cheque/postal order made payable to St Jude's Church)

CREDIT CARD PAYMENT

I prefer to donate by
Switch/Delta/MasterCard/Visa/Amex/
Diners Club/CAF Card
(please delete as appropriate)

Amount: _____

Card Number

_ _ _ _ _ _ _ _ _ _ _ _ _ _ _ _

Issue number _ _
Valid from _ _/_ _

Expiry Date _ _/_ _
Today's date _ _/_ _/_ _

Signature

_____

Please post this form/envelope into the
donation box in church OR deliver to
the church office ——— OR post to:
St Jude's Church Appeal, St Jude's
Church, High Street, Hightown.

If you would prefer to receive no further
communication from our appeal office
please tick this box. ☐ We will,
however, send you a thankyou letter.

To make a STANDING ORDER from
your bank account:

To the Manager . . . .
.. . . Bank (your bank)
(address) . . ..
.. . . .Branch
Sort Code _ _ _ _ _ _ _

Please pay to the account of the
Parochial Church of St Jude's
Church, Hightown at the [———]
Bank plc [———] bank address

Sort Code: [———]
Account number: [———]

On the . . . .. . day of . . ..
200. . .
And thereafter at regular monthly
intervals until further notice, the sum
of £. . .. . .. (figures)
. . . .
.. . . (words)

Please debit my account number
. . ..
with each payment made.

Signature

_____

Appendix 10: Option analysis for a building project

Options scored out of 5, with 1 being the lowest score

Option	Suitability to present needs	Provision for future needs for mission	Cost of building works	Income potential to help sustain mission	Total
Major repair programme					
Demolish and rebuild					
Rebuild with social housing					
Rebuild with developer					
Sell, share premises with another church					

Appendix 11: Option analysis for a business plan

Option		Are skills available?	Is time available?	What is the cost potential?	Preference
Hall letting	Volunteers to manage?				
	Clergy to manage?				
	Employ part-time hall manager?				
Letting social housing	Clergy to manage?				
	Volunteers to manage?				
	Housing association to manage?				
Other manage-ment options					

Appendix 12: Two models for a statement of context

Model One

Context of St George's Church

Sociological

Bloomsbury ward, in the London Borough of Camden, is in the bottom 2 per cent of the country with regard to quality of housing. Among local children, 49 per cent live in low-income families. Unemployment runs at 13 per cent and incomes are in the bottom 25 per cent nationally.[32]

The figures reflect the local mixture of Georgian and Victorian housing, with small independent shops at street level, that has an air of surviving rather than thriving.

Poverty of housing provision indicates a pressing need for meeting and for social space. The needs of children in families living on low income and in poor homes are pressing, yet the standards of education are above the national average. Increased engagement with schools as well as community groups is therefore sought.

Economic

The London Borough of Camden is one of the poorer of London's boroughs. Regeneration and neighbourhood renewal strategies are focused on revenue programmes for local community initiatives. The borough does not have resources to invest in capital works on churches.

The Parochial Church Council has over the past five years established income to cover its running costs and pays a full share of the Common Fund of the Diocese. Once the building is repaired, the Parochial Church Council has identified a financial strategy that will provide for its future maintenance and repair.

At present the church and nearby streets are blighted by a drugs problem, and work with the police continues to try to diminish the activity. Those whose lives

[32] Information from the Indices of Multiple Deprivation 2000 published by the Office of the Deputy Prime Minister.

are most affected by drug and alcohol abuse are often rough sleepers, and because of the damage caused the church is actively seeking to discourage such activities on the church site.

Environmental

St George's Church is on the tourists' walking route from the British Museum to Covent Garden. Nearby are the historic squares: Bloomsbury, Bedford and Russell Squares.

Refurbishment of the Ministry of Defence building opposite the church on Bloomsbury Way will greatly improve the streetscape. The restoration of the portico and approach to St George's will add to this.

With its closeness also to the commercial centres of Oxford Street and Tottenham Court Road, St George's Church is well served with buses and tube.

Cultural

St George's Church has an ethnically mixed congregation. The church has good relationships and partnerships with other faith groups and people from all ethnic backgrounds in the area.

The visitors to St George's are as diverse as the spectrum of visitors to London: of many nationalities, races and cultures.

The local economy of small businesses and cafés brings both residents and a workforce that tends to be very mixed and transitory. The church works with local residents and tenants' organizations and with local businesses in developing a sense of local responsibility and pride.

The story, the quality and the processes of restoration will have the potential to bring many visitors to explore the church. It is part of the ongoing strategy that provision of displays and photos of the process will open up the heritage of St George's to people of all backgrounds, faiths and races. Work with local schools will be targeted to encourage children's sense of ownership, knowledge and pride in their neighbourhood and its heritage.

Limitations

As a Grade I listed building and a church, the use, modification and repairs must be of the highest quality. The requirements of protecting and preserving the architectural and historic quality of the building are respected alongside recognition that the building serves the living tradition of being a parish church. Additional uses are bound by both these parameters that will be addressed in the detailed policies and principles of adaptation, management, repair and additional uses.

The running costs of the building will need to be met from its income, as they are now. This will include an increased budget for maintenance and a Sinking Fund for future repairs.

Model Two

The Area Analysis

Demographic information would have greater significance to the ministry of the Guild Church Council if St Andrew's were bound by a parish identity. The remit of the St Andrew's Charities carries the concerns of the church into three council wards in south Camden and to the City. Statistics for the Camden area indicate that while education standards are moderate, in several other ways this area is extremely deprived. In King's Cross ward the housing is in the worst 0.5 per cent in the country, and child poverty is a pressing factor with all three wards being in the worst 10 per cent or in the case of Bloomsbury ward on the edge of it.

St Andrew's does not function pastorally for these residents, but through the Charities can make a major impact on the deprivation in the lives of individuals and organizations. The continuing support of the Charities by St Andrew's, even though the Charities are each independently functioning, is important to both.

Economic trends in the business sector have significant effects on the lives of local workers. There are cycles of downsizing that are stressful for those losing their jobs and for those staying. Long hours and extreme work pressure require individuals to cope with enormous personal pressures. With the City increasing its strength and profile among banking centres in Europe this is not going to reduce.

St Andrew's pastoral function in being a gathering-point for September 11th or similar events, alongside offering individual support through counselling and therapy, is significant.

The European pressure-point of the current flood of economic refugees and asylum seekers from Eastern Europe is not of particular significance to St Andrew's, as very little refugee housing could be available in the immediate environs. There is housing for refugees in the areas served by the Charities, and many small grants are made to meet their needs.

In the event of a major economic downturn or recession, the Guild Church Council should note that restaurants and cafés do better than most businesses in a boom and drop further than most in a recession. The implications are that taking on a restaurant tenant could mean some stress in a recession, and the Guild Church Council would be wise to build up a revenue reserve to cover the possibility of a restaurant tenant failing and there being a void in rental income till a new tenant is found.

The key Environmental factor affecting St Andrew's development is the Partnership of local businesses and the Corporation of the City of London that is reviewing Holborn Circus and the surrounding areas with a view to street-level improvements. Fundamentally, the area is unfriendly to pedestrians and lacking in services such as refreshment and retail that give a warmer and more welcoming 'feel' to streets. Additionally, the Circus itself is designed for vehicles, and pedestrians struggle to find a place. The new strategies and layouts include better pedestrian services, crossings, open spaces and refreshment opportunities. The most recent draft plan for the Partnership includes 'opening up' the green spaces more and creating a refreshment point in the garden between St Andrew's and the Circus. This need can easily be met by the opening up of St Andrew's west end and the provision of café or similar facilities at ground level. This ties St Andrew's into the development plan, and a timely consultation with the Corporation as the Partnership develops could result in a potential joint project.

At present, from the Circus the church looks locked off by the wall and trees, and very private. If Cross-Rail happens, and if it finally comes through Farringdon station this will place St Andrew's on the pedestrian route of many more local workers, and the increased openness and facilities will have new relevance.

The *Political factors* of significance to St Andrew's are on three sides. Firstly, government itself does not appear to be going in a direction that could damage the development in the foreseeable future. Some of its directions may help. The heritage strategy is inclusive of an English Heritage strategy called Pride of Place. This is a medium-term strategy to engage local people in their local heritage – to become proud of their locality and its heritage. Similarly, regeneration strategies and town-planning, including those of the Greater London Authority, are increasingly concerned to create people/pedestrian-friendly environments, including more green spaces and city squares. Further checking will be undertaken, as the building of Cross-Rail involves ten years of building sites on open spaces right across the City. At present we can only hope this construction work has little or no impact on the Circus, although it may impact on traffic levels. In places the sites will look like the redevelopment by King's Cross, at present causing major problems.

The Diocese and the Diocesan Advisory Committee are likely to approve the church's overall strategy as far as it impacts on them. There are likely to be continuing challenges, from English Heritage and possibly the Diocesan Advisory Committee, to change on the building itself. The development of new buildings in the grounds is likely to be highly contentious with them and with the Corporation, from whom listed building consent and planning permission will be needed. This, however, does not stop the church from being very persistent and committed to the project on the basis of essential ministry development.

Technical or technological developments at present are not likely to threaten the St Andrew's development. As there are gradual changes in working patterns as a result of new technology, the impact should be monitored and programmes reviewed. Since so many local corporate buildings are already the focus for international activity it is likely to change only if technological developments reduce the need to centralize aspects of business. This, for an area such as Holborn, might bring a temporary local 'recession' but with minor impact on the church's ministry. This is an issue for strategic development in the very long term.

Appendix 13: An example of SWOT analysis

STRENGTHS

Restoration project

The £5,000,000 gift of the estate of ———

Skills of the Parochial Church Council for delivering the project

Very skilled design and project management team

Ongoing engagement of the ——— in fundraising and management

Support of the Bishop and Diocesan Advisory Committee

Ongoing strategy

Well-established programmes for church, community and visitors

Experience of the Parochial Church Council over a number of years in maintaining revenue viability

Well established partnerships with local community organizations

Inclusion in guidebooks and ongoing marketing has produced a considerable and growing stream of visitors

---

OPPORTUNITIES

Restoration project

The ——— gift

The Heritage Lottery Fund targeting projects that will increase education and community use of heritage buildings, and those tackling social exclusion

Contemporary interest in Hawksmoor's architecture

Ongoing strategy

Reviews by the London Borough of ——— of pedestrian provision and the streetscape may result in benefit

Transport links are excellent, with many bus routes stopping outside the church, local tube, and pedestrian routes between local attractions

Local community, residents and business partnerships and links in place and growing

WEAKNESSES

Restoration project

Very tight time-scale imposed with the ——— gift

Church has never undertaken a programme of this magnitude before

The time available for intervention/conservation, before a catastrophic failure in the fabric, is decreasing so that the present opportunity is increasingly pressing

Challenges to overcome include the most appropriate location of new works, especially disabled access on a Grade I listed building with world monument status

Money to match the ——— gift has still to be raised

Ongoing strategy

The Parochial Church Council includes volunteers who are professional people with relevant skills, but their time for the project is limited by their work

Present lack of administrative staff poses a challenge to the maintenance of ordinary functions such as site security/opening hours, maintaining marketing strategy. *This is being addressed in the strategy for the future.*

THREATS

Restoration project

The failure to raise the money to match the ——— gift by the required time. This would have a catastrophic effect, cutting off the construction programme mid-way.

Time involved in gaining essential permissions – faculty and listed building consent – is not in our control

Ongoing strategy

Congestion charging for cars in London could adversely affect parking income. However, the future income with crypt use is adequate without car parking.

The changes to the local area in the medium term, residential and business, will require ongoing monitoring and modification of communication and marketing strategies.

Appendix 14: Indicative budget for capital works

Preparatory Work

Strip out basement and carefully remove pews etc.	£ 16,000	
Protect organ, bell and ceiling	£ 32,000	£ 48,000

Stabilize building

Brace windows & support balcony	£ 40,000	
Excavate basement & underpin	£ 185,000	
Allowance for archaeological dig	£ 50,000	
Allowance for removing 200 graves	£ 150,000	
Flight auger piling	£ 183,000	
Form basement floor	£ 58,000	
Form ground floor	£ 86,000	
Permanent support to galleries	£ 19,000	
Remove propping and temporary work	£ 6,000	£ 777,000

Building repair

Re-roof church with copper & slate	£ 150,000	
Line rainwater downpipes	£ 3,000	
Minor repairs to flashings	£ 2,000	
Stone	£ 50,000	
Structural	£ 20,000	
Windows	£ 6,000	
Doors	£ 5,000	
Internal stairs	£ 500	£ 236,500

Finishes

Church	£ 184,000	
Refurbish and reinstall church woodwork (pews etc)	£ 50,000	
Remaining rooms (exc. basement)	£ 14,000	£ 248,000

New Services

Electrical & specialist	£ 35,000	
Plumbing	£ 5,000	
Lightning conductor	£ 4,000	
Heating	£ 40,000	£ 84,000

Basement

Fit-out	£ 143,000	
Lift	£ 60,000	£ 203,000

Entrance

Allowance	£ 75,000	£ 75,000
	Sub-total	£ 1,671,500

Preliminaries @15%	£ 250,725
	£ 1,922,225
Contingency @ 10%	£ 192,223
CONSTRUCTION TOTAL	**£ 2,114,448**
VAT on 66% of works	£ 244,219
TOTAL	**£ 2,358,667**
Professional fees @ 20%	£ 422,890
VAT on fees	£ 74,006
	£ 2,855,562
Allowance for inflation since June 1999 to start of work @ 7.5%	£ 214,167
Church Building Insurance	£ 5,000
PROJECT TOTAL	**£ 3,074,729**

Appendix 15: Risk assessment for St Jude's project strategy

Risk	Probability of Occurrence	Impact of Occurrence	Mitigating Planning and Action
Failure of maintenance programmes	The building has not had a challenging maintenance programme in the past, so managing an effective programme is new and significant. Low probability of problems	Failure of maintenance contracts on the lift and similar critical facilities could have immediate effect on the licensed status. High impact on financial plans Failure of routine maintenance on minor items, redecoration and similar items will reduce letability. Medium and increasing impact on financial viability	Maintenance is a key element in the financial and facilities management that has resulted in the present strategy for viability. Within the church council, there are people with the skills to ensure the establishment of a programme that fulfils the work of the Ten-Year Maintenance Plan. The church council will address maintenance through regular reports from the administrator and churchwardens on maintenance and repair programmes; reports and spot checks on facilities will be undertaken; reports on standards of similar premises will inform upgrading in future years. Financial planning now includes adequate funds to maintain and repair the building.

Risk	Probability of Occurrence	Impact of Occurrence	Mitigating Planning and Action
Failure of repair programmes	The building has had no major repairs in recent decades. Quinquennial repairs are not expected to be major in the near future, but regular repair will be needed. This will include items from the Ten-Year Plan, plus items identified in quinquennial reports. Over the next fifty years major works will be needed to high levels and this is inevitable. Low probability of occurrence	Quinquennial repairs in the medium term are not expected to have high impact. Long term: some repairs will have high impact eventually with a high cost.	It is crucial that long-term planning prepares for both minor and major repairs. This is a critical element of the financial planning, and the establishment of a Sinking Fund for repairs is planned from the outset. An annual review of designated and restricted repair funds will be undertaken to affirm that the accrual of funds is adequate for future works as far as can be anticipated.

continued

Risk	Probability of Occurrence	Impact of Occurrence	Mitigating Planning and Action
Loss of key staff	The management of high quality facilities, with high level of use in a Grade I building, requires staff with considerable relevant experience and commitment, both volunteer and paid staff. Loss of such staff once in post is of low probability in the immediate future.	Medium impact.	The church council takes full responsibility for the overall strategy and will develop more detailed contingency plans including for staff holidays, illness, absence and loss. This will allow for the shortest possible break in service or interruption in programmes. Plans will be made for an interregnum between clergy to have minimum possible impact on the building, its programmes and its maintenance.
Failure of security and safety of staff and public	Given the location and being open every day, St Jude's Church will need continuing vigilance over security and safety. All staff are at risk from verbal and physical attack (statistics of the Diocese of London). Medium probability	Medium impact if comprehensive policies and procedures are operated and all staff are well-trained.	Ongoing staff training in practical aspects of alarms, fire and all other hazards. Training on dealing with all visitors. Training on dealing with difficult and abusive members of the public. Training on dealing with emergencies and in First Aid.

Risk	Probability of Occurrence	Impact of Occurrence	Mitigating Planning and Action
Failure of income	Failure or loss of targeted additional sources of income from outside groups. Arts and community groups and commercial office letting. Inevitable changes in day-to-day lettings. Medium probability	High impact	Early establishment of marketing programme to find suitable users and tenants before works are complete. Regular monitoring of letting frequency to facilitate tackling problems early. Contingency planning to be undertaken to allow for financial accrual to cover voids and for quickly finding new tenants and partner projects.
Excess of expenditure over income	There are a number of unchanging overheads such as insurance and staff costs that will be expended regardless of fluctuating programmes. Others such as lighting will be less if the programme reduces. The possibility of expenditure exceeding income is a high probability.	High impact	Immediate action required to identify or raise working capital to create viable cashflow from day one of reopening. Vigilance through the staff producing monthly reports on finance so that problems are anticipated and dealt with quickly by the church council. Development of contingency fund that is able to absorb ups and downs in cashflow.

continued

Risk	Probability of Occurrence	Impact of Occurrence	Mitigating Planning and Action
Loss of commercial tenant	Medium probability	Low impact	To minimize the impact of a tenancy change, the church will secure a rent deposit from incoming tenants and have contingency plans ready for action as soon as a tenant gives notice to quit.
Loss or failure of Community Project/Arts Project tenant	Low probability	Medium impact	The church will ensure that all agreements are thoroughly established on a professional basis so that clear decision-making processes are in place. While the rental level is appropriate to a community project, in all other ways this will be managed in exactly the same way as the commercial lease. Contingency plans will be set.

Appendix 16: Critical path diagram for St Dunstan in the West

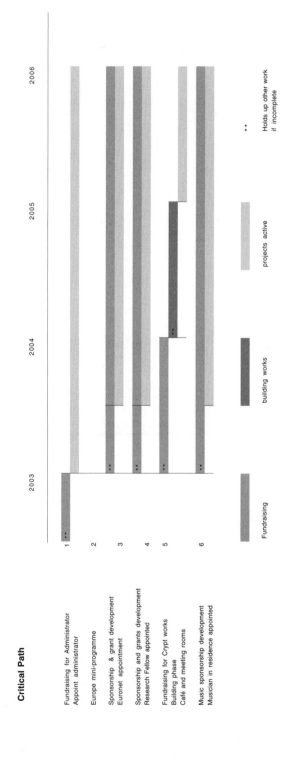

Appendix 17: Two examples of revenue budgets

All Saints Hall Projected Income and Expenditure

	2002	2003	2004
Income			
Counselling Office	£ 1,700	£ 1,700	£ 1,700
Deanery Office	£ 1,700	£ 1,700	£ 1,700
Regular groups letting	£ 3,500	£ 5,500	£ 5,500
Occasional letting	£ 2,000	£ 2,000	£ 2,000
Bank interest	£ 200	£ 200	£ 200
TOTAL INCOME	£ 9,100	£ 11,100	£ 11,100
Expenditure			
Insurance	£ 1,122	£ 1,122	£ 1,122
Gas	£ 500	£ 500	£ 500
Cleaning materials	£ 100	£ 100	£ 100
Electricity	£ 600	£ 600	£ 600
Caretaking	£ 2,000	£ 2,000	£ 2,000
Administration	£ 500	£ 500	£ 500
Fire extinguishers	£ 100	£ 100	£ 100
Sundries	£ 300	£ 300	£ 300
Water charges	£ 500	£ 500	£ 500
Repairs	£ 1,500	£ 1,500	£ 1,500
TOTAL EXPENDITURE	£ 7,222	£ 7,222	£ 7,222
OPENING BALANCE	£ 5,600	£ 7,478	£ 11,356
carried forward	£ 7,478	£ 11,356	£ 15,234

Community Centre Budget Projections

	1999/2000	2000/2001	2001/2002	2002/2003	2003/2004
Revenue Income					
Fundraising	3,000	3,090	3,183	3,278	3,377
Borough grant	67,746	69,778	71,872	74,028	76,249
Premises hire	9,000	9,270	9,548	9,835	10,130
Play scheme grants	12,000	12,360	12,731	13,113	13,506
Activities fees	42,000	43,260	44,558	45,895	47,271
Bank interest	500	515	530	546	563
TOTAL REVENUE INCOME	134,246	138,273	142,422	146,694	151,095
Revenue Expenditure					
Office costs					
Postage	600	618	637	656	675
Phone	1,995	2,055	2,116	2,180	2,245
Stationery	1,500	1,545	1,591	1,639	1,688
Building costs	0	0	0	0	
Rent	2,677	2,757	2,840	2,925	3,013
Rates		0	0	0	0
Maintenance	7,000	7,210	7,426	7,649	7,879
Activities					
Programmes	30,000	30,900	31,827	32,782	33,765
Summer programme	12,000	12,360	12,731	13,113	13,506
Hospitality	700	721	743	765	788
Travel/expenses	500	515	530	546	563
Trips and holidays	12,000	12,360	12,731	13,113	13,506
Utilities	0	0	0	0	
Electricity	2,200	2,266	2,334	2,404	2,476
Gas	1,015	1,045	1,077	1,109	1,142
Water rates	630	649	668	688	709
Insurance	2,500	2,575	2,652	2,732	2,814
Staff Costs					
Salaries	55,605	57,273	58,991	60,761	62,584
Salary administration	500	515	530	546	563
Equipment repair and renewal	500	515	530	546	563
Equipment	1,000	1,030	1,061	1,093	1,126
Miscellaneous	250	258	265	273	281
Subscriptions	100	103	106	109	113
Audit and accounts	575	592	610	628	647
Bank charges	200	206	212	219	225

New Activities

Equipment and materials			5,000	5,150	5,305
Internet training costs			2,000	2,060	2,122
Co-ordinator for Youth & Play			23,000	23,690	24,401
Facilities administrator			12,000	12,360	12,731
Administration			3,000	3,090	3,183
Sessional youth work					
Group Tutors					
Operating Reserve			10,000	10,000	10,000
TOTAL REVENUE EXPENDITURE	134,047	138,068	197,210	202,827	208,612
Revenue fundraising			55,000	56,350	57,740
Operating reserve			10,000	20,000	30,000
Balance	199	205	211	217	224

Appendix 18: Projected revenue budget and cashflow for St Dunstan's

St Dunstan's Projected Revenue Budget and Cashflow

	2002	2003	2004	2005	2006	2007
Opening Balance		£31,643	£20,410	–£6,818	£4,954	£19,226
Income						
Donations	£11,335	£11,335	£11,335	£11,335	£11,335	£11,335
CPC for clergy salary p.t.		£10,000				
Rents						
St Helen's	£3,000	£3,000	£3,000	£3,000	£3,000	£3,000
Charity Cards	£3,000	£3,000	£3,000	£3,000	£3,000	£3,000
Cordwainers	£1,500	£1,500	£1,500	£1,500	£1,500	£1,500
Church Rate	£310	£310	£1,000	£1,000	£1,000	£1,000
Romanian church	£1,250	£1,250	£2,500	£5,000	£7,500	£10,000
	£20,395					
Capital Income for Major Repairs						
Projected Income						
Flats	£25,000			£25,000	£25,000	£25,000
Church for Europe grants and sponsorship	£100,000		£100,000	£100,000	£100,000	£100,000
Café	£15,000			£15,000	£15,000	£15,000
Crypt lettings	£15,000			£15,000	£15,000	£15,000
Sponsorship for Music Programme	£15,000		£15,000	£15,000	£15,000	£15,000
Euronet grants and sponsorship	£65,000		£65,000	£65,000	£65,000	£65,000
	£255,395	£30,395	£202,335	£259,835	£262,335	£264,835

Expenditure	2002		2003	2004	2005	2006	2007
Quota	£4,306		£5,000	£5,500	£10,000	£10,000	£10,000
Repairs and Maintenance	£2,000		£2,000	£ 5,000	£ 5,000	£ 5,000	£ 5,000
Heat, Light, Cleaning and Rates	£2,565		£2,565	£ 5,000	£ 5,000	£ 5,000	£ 5,000
Insurance	£157		£157	£157	£157	£157	£157
Admin and Office	£1,372		£1,372	£1,372	£1,372	£1,372	£1,372
Entertaining	£201		£201	£201	£201	£201	£201
Clergy	£1,493		£1,493	£1,493	£1,493	£1,493	£1,493
Audit	£940		£940	£940	£940	£940	£940
Music	£700		£700	£700	£700	£700	£700
Sundries	£200		£200	£200	£200	£200	£200
		£13,934					
Projected Expenditure							
Salaries							
Director/Vicar	£26,000		£10,000	£26,000	£26,000	£26,000	£26,000
office	£5,000			£5,000	£5,000	£5,000	£5,000
Manager/ Administrator	£23,000		£12,000	£23,000	£23,000	£23,000	£23,000
office	£5,000		£5,000	£5,000	£5,000	£5,000	£5,000
Church For Europe							
Research Fellow	£40,000			£40,000	£40,000	£40,000	£40,000
Admin, Promotion and Event costs	£30,000			£30,000	£30,000	£30,000	£30,000
Lettings							
Promotion and Running costs	£6,000				£6,000	£6,000	£6,000
Concerts							
Music Fellow	£10,000			£10,000	£10,000	£10,000	£10,000
Administration and Promotion	£5,000			£5,000	£5,000	£5,000	£5,000
Euronet Hub							
Hub Manager	£35,000			£35,000	£35,000	£35,000	£35,000
office	£5,000			£5,000	£5,000	£5,000	£5,000
Equipment and Maintenance	£25,000			£25,000	£25,000	£25,000	£25,000
Sinking Fund	£8,000				£8,000	£8,000	£8,000
	£236,934		£41,628	£229,563	£248,063	£248,063	£248,063
Closing Balance			£20,410	–£6,818	£4,954	£19,226	£35,998

NOTE: no inflation is included

Appendix 19: Projected revenue budget and cashflow for St Jude's

Projected Revenue Budget and Cashflow

		budget annual 2002	2002 Jan-Mar	Apr-Jun	July-Sept	Oct-Dec	2003 Jan-Mar	work commences Apr-Jun	July-Sept
Opening Balance	1		£42,267	£41,892	£41,518	£41,143	£40,769	£37,461	£37,054
Income									
Church voluntary income	2	£16,300	£4,075	£4,075	£4,075	£4,075	£4,075	£4,075	£4,075
Vestry upper floor	3	£20,000	£5,000	£5,000	£5,000	£5,000	£5,000	£5,000	£5,000
Vestry lower floor	4	£11,730	£2,933	£2,933	£2,933	£2,933			
Crypt	5, 6	£400	£100	£100	£100	£100	£100		
Car parking	7	£30,000	£7,500	£7,500	£7,500	£7,500	£7,500		
Other ordinary income	8	900	£225	£225	£225	£225	£225	£225	£225
Investment income	9	£21,400	£5,350	£5,350	£5,350	£5,350	£5,350	£5,350	£5,350
Income generation during construction	10							£9,000	£9,000
		£100,730	£25,183	£25,183	£25,183	£25,183	£22,250	£23,650	£23,650

Expenditure		budget 2002	2002 Jan-Mar	Apr-Jun	July-Sept	Oct- Dec	2003 Jan-Mar	Apr-Jun	July-Sept
Ministry/clergy expenses	11	£2,350	£588	£588	£588	£588	£588	£588	£588
Church and services	12	£7,200	£1,800	£1,800	£1,800	£1,800	£1,800	£1,800	£1,800
Management & administration	13	£24,700	£6,175	£6,175	£6,175	£6,175	£6,175	£6,175	£6,175
Running costs	14	£13,500	£3,375	£3,375	£3,375	£3,375	£3,375	£3,375	£3,375
Publications and promotion		£250	£62	£62	£62	£62	£62	£62	£62
Vestry house and business rate		£6,200	£1,550	£1,550	£1,550	£1,550	£1,550	£1,550	£1,550
Prof. fees		£5,400	£1,350	£1,350	£1,350	£1,350	£1,350	£1,350	£1,350
Diocese and deanery		£33,830	£8,458	£8,458	£8,458	£8,458	£8,458	£8,458	£8,458
Charitable donations		£800	£200	£200	£200	£200	£200	£200	£200
Repair	15	£8,000	£2,000	£2,000	£2,000	£2,000	£2,000	£500	£500
Sinking Fund	16		£0	£0	£0	£0	£0	£0	£0
		£102,230	£25,558	£25,558	£25,558	£25,558	£25,558	£24,058	£24,058
Closing Balance			£41,892	£41,518	£41,143	£40,769	£37,461	£37,054	£36,646

NOTE: no inflation is included

on site

	2004				2005				2006
Oct-Dec	Jan-Mar	Apr-Jun	July-Sept	Oct- Dec	Jan-Mar	Apr-Jun	July-Sept	Oct- Dec	Jan-Mar
£36,646	**£36,239**	**£30,831**	**£25,424**	**£20,016**	**£19,609**	**£22,001**	**£24,394**	**£26,786**	**£29,179**
£4,075	£4,075	£4,075	£4,075	£4,075	£4,075	£4,075	£4,075	£4,075	£4,075
£5,000				£5,000	£5,000	£5,000	£5,000	£5,000	£5,000
					£7,000	£7,000	£7,000	£7,000	£7,000
					£8,500	£8,500	£8,500	£8,500	£8,500
£225	£225	£225	£225	£225	£225	£225	£225	£225	£225
£5,350	£5,350	£5,350	£5,350	£5,350	£5,350	£5,350	£5,350	£5,350	£5,350
£9,000	£9,000	£9,000	£9,000	£9,000					
£23,650	£18,650	£18,650	£18,650	£23,650	£30,150	£30,150	£30,150	£30,150	£30,150

	2004				2005				2006
Oct- Dec	Jan-Mar	Apr-Jun	July-Sept	Oct- Dec	Jan-Mar	Apr-Jun	July-Sept	Oct- Dec	Jan-Mar
£588	£588	£588	£588	£588	£588	£588	£588	£588	£588
£1,800	£1,800	£1,800	£1,800	£1,800	£1,800	£1,800	£1,800	£1,800	£1,800
£6,175	£6,175	£6,175	£6,175	£6,175	£6,175	£6,175	£6,175	£6,175	£6,175
£3,375	£3,375	£3,375	£3,375	£3,375	£3,375	£3,375	£3,375	£3,375	£3,375
£62	£62	£62	£62	£62	£62	£62	£62	£62	£62
£1,550	£1,550	£1,550	£1,550	£1,550	£1,550	£1,550	£1,550	£1,550	£1,550
£1,350	£1,350	£1,350	£1,350	£1,350	£1,350	£1,350	£1,350	£1,350	£1,350
£8,458	£8,458	£8,458	£8,458	£8,458	£8,458	£8,458	£8,458	£8,458	£8,458
£200	£200	£200	£200	£200	£200	£200	£200	£200	£200
£500	£500	£500	£500	£500	£2,000	£2,000	£2,000	£2,000	£2,000
£0	£0	£0	£0	£0	£2,200	£2,200	£2,200	£2,200	£2,200
£24,058	£24,058	£24,058	£24,058	£24,058	£27,758	£27,758	£27,758	£27,758	£27,758
£36,239	£30,831	£25,424	£20,016	£19,609	£22,001	£24,394	£26,786	£29,179	£31,571

see notes overleaf

Please note that St Jude's Church makes no charge to visitors and plans not to do so in future.

1. Opening balance from the most recent church council accounts.
2. Church budget for 2003.
3. Based on 2001 & 2002.
4. Current rental which after building works will rise to commercial rate of local letting agents.
5. Crypt: present income from storage use by community group.
6. Parish room and Community Project income rates set by comparison with similar spaces in London churches.
7. High source of income at present *but* target is to have minimum car parking in future with income replaced by better letting of vestry house and crypt.
8. As at present.
9. As at present.
10. Temporary income from targeted advertising on the scaffolding.
11. As at present.
12. As at present.
13. As at present, with slightly changed job structures.
14. Changes after works, with system of heating and lighting that is effective and in more areas.
15. Based on increased annual maintenance costs, for example for lift contract, electrical checks, gutter clearance, etc.
16. Sinking fund (see separate sheet) to accrue funds for minor and major repairs in the medium and long term.

No inflation is shown on the budget and cashflow projections.

Appendix 20: Projected sinking fund targets

YEARS	Cycle of repair	cost per cycle	5	10	15	20	25	30	35	40	45	50	cost over 50 years
Capital													
Lighting repair & upgrade		£40,000					*					*	£80,000
Heating and boiler upgrade		£45,000					*					*	£90,000
Kitchen and toilets upgrade		£12,000		*		*		*		*		*	£60,000
Ventilation system		£10,000			*			*			*		£30,000
Fire alarms/Safety		£15,000			*			*			*		£45,000
Vestry House redecoration	5 years	£7,000	*	*	*	*	*	*	*	*	*	*	£70,000
Church redecoration	25 years	£250,000					*					*	£500,000
Sacristy	7 years	£3,000	*		*	*		*	*	*		*	£21,000
Lead roof	40 years repair / 75 years replace									*			not priced
Maintenance													
Gutters	twice per annum	£2,000											annual budget item
Timber waxing reredos	10 years	£1,000		*		*		*		*		*	£5,000
Quinquennial items	5 years	£6,000	*	*	*	*	*	*	*	*	*	*	£60,000
Churchyard paving	10 years	£2,500		*		*		*		*		*	£12,500
Churchyard railings	5 years	£2,500	*	*	*	*	*	*	*	*	*	*	£25,000

Sinking Fund requirement	£998,500
Annual accrual	£19,970

* Refers to the year in which work will need to be repeated, so lighting upgrade happens twice in 50 years, therefore the cost is double that listed in the cost per cycle column.
Similarly Vestry House redecoration will take place every five years at the cost of £7,000 and will total £35,000 (excluding VAT and inflation).
The Sinking Fund represents all the money that will be spent on repairs in the next fifty years (excluding VAT and inflation). Hence the church needs to save the Annual Accrual of £19,970 to provide for all these predictable repairs.

Appendix 21: A fundraising programme outline

Funding source	Date for action	Historic church repairs	Church new works	New organ	Lift, crypt and hall facilities	Specific items	Outside areas
EH & HLF Repair Scheme	Apr	x					
Trusts for repairs	June	x					
Trust for organs	June			x			
Local donations	& Nov now	x	x	x	x		
Concerts and events	ongoing	x	x	x	x		
Heritage Lottery Fund Main Grant Scheme	June				x		
ICBS and other new build trusts	June		x		x		
Lottery Community Fund	June				x		
Heritage Lottery Fund 'Your Heritage'	June					x	
Big Names as advocates and patrons	Now?						
A Sainsbury to get an opening with the Monument Fund	Now?	x	x	x			
Memorials: to attract gifts for specific items	Now/June	x				x	
Landfill Tax: Western Riverside Environmental Fund	Now						x
Groundwork Lambeth	Now						x

Appendix 22: Legacy information

Would you consider making a legacy to help the St James's Appeal?

If you haven't already included a charity in your Will perhaps you'll be kind enough to consider leaving a legacy to St James's Church.
There are four main types of gift you can make in your Will:

1 Pecuniary legacy – a gift of a specific amount of money.
2 Residuary legacy – a gift of part of your estate after all costs and other gifts have been paid.
3 Reversionary legacy – a gift left to someone with instructions that it is to pass to another person on the death of the first person.
4 Specific legacy/bequest – a gift of a particular item, such as a painting, jewellery, portfolio of shares or the whole of your estate.

Residuary Bequests

If you are unsure how best to help St James's Church in your Will, leaving a share of your estate is often the easiest option. This is called a residuary bequest and is a gift made from the residue of your estate after all your loved ones have been provided for.

Your Legacy and Legal Advice

If you would like to make a gift to the St James's Church Appeal in your Will, you should get professional advice, usually from a solicitor. An existing Will can easily be changed by the addition of a Codicil. Although your bequest to a charity such as St James's is exempt from Inheritance Tax, your solicitor will also be able to advise on your overall tax liability. If you decide to do so your solicitor might find the following wording useful:

For a new Will

I give to St James's Church, *address*
*All the residue of my estate.
*One ...... (enter the fraction) share of the residue of my estate.
*The sum of £......
*An item or items of value (please give an accurate description) to be used by St James's Church for its building repair or general purposes and I direct that the receipt of the Hon. Treasurer or other duly authorized officer shall be sufficient discharge of the said legacy.

For an existing Will

If you have already made a Will, you can make a simple addition to include St James's Church. This is called a codicil. Please see the form overleaf.

Want to know more?

Thank you for reading this sheet and summary of how to go about making or changing your Will. We strongly advise that you visit a solicitor to make or update your Will – he or she can ensure that it is legally binding, thus saving your family and friends unnecessary stress.
If you intend to support St James's Appeal by making a gift in your Will, we would invite you to complete the form and return it to the church office.

It would help our planning if you are able to return this form to us

I intend to remember the St James's Appeal in my Will.

Type of bequest:

O **Residuary legacy**

O **Pecuniary legacy**

O **Specific legacy**

Title (Mr/Mrs/Miss/Ms/other)

Name..

Address..

Post Code...

E-mail..

Do you have any specific requirements with regard to your pledge?

I wish to make a donation now of _____ (please make cheques payable to: 'PCC of St James's Church'

Return this form to: St James's Church (*address*)
Tel: **Website: www.st-james**

Codicil Form

You can use this codicil form to leave a legacy to St James's Church, if you have an existing Will. Once you have decided what you wish to bequest to St James's Church, take this form to your solicitor with your Will.

Your solicitor will check that your codicil does not conflict with your Will or any other codicils you may have made, and will ensure that you sign your codicil in the presence of two independent witnesses. The witnesses must sign your codicil at the same time as you do.

MY CODICIL INSTRUCTIONS ARE:

Name: _____

Address: _____

_____

Postcode: _____

I would like to change my Will to bequest St James's Church, The Heart of Piccadilly Appeal, 197 Piccadilly, London W1J 9LL the following (please tick relevant boxes):

❑ The sum of £_____

❑ And/or _____% of my estate

(please enter the fraction/percentage share in words)

To be used by St James's Church for its building repair or general purposes and I direct that the receipt of the Honorary Treasurer or other duly authorized officer shall be sufficient discharge of the said legacy.

In all other respects I confirm my Will.

I _____

The Testator declares this to be a

_____ (first, second, etc)

Codicil to my Will dated

_____ (in words)

and that this Codicil was signed in the presence of both my witnesses

Signed

Date

Signed (witness 1)

Date

Signed (witness 2)

Date

Glossary

Archdeacon: a middle manager in the Church of England system to whom local churches relate over issues of buildings, finance and resources.

Beneficiaries: all the people who benefit from the presence of the church, including churchgoers, local residents, people who use the church hall or facilities, and local organizations that the church helps, such as schools.

Branding: a method of creating the image that the church wants people to have in their minds when they think of the church and its ministry.

Building works:

Architect: designs the architectural work needed and leads the design team.

Design team: the group of professional advisers who are appointed by the church for their different areas of design expertise and meet regularly with the building contractor during a major building project.

Indicative budget: the quantity surveyor's considered assessment of what the architect's designed works will cost.

Mechanical and electrical designer: designs electrical and other utilities provision in the building.

Preliminaries: the cost of the builder being on site, from scaffolding to insurance.

Project manager: has special responsibility for organizing the other professionals (including the architect) to achieve the targets of the church, quality, time and cost.

Quantity surveyor: has responsibility for assessing the cost of building works, including everything from stone, work hours and site access, to insurance and skips. Also values the work achieved at monthly intervals during the work programme.

Structural engineer: designs or assesses the structural elements from roof beams to stone arches. Often consulted when churches suffer subsidence.

Business Plan: using a model from the world of commerce, this is a method of illustrating how the church or charity is going to use its resources to fulfil its mission over three to five years.

Champion: the person who will campaign inside and outside the church for the particular project and champion its progress.

Church council: the group legally responsible for the ongoing life of the church. For some churches this may have another name such as Elders or Deacons.

Critical path analysis: (Business Plan) a method of highlighting the order in which activities need to be undertaken before a target can be achieved. Some activities have to be completed before others start.

Diocesan Common Fund: the money that many denominations have to pay to the central church administration to cover costs of staff and other centralized provision.

Excepted charity: many churches are registered charities but do not have a registration number from the Charity Commissioners. However, they are still legally controlled by the rules and principles of the Charity Commissioners.

Faculty: for the six main church denominations, building works are controlled primarily by internal systems rather than the listed building consent process of local authorities. The legal permission for work to a listed building is for these churches called Faculty.

Footfall: this is widely used description of the numbers of people visiting a building, regardless of whether some are regular visitors. Every time someone visits, it registers on the 'footfall' total.

Gift Aid: the money that donors have previously paid in income tax that can be reclaimed by charities to whom they make a donation.

Imprest system: the method of running a petty cash system in which a float is topped up as receipts are produced for the treasurer.

Mission plan: the strategy the church has for its mission activity over the next three to five years.

Quinquennial report: the regular five-yearly architect's report on the state of the church building.

Stakeholders: all those holding an interest in the church building – those who use it, those who own it, those in the church hierarchy responsible for ensuring its proper care, those who have or might contribute funds, local authority and others.

Match funding: when a church receives a partial grant towards their project that is conditional on further funds being raised, this further funding is referred to as match funding.

Option analysis: a report on the various solutions a church has considered to its problem or provision, with the reasons for choosing its preferred solution.

Sinking fund: the money set aside for future repairs to a building – a special form of reserve that will be described as Sinking Fund or Repair Fund in the annual accounts.

SMART objectives: very specifically achievable objectives detailed more fully in the Business Plan.

Strapline: a key phrase or sentence flagged across promotional material that grabs people's attention with the key quality of the church or project being promoted.

SWOT analysis: the church's analysis of its internal strengths and weaknesses that are within its control, and of the opportunities and threats from outside that are beyond its control.

Resources and Connections

Useful books

Sources of Grants for Building Conservation, Cathedral Communications Ltd, The Tisbury Brewery, Church Street, Tisbury, Wilts SP3 6NH

Funds for Historic Buildings, Architectural Heritage Fund, Clareville House, 26–27 Oxenden Street, London SW1Y 4EL

The Directory of Social Change produces many fundraising and other books for the voluntary sector. They also stock the books and guides of the Charities Aid Foundation. Their catalogue is available from Kings Hill, West Malling, Kent ME19 4TA. I use a few of their books regularly: *Guides to Major Trusts*, vols 1, 2 and 3. Also the *Guide* to the part of the country, for example, *Guide to Local Trusts – Midlands*. These guides are updated regularly.

The Diocese of Southwark Communications Department produces an excellent model for a Hall Handbook in its Purple Packs, as well as good material on *Developing a Community Project*. The Purple Packs are available from Diocese of Southwark, Trinity House, 4 Chapel Court, Borough High Street, London SE1 1HW.

Managing your Community Building, Community Matters, 8/9 Upper Street, London, N1 0QP

The Charities Act 1993 and the PCC (2001), Church House Publishing, Great Smith Street, London SW1P 4AZ. This outlines all the accounting and reporting requirements of charity law as applied to churches.

CD-Roms

The *Grant Making Trusts* CD-Rom from Charities Aid Foundation, Kings Hill, West Malling, Kent ME19 4TA

FunderFinder, 65 Raglan Road, Leeds, West Yorkshire LS2 9DZ

Webpages

Council for the Care of Churches gives guidance on fundraising and a useful selection of trusts on www.churchcare.co.uk

Directory of Social Change for books, information and training: www.dsc.org.uk and www.trustfunding.org.uk

National Lottery Community Fund: www.biglotteryfund.org.uk

Information on sources of funds:
    Funderfinder and Budget Yourself, at www.funderfinder.org.uk
    Architectural Heritage Fund, at www.ahfund.org.uk
    Entrust for Landfill Tax information, at www.entrust.org.uk
    Government funding, at www.governmentfunding.org.uk
    Grants to offset VAT, at www.lpwscheme.org.uk
    Heritage Lottery Fund, at www.hlf.org.uk (other lottery funders each have
    their own sites)
    The Church Urban Fund on funds and lots of other useful information, at
    www.cuf.org.uk
    Funds from a variety of sources, at www.fundingcentral.org.uk

The statistics from the 2001 census are being published on www.statistics. gov.uk/census2001

Trusts that now have webpage information and application forms include:

National Churches Trust, at www.nationalchurchestrust.org
Allchurches Trust, at www.allchurches.co.uk

Other useful sites are:
    The Office for National Statistics, at www.neighbourhood.statistics.gov.uk
    (enter your postcode)

National Association for Voluntary and Community Action, at www.navca.org.uk

Voluntary England, at www.volunteering.org.uk

Training

The Directory of Social Change runs a major annual event, *Charity Fair*, in London each April when seminars and workshops include fundraising, books are on sale and many agencies serving the voluntary sector have stalls and advice.

Index